TAXI!

Cabs and Capitalism in New York City

BIJU MATHEW

ILR Press
an imprint of
Cornell University Press

Ithaca and London

First published in cloth 2005 by The New Press
Published by arrangement with The New Press, New York
First printed, Cornell Paperbacks, 2008

Printed in the United States of America

Library of Congress Cataloging-in-Publication Data

Mathew, Biju.
    Taxi! : cabs and capitalism in New York City / Biju Mathew. — Cornell ed.
        p. cm. — (Cornell paperbacks)
    Includes bibliographical references and index.
    ISBN 978-0-8014-7439-2 (pbk. : alk. paper)
    1. Taxicabs—New York (State)—New York.   2. Taxicab drivers—Labor
unions—New York (State)—New York.   3. Strikes and lockouts—Transport
workers—New York (State)—New York.   I. Title.   II. Series.

    HE5614.4.N7M38   2008
    388.4'13214097471—dc22   2008012852

Cornell University Press strives to use environmentally responsible
suppliers and materials to the fullest extent possible in the publishing
of its books. Such materials include vegetable-based, low-VOC inks
and acid-free papers that are recycled, totally chlorine-free, or partly
composed of nonwood fibers. For further information,
visit our website at www.cornellpress.cornell.edu.

Paperback printing   10 9 8 7 6 5 4 3 2

For my mother, Baby Mathews, who continues
to teach me how not to give up
and
in memory of two organizers who left us too early,
Agha Saleem Osman and Malik Majid.

CONTENTS

Three significant events have happened since 2005 when this book was first published. (1) Starting in 2004, the city of New York began advancing the Taxi Technology Enhancement Program (TTE), which would require every yellow taxi in NYC to be fitted with a non-navigational Global Positioning System–based tracking system. Driver opposition to this system grew over the next three years, leading up to a series of strikes in September and October 2007. Even as we go to press, this battle continues. (2) In early 2007, the New York Taxi Workers Alliance (NYTWA) became the first independent labor union to become a full member of the New York State Central Labor Council, a historic development with tremendous significance for the labor movement. (3) Finally, based on burgeoning interest and several taxi-organizing initiatives emerging throughout the United States, NYTWA along with the Taxi Workers Alliance of Pennsylvania organized a founding meeting of the Taxi Workers International (TWI) in March 2007.

All three dramatic events promise long-term effects. In many ways the intertwined nature of these events has given me a more complete understanding of the challenges the contemporary labor

For this edition I would like to acknowledge the debt I have gathered over the last three years. My deepest gratitude goes to the new members of the NYTWA Organizing Committee who joined us between 2004 and 2008: Beresford Simmons, Lakshman Abesekhare, Thomas Osam, Victor Salazar, and Mor Thiam. Also, a special thanks to Abdul Qayyum and Tipu Sultan for always being there for battle.

movement faces. Accordingly, this Cornell edition carries a new epilogue that not only describes these events and the actions that surrounded them but also attempts to synthesize them theoretically. The result, I hope, is a compelling conclusion to the book that will open up fresh debates within the labor movement.

DEDICATION: TWO HEROES

Since this book first appeared, we lost two of our most beloved organizers—Kevin Michael Fitzpatrick and Yilma Wolde Mariam. To both of them—a special shout out—Inquilab Zindabad! We have not yet learned how to walk without you.

Yilma Wolde Mariam was mercurial, erudite, hungry to debate, always on the prowl for the next person to awe with the sheer depth and perceptiveness of his incessant questions. A few months before he left us, Yilma rocked the organizing committee of the Alliance with an electrifying analysis of nihilism in the American working class—explicating through a series of vivid images the contemporary problems of the relationship between the white and new immigrant working classes. The pictures he painted were always larger than life.

Kevin Michael Fitzpatrick was dramatically different. His approach to life was somewhere between phlegmatic and sanguine—an approach captured so aptly in the lines Bhairavi Desai wrote after Kevin passed away: "May you be, beloved Kevin, where the poet meets the scientist to talk revolution." Kevin *knew that he knew*, and it wasn't that nothing fazed him but that nobody fazed him.

If Yilma's wit was sharp, Kevin's was sardonic; if Kevin carried people with him, Yilma hung back and listened. Yilma was our champion phone-banker. He could disarm anyone on the phone, and all of us sitting around would be either dumbstruck by the brilliance of his responses or keeling over in laughter. That capacity to arm and disarm, irrespective of culture or language, was how we will remember Yilma. In today's fragmented and utilitarian world, Yilma was possibly one of the last true working class internationalists.

A whole generation of NYC taxi drivers knew Kevin as their FEMA hero when, after 9/11, he shouldered much of the work to help drivers get FEMA relief. He knew what it meant to stay in the battle for the long haul. The two books at his bedside when he passed away—one a commentary on Hegel and the other a book on the peoples' history of science—tell us much about him. His hunger for knowledge and his dedication to the liberation of the working class have few parallels. This book would never have been written without him, and in many ways, it is one he should have written himself.

There is a way in which the hurly-burly of politics and the rigors of a campaign don't allow us to stop and mourn fully, don't allow us to reconcile with this loss. Kevin and Yilma led the Taxi Alliance to the doorstep of a tremendous transformation and participated in it until their very last days. *Alvida*, comrades. A thousand flowers will bloom from the memories you have left behind.

ACKNOWLEDGMENTS

This book owes its existence entirely to the New York Taxi Workers Alliance and Bhairavi Desai, who has led the organization with rare vision and brilliance for all of its years of existence. It is not often that one has a chance to work with an organizer of such political clarity and intellectual depth and I am incredibly thankful for all that I have learned from her. In lockstep with Bhairavi have been a range of tremendously courageous and creative organizers—members of the Alliance's Organizing Committee, past and present, whom I have no proper way to thank: Rizwan Raja, Kurshid (Amer) Khan, and Tahir Sheik for teaching me to think about the taxi industry; Kevin Fitzpatrick for being what he is—a walking, talking organic New York City history book; Kulwinder Singh, Ghulam Rabbani, Abdul Qayyum, Sharanjit Singh, Akhtar Choudhury, Imran Hossain, Abdul Farooq, and Manjit Singh for the patience with which they took me along in the early days when I knew nothing of the industry; Saeed Ahmed, Mamnun Ul Huq, Ilyas Khan, Moiuddin Ahmed, and Javaid Tariq for the strength and conviction with which they led us during the years of early instability into the days of the strike; Mohammed Kazem, Nauroz Wein, Yilma Wolde Mariam, Agha Saleem Osman, Tahir Siddiqui, Kasif Akhtar, and Chidibere Kamalu for keeping the connections between global politics and laboring in New York City alive in my mind all the time; Tasleem Khan, Maged Gabriel, Vivian Borges, Mohmmed Ahmad, Surinder Walia, and Malik Majed for leading me deeper into the intrigue that lies behind the

TLC, garages, and brokers; Shomial Ahmad, Osman Chodhury, Chaumtoli Huq, and Bill Lindauer for keeping so many balls in play in the office and outside. But this list of names conveys little of the life that all of us created. A new world into which I would so gladly wake up each morning (or rather afternoon!). Bhairavi and the Organizing Committee have not just built a militant labor organiztion but a sensitive and nuturing space—one that so easily became my home.

There is always more than one story to tell about a book. The community of friends and comrades who have engaged me and created a world with me is too vast to name. And yet, there was a moment in 1997 when I thought I would never write this book— when I thought my days of reading and writing had come to an end because of a serious eye ailment. Raza Mir, Vamsi Vakulabharanam, Vijay Prashad, Lisa Armstrong, Sekhar Ramakrishnan, Sue Sussman, Maya Yagnik, Farah Hasan, Rahul De and Sharmila Chakravarty, Raju Rajan, Syeda Fatima, Kuldhir Bhati, Mona Chopra, Vivek Bald and Kym Ragusa, Gautam Premnath and Kasturi Ray, Himadeep Muppidi and Nellie Prabhu, Jagdish Parikh, Srikanth Bollam, Smriti Rao, Balaji and Suba Krishnan, Svetlana Vilanskaia, and Chris Chekuri and Radhika Lal saw me through the worst crisis in my life. Week after week they were there to talk, to read to me, to write and manage my e-mail, and just there to surround me. But there are two friends who took this task of "being there" far beyond any ordinary call of friendship. Hussain (Ali Mir) was there with me at every turn during that crisis and since. Thanks, Bhai. And later there was Pilar Hernandez, who refused to accept that I would not write. Every week she drove forty miles back and forth to sit me down and force me to record this book on tape. It was Pilar's determination that made me take the idea of writing seriously again.

I have no idea where the process of recovering from an illness ended, if it ever did, and where political reengagement began. The unflinching demand for a more complex politics that came from Aley Mathew, Ragini Shah, Prerana Reddy, Amita Swadhin, Prachi Patankar, Anjali Kamat, Sonia Arora, Svati Shah, Surabhi Kukke, Tejasvi Nagaraja, Nidhi Mirani, Linta Varghese, Marian Thambinayakam, Junaid Rana, Maya Sen, Satish Kolluri, Sangeeta Rao, Jawad Metni, Anand Roop Roy, Ayaz Ahmad, Prantik Saha, Saadia Toor, and Sonali Sathye has made me politically richer and given me a bunch of lifelong friends. At the same time the struggle against Hindutva outside India, which seemed so hopeless through the 1990s, was given new shape and direction by Mubeen Bolar, Girish Agarwal, Raja Harish Swamy, Kamala Visweswaran, Ra Ravishanker, Kamayani Swami, Chetan Bhatt, Anant Maringanti, Jayant Eranki, and Angana Chaterjee, with tremendous leadership from Shalini Gera. I have learned so much from all of you. In Amherst, Massachusetts, a new community of friends in Srirupa Roy and Lalit Vachani, Usha Zacharias, Nirupama Ravi, and Paula Chakravarty turned what would otherwise be a sterile space of granola-infested living into one charged with political engagement and camaraderie. At the Brecht, Liz Mestres, Sam Anderson, Merle Ratner, Liz Roberts, Nan Rubin, and Lincoln Van Sluytman opened up the world of universalist struggles that had been missing for so long. Liza Featherstone, a Brecht Forum comrade, was also the most engaged reader of this book and her contribution, along with that of Colin Robinson, to its final shape is huge. Also among those who helped read and edit the book and bring it to where it is now are Laura Secor, Samita Sinha, Lizzie Seidlin-Bernstein, Sarah Fan, and Nicole Lebo, and I thank them all for their help.

And as this community grew around me, there were some among them who became the cornerstones of intellectual and social sustenance: Saba Waheed, who became my most consistent interlocutor and helped shape so many ideas; Rupal Oza and Ashwini Rao, who have been part of thinking though so many projects in diasporic politics; Shabnum Tejani, who never allowed the desire for community to die by reminding me of what honest intellectual work along with deeply held relationships could mean; Deepa Fernandes, who gave me a new world by teaching me how to create conversations from behind a microphone; and Ayca Cubukcu, who brought me back to the live connection between political theory and the daily work of social justice struggles.

Support came from India too—close friends and political comrades who, in the midst of lives in upheaval, still found the time to support me. Pradip Prabhu, Shiraz Balsara, Madhu, Dhodi, Brian Lobo, Priya Sreenivasa, and Meena Dhodade from Kashtakari Sanghtana; Aruna Roy, Shankar Singh, and Nikhil De of MKSS; Madhava Prasad and Janaki Nair, Gita Ramaswamy, Shabnam Hashmi, Anand Patwardhan, Simantini Dhuru, Humaira and Ashar Farhan, Vinod Pavarala and Aparna Rayaprol, Elahe Hiptoola, Azam and Asea Khan, Javed Anand, Teesta Setalvaad, Amirullah Khan and Saleema Rizvi, Jharana Jhaveri, Surinder and Sneha Jodhka, and Anuraag Singh were never too far away. And from different corners of the world, other old friends: Deepa and Pahai Kuo; Shubhra Gururani; my sister Binu and her family, Neaan, Nicole, and Pramod; my mum and Leela aunty; and my other family in Bangalore—Shruti, Madhu, Supriya, Prashant, Praveen, Baba, and Aayi—have all given such wonderful support.

And in the end, every person is easy to thank, except one's partner. There is nothing I can write here that will say everything that I feel for Sangeeta Kamat and what she has meant for me over the last eight years. She has been at the heart of it all—every discovery and every crisis, every struggle and moment of caring. To her, I owe a large part of what I am today.

MAY 5, 2004. Lahore Deli, Houston and Crosby Streets, New York City. 11 P.M.

"Aare yaar yeh ho hi nahi sakta," exclaimed Bashir Ahmed, with a look of disbelief. "This is simply impossible!" His short, stocky frame half rested on the door of his yellow cab, but his hands moved furiously.

"Kyon Bhai, mazaa aa raha hai?" "Hey, brothers, so has it been good?" Rizwan asked the small crowd that was gathered on the sidewalk outside the deli drinking chai — a brief break in the night shift, which had begun more than six hours ago.

Bashir looked at Rizwan. *"Ohhw! O bhai. Aap tho union wale hai. . . ."* he said, as he recognized Rizwan as a member of the New York Taxi Workers Alliance (NYTWA).[1] Bashir approached Rizwan and pumped his arm. The small crowd followed — some smiling at Rizwan, others shaking his hand or fraternally thumping him on the back.

The Alliance had just won a major victory: after eight months of negotiations with the mayor's office, the drivers had not only scored the fare increase they wanted, but they'd done so on advantageous terms. The drivers would likely take home 70 percent of the additional revenue, compared to the owners' 30 percent. It was the best split drivers had won since 1967. The previous fare hike had gone to the owners by 86 percent, with only 14 percent reaching the drivers' pockets.

Sadiq, a young man with the demeanor of one much older, was

the last of the group to reach Rizwan. He knew the Alliance well. "Brother," he began, "please thank Bhairavi on our behalf. . . . She is truly amazing."

Rizwan smiled at the way Sadiq said "Bhairavi": perfectly Punjabi, dropping all the heavy sounds, her name rolling off his tongue with a lilt. Bhairavi Desai was the director and lead organizer of the Alliance and one of its founding members. Rizwan nodded. "You're right," he said. "She has such a vision."

"And sheer hard work and dedication. . . . All of you in the Alliance deserve our gratitude," continued Sadiq, who viewed the fare increase as his due but knew well that it had come about only thanks to the Alliance's sustained battle with ownership and its allies.

Bashir was getting agitated. He had lost Rizwan's attention and he had questions. Fidgeting, he pointed in the general direction of his cab. *"O yaar . . . ye dabba daud raha hai . . . galti tho nahi. . . ."* He was worried, and his face showed it. The meter, he was saying, is running too fast. Are you sure there is no error? Rizwan's smile grew wider. *"Na . . . nahi,"* he replied, "there is no error. . . . It's just as it should be." He turned to the rest of the crowd and explained his logic.

"See, we used to start at $2.00 and go up 30 cents every fifth of a mile. So by the time your meter went past the $3.00 mark you had traveled almost a whole mile. Now you start at $2.50 and the meter goes up 40 cents every fifth of a mile. And so you have just started your run and it's way past $3.00. It feels incredible to those of us who have seen the old meter. It's the combined effect of a hike in the base fare and the per-mile rate."

Harjit, an old, lean Sikh driver who had followed Rizwan's logic to the end, nodded. *"Aap log sab union member hai?"* he asked, turning and surveying the crowd, which was growing in size, to see how many of them would acknowledge membership in the Alliance.

"This is their second big win. First they got us the FEMA money, now the fare hike. We should not just be thanking them, we should be joining them in droves." His gaze rested on Rizwan after lingering for a moment or two each on those who had not said they were Alliance members. "How many members are we?" he asked.

"Just over five thousand," Rizwan answered. "And thank you, brother, for mentioning the FEMA victory. Everybody forgets about it."

Harjit and Rizwan referred to the mass mobilization of taxi drivers in the aftermath of the attacks of September 11, 2001. The city had shut down from Broadway to the airports. Tourism had died and swaths of Manhattan were closed to traffic. In the first four months after September 11, most drivers lost between 60 and 80 percent of their daily income. Suddenly, basic necessities—rent, medical care, car payments—slid beyond reach. Bankruptcy was widespread among the drivers. An Urban Justice Center (UJC) survey found that six out of every ten drivers surveyed had amassed debt between $5,000 and $10,000 as a direct result of September 11. Yet, following the lead of then-mayor Rudolph Giuliani, the Federal Emergency Management Agency (FEMA) declined even to entertain disaster assistance claims from taxi drivers.

Refused entry into the Disaster Assistance Center set up on the piers in Manhattan, driver after driver came to the Alliance office to complain. Their exclusion from the city's assistance programs was baffling. They had lost an enormous amount of business, suffering the impact of the closure of a number of sectors of New York City life.[2] By December 2001, when statistics became available, almost every taxi garage and broker had collected emergency assistance but drivers still had not.

The disparity reflected something larger about the country's response to tragedy. The spoils, at least as far as the taxi industry was concerned, had been grabbed by the white middle class and elite.

The wave of random arrests and detentions that was unleashed across America, and especially in urban centers like New York, clearly targeted South Asian and Middle Eastern working-class men. It was also this specific segment of the working class—the immigrant driver—that had been excluded from disaster assistance.

Slowly, the drivers began to mobilize. Their effort picked up steam in early 2002 as the drivers' anger overtook their fear. In March 2002 the Alliance organized a public hearing at Hunter College to which it invited FEMA officials along with a variety of public and private charity officials. The 300-seat auditorium was full an hour before the hearing began. One driver after another described his post–September 11 experience. By the end of the hearing, a crowd of close to 4,000 drivers had gathered, overflowing onto the street. FEMA and Taxi and Limousine Commission (TLC) officials looked stunned. Within weeks, FEMA announced that it was reopening the application process for an all-new Rental and Mortgage Assistance program. The Alliance held a series of FEMA clinics at the airports and at its office on how to apply for assistance. More than 2,000 drivers participated. It was the first successful mobilization against the post–9/11 American state, and it was planned and executed by an almost entirely immigrant workforce union.

Building on the momentum and success of the FEMA mobilization, the Alliance began to develop its livable wage campaign. The economic logic of this campaign for the taxi industry was simple. Drivers do not own the right to put a taxi on the street; that right is almost entirely monopolized by fleet garages and brokerage houses. Drivers lease taxis from these fleets and brokers, and then they drive to pay the rent on their cabs. Only after they make the rent in fares do drivers begin to earn money for themselves. This was hard enough to do pre–9/11, but, in early 2003, close to a year and a half after the September 11 attacks, most drivers estimated that business was still down by around 10 percent to 20 percent. At an average, drivers earned less than $500 per week—working in excess of 72 hours each week—while the garage owners and brokers collected, again at an average, in excess of $1,000 per week on each cab. A driver thus earned barely above minimum wage levels for a twelve-hour workday; the fundamental reason for this was simply that owners took away too large a chunk of the revenue earned by drivers through their lease and car payments.

Since the late 1960s, when the AFL-CIO union representing taxi drivers sold out workers' interests to the bosses, the drivers had been getting a raw deal on wages. Whenever the owners sought to impose a fare hike, they would launch a public relations campaign arguing that "hard-working drivers need a raise," but then they would pocket the proceeds of the fare hike by dramatically raising the lease on cabs.

In mid-2003, the Alliance made its final decision on its livable wage position and submitted a "petition for rule making" to the TLC. The demand was simple: a fare hike along with a reduction in the lease rate. This strategy, the Alliance explained at a press conference in September 2003, was the only way to create a livable wage for drivers; raising the fare alone would do nothing. The Alliance backed up its demands with a detailed report on lease rates as of April 2003 and followed this up with a survey establishing average base driver incomes for the industry. The survey report, called "Unfare," was published by the Urban Justice Center.[3] Meanwhile, as winter approached, the mobilization gathered momentum with large-scale outreach at the airports and during shift changes. The Alliance threatened to strike, and drivers girded up for a long one. No start date had been announced, but the rumor mill spun and the press began hinting at an impending Thanksgiving Day strike. Worried, the mayor's office called the Alliance.

The city regulates the amount of rent that owners can charge drivers with something called a lease cap—a set maximum a fleet or broker can charge a driver to lease a cab. The Alliance would not discuss a fare hike with the city unless a reduction in the lease cap was on the table. By late December, both sides had more or less agreed upon the rate of fare increase—26 percent—but the negotiations were stalled on the point of the lease caps. The owners had proposed a 23 percent fare increase and 23 percent lease cap increase—an offer unacceptable to the Alliance.

By late 2003, it was not just the negotiations that were stalled. There appeared to also be a limit to how the issue would be reported by the media. A large number of stories about the negotiations had appeared both in print and on television. Without exception, all of these reports followed the same story line: an image of a hard-working immigrant driver who deserved a raise, and a range of passenger opinions—some of which endorsed the idea that drivers deserved a raise and others which stated that the increase would hurt the average passenger. One television reporter even told the Alliance off the record that she had to search for more than half an hour to find a passenger who didn't support the increase but had to do so to make the story "balanced."

More important, there was a third element of this story that was just not being reported—that the owners charged a rent and that if the rent were to go up with the fare, then drivers would get nothing. This silence was inexplicable given the fact that the Alliance never held back in specifying this relation between the lease rate and the fare increase as its most critical issue, but the media seemed to prefer blocking it out. Something had to be done.

The Alliance went back to the drawing board and again began an intense driver mobilization effort. In a rain-soaked demonstration outside the TLC's offices on Rector Street in October 2003, driver anger at the commission and the mayor's office welled up.

The Alliance renewed its call for a strike if necessary. The first signs of a change in the media's stance came in a story in *Newsday* that acknowledged the link between lease rates, fare increases, and driver incomes. This was followed by an editorial in the *Daily News* that surprised everyone. The paper, thus far an unlikely ally of immigrant workers, called for a fare increase with "every penny of the increase going to the drivers."[4] The *New York Times,* in contrast, called for a fare increase that it conceded hard-working drivers deserved, but insisted that owners should be permitted to raise their rents as well, by an unspecified amount.[5]

With the strike call renewed and with the question of lease rates forced into public debate, the negotiations began to move forward again. In the end, on April 23, 2004, the Alliance agreed to a 26 percent fare increase with an 8 percent lease cap hike. The margin between the lease cap hike and the fare hike was sufficient to ensure an average 70–30 split in favor of the driver. Drivers and organizers knew there would still be battles to fight, especially with the fleet garages, who would try to squeeze this split into something closer to 50–50. But the favorable terms of the agreement would send the Alliance into battle with strong odds.

The FEMA settlement and the recent fare hike were dramatic successes for the Alliance, but they were not the union's first endeavors. The Alliance actually cemented its reputation as a quick and aggressive mobilizer with a series of strikes that brought New York City to a halt in May 1998. At that time, the Alliance was a fledgling organization with approximately 500 members. Though the strikes were in large part a success, the results were less clear.[6] The Alliance had not yet built its capacity to sustain a mobilization. Six years and five thousand members later, the Alliance has won two successive victories—one against a federal agency and the second against the taxi industry's ownership and the mayoral agency that oversees the industry, the Taxi and Limousine Commission. During those six years, the foundations laid by the 1998 strikes had been consolidated, built on through many campaigns, large and small.

When I began working with the Alliance in 1996, I had no understanding of the industry. Over the last eight years, different pieces of a complicated picture have come together. One is the story I started with in 1996—one that you may also have constructed as you sat in the backseats of yellow cabs, having quick and fragmentary conversations with drivers. Slowly parsing the names you see on the hack licenses displayed in the Plexiglas partitions of cabs, you may have noticed that most drivers in New York are Third World immigrants from Pakistan, Haiti, Bangladesh, Egypt, Senegal, India. From fleeting conversation, you may have gathered that most drivers don't own their taxis but instead lease them from garages and brokers for more than $100 a day, and that they are required to have two licenses—one a chauffeur license issued by the Department of Motor Vehicles, and one a "hack license," issued by the Taxi and Limousine Commission. (To earn a hack license, which a driver is required by law to display in his cab's partition, the driver must submit to eighty hours of classes and testing in map reading, English, etiquette, and taxi industry rules.)

If you are particularly curious, you might have also asked a driver what he or she thinks of the TLC or the garage owners. You would most likely have been told that the TLC is fundamentally antidriver, that the fleet bosses are millionaires, that the TLC courts are a sham, and that the garage owners are cheats.

From these passing conversations you may have put together the story of New York City yellow cabs: a fast and efficient transport system symbolic of the city, driven by Third World immigrant drivers looking for better lives than the ones available in their countries of origin. You may have concluded that, like their predecessors, the Italian or Irish drivers, these immigrants can expect to save money over a few years and move on to greener pastures. This is in fact the official story—one that allows us to recognize in the person behind the wheel of our taxi a shared aspiration to success and the simple dictums of hard work and diligence.

This book tells the other story, framed by two key moments in the history of taxi drivers' organizing work. It begins on May 13, 1998, when 24,000 New York yellow cab drivers went on strike, and it ends on May 3, 2004, when the New York Taxi Workers Alliance secured the biggest victory for drivers in over three decades. In recording this story of the evolution of driver power in the industry, my message is a simple one: that political victories are always won by long-term and sustained work, by building organizations and their bases brick by brick. In some part, then, this is the story of that incremental construction.

In describing the Alliance's organizing work, however, other stories emerge from the background, demanding to be told. If we can answer the question of why Mayor Giuliani and the rest of the city were able to ignore the collective call of drivers in 1998, maybe then we can understand why Bashir Ahmed finds it difficult to believe that the fare hike is real. Maybe we can really discover why a particular driver is in the United States rather than in his native Pakistan, and why it is that nearly all of New York's taxi drivers, restaurant workers, and parking lot attendants are Third World immigrants. Maybe we can figure out what exactly Giuliani was doing to New York City during the eight years of his mayorship. And maybe we can understand why Third World immigrant labor patterns are more aptly compared with those of African Americans than with Italian or Irish Americans. Maybe we can decide if multiculturalism, that wonderfully colorful umbrella under whose shade we welcome all the immigrants, is a reality or a fiction.

Maybe we can fathom why so many of us are silent when the INS and FBI tear down the doors of hundreds of impoverished and innocent immigrants in Midwood, Brooklyn. A hundred maybes. Maybe we can decide on the political choices we need to make and the future we want to construct.

ROOTS OF VICTORY:
THE TAXI STRIKES OF 1998

A LITTLE AFTER 1:00 P.M. on May 3, 1998, Saeed Ahmed, an organizer for the New York Taxi Workers Alliance (NYTWA), pulled into LaGuardia Airport's Delta–US Airways taxi holding lot. Nestled between the Delta and US Airways terminals, the holding lot is hidden from public view by the looming terminal buildings and the elevated ramps that connect the departure levels to the road below. To a passenger stepping off the line and into a cab, which then speeds through the airport complex's many ascending and descending ramps, the holding lot appears only as a passing peal of bright yellow down below. But it is from lots like this one that cabs appear, as if by magic, in front of the terminals just as passengers arrive.[1]

As Saeed eased his cab into the Delta holding lot, he noted that it was full: sixteen columns of yellow cabs, some 150 drivers, waiting for passengers. He parked his car and walked to the front of the lot, where he silently handed flyers to the drivers getting coffee at the food truck. The flyers had a simple message printed in big bold letters under the banner of the New York Taxi Workers Alliance: 24-HOUR STRIKE. Below that, in smaller print: May 13, 1998. As Saeed walked up and down the columns of cars dispensing flyers, a cheer rose. The drivers who had gathered around the food truck began calling for a longer strike.

"*Oye Saeed,*" an older driver from Faisalabad, Saeed's hometown in Pakistan, yelled across the lot in a Punjabi full of the tonal lilt so peculiar to that part of the subcontinent, *"yeh ek din da strike ki hai?"* ("Is it just a one-day strike?")

Saeed nodded. "Just one day, yes. For now."

He spoke to drivers standing in clusters of three or four, urging them not only to go on strike but to help get out the word. "Come by the office," he urged them. "Pick up as many flyers as you need."

In less than ten minutes the lot was abuzz with animated conversation, as drivers who had never before spoken to one another reflected together on the possibility of a strike.

HOLDING CONVERSATIONS

The holding lot is normally a quiet place, and sometimes the silence is a despairing one—especially on days like this one, when a few delayed flights combined with the routine mid-afternoon lull leads to a surfeit of cabs. Drivers find themselves waiting an hour, sometimes even two, for passengers. A couple of lost hours can cost a driver dearly, but such risks are a fact of daily life. Many drivers use the downtime to stretch their legs or grab a snack at the food truck, which serves overpriced, dried-out samosas and rolls sticky with stale oil from sitting on a hot plate for hours. The drivers sometimes joke that if anybody ever invented a way of screwing up a tea bag, the holding lot food truck would probably patent it. But, stuck in the lot, many drivers grudgingly shell out a dollar for bad coffee. Some prefer to stay in their cabs for a quick nap in the backseat if the day is not oppressively hot or bitingly cold. If it's not too windy, others will step out of their cars and spread newspapers across their hoods to read. The holding lot is like a badly maintained public park without the shade of the trees, a place where drivers who would rather be working have little choice but to relax and catch up with each other. And if the moment of asking after each other lasts too long and the lines don't move, it can become a deeply depressing place.

An hour into Saeed's work in the holding lot, two more Alliance organizers, Javaid Tariq and Bhairavi Desai, arrived. Bhairavi's arrival created a stir. Many drivers knew her as the one person they could talk with, someone who could answer their questions. In the two years she had been working as the Alliance's only full-time organizer, Bhairavi had built a powerful reputation among drivers as a fearless, effective, and committed organizer.

Discussions grew more animated as the crowd swelled around Bhairavi. Within minutes she was relieved of more than half of the five hundred flyers she had brought into the lot. Drivers came up and took them in stacks. "For my garage this evening," a driver would say, taking charge of fifty flyers. By late afternoon Alliance organizers began arriving in groups. The lines were moving now, but every driver entering the lot was leaving with a flyer.

"*Idea tho sahi hai,*" a frail sardar driver told Saeed, "*lekin, yeh sab karenge* strike?" His eyes moved across the lot as he asked whether Saeed believed that all the drivers would strike. Saeed nodded.

Amid the excitement, there were also many drivers whose only reaction to the flyer was silence. They watched and listened as their fellow drivers worked the idea through: Why should we strike? What will the strike bring us? For how many days should we take action? Is one day enough? The silence was a sign that not everybody was engaged enough to offer an opinion. "It's our responsibility . . . to each other," Saeed answered. Later, reporting back at the Alliance office, he said "*Kaam shuru hua hai . . . kuch mat poochau ki kya hoga,*" explaining that at the end of day one, everything was still up in the air.

Back in Manhattan, Javaid Tariq and I met up just before his shift ended. Our task was to monitor the CB radio. Javaid had just come into Manhattan after his brief visit to the LaGuardia holding lot. His face was flushed with excitement. *"Aare Biju Bhai, kafi shor mach gaya hai,"* he said, as he told me about the lively discussion that had unfolded at LaGuardia, especially after Bhairavi had arrived.

Javaid had been driving yellow taxis for six years when he first came to an Alliance meeting. An occasional photographer, an undying romantic, and a terribly gentle soul, he wore a sixties-style ponytail. I had joined the Alliance as a volunteer organizer a few weeks after Bhairavi had started full time. Javaid, Kulwinder, Tahir, Yunus, Manjit, Moiuddin, and Kursheed had all come in the immediate months that followed.

I'm sure that for many of the founding activists, my interest in organizing immigrant yellow-cab drivers was a bit of an enigma: a professor of business whose specialty was computers didn't fit the standard image of a labor organizer. Many of the early conversations focused on building trust more than anything else. Bhairavi's commitment, her capacity to create spaces where such conversations were possible, and her clear vision for the organization had been critical in forging these early relationships.

Javaid hesitated a moment before continuing his summary. "It's a good start, really good, but you will hear, there is some confusion too," he said, then turned up the volume on his CB radio. For a brief moment it was only static. Then the CB crackled and we landed in the middle of an ongoing conversation. A raspy voice burst out in Punjabi: *"Oye beerya . . . chotta da haalat karab hai. . . ."* A pause and then he continued, *"Bas strike di baat chalriai. . . ."* I looked to Javaid for a translation. He smiled, knowing what had confused me. *Chotta* just means small, so the driver's statement that things were not good at *chotta* made little sense to me. "*Chotta* is LaGuardia," he explained, "and *Badda* (big) is JFK." It was apparent that in the crowded lots at LaGuardia the strike was the biggest discussion piece.

Another voice cut in: *"Haan ji . . . kuldip . . . main bhi uthe aa raha hun . . . ye strike da kya kissa hai. . . ."* The newcomer had apparently just begun his shift and had heard nothing of the strike yet. Immediately the channel exploded into conversation about the purpose of the strike. A few voices were speaking in Punjabi, some in Urdu, and others in English. Javaid recognized one of those giving answers—"There," he said, "that's Ilyas." Ilyas Khan, another Alliance organizing committee member, was plugging the strike in English, knowing that there would be drivers on the channel who wouldn't understand either Punjabi or Urdu. (CB channel 31 was unofficially called the "international channel." Of all the driver CB stations, it had the largest number of users and was the prime channel for disseminating information. Every driver with a CB tuned in to check out how the city was doing. Haitians and Bengalis, Colombians and Egyptians, all understood the codes: *Babba,* though Punjabi for "old man," also meant Lincoln Center, for example, and *Billi* was a reference to the Broadway musical "Cats." The codes on 31 moved between languages freely.)

Ilyas was providing a quick but detailed summary. He spoke like a seasoned CB user, his voice low-pitched and unexcited, an almost perfect monotone. Too many voice modulations can produce static and variable receiving strengths. Ilyas was one of the older drivers in the industry. His age and experience gave him a status on the CB that a new driver could never have.

"But who is calling the strike?" another newcomer asked. Javaid waited to see if Ilyas would respond. He didn't, probably lost in some static at his end. Javaid picked up the mouthpiece, hit the button, and said in his own seasoned CB monotone, *"Bhaiyon . . . strike Taxi Workers Alliance de naal organize hondi hai."* He looked at me to see if I wanted to join in, but I shook my head. He introduced himself as part of the organizing committee of the Taxi

Workers Alliance and explained that the strike was to last all day on the thirteenth of the month.

Ilyas came back in to acknowledge Javaid: *"Haan ji bhai Javaid . . . sadde pas flyer hai."* Javaid was quick to pick up on the opening Ilyas had offered him: "Hey, brother, do you have any flyers on you?" He announced, this time in English, that flyers for the strike were available at the Alliance office, and gave out the organization's address and phone number.

Another burst of conversation followed. Some drivers ignored the strike announcement, asking instead how JFK was doing or how bad traffic was on the Brooklyn Bridge. Maybe they had heard about the strike already. Maybe the possibility of being stuck on the Brooklyn Bridge was a more immediate problem than a strike some days away. Maybe they were among the many at this point who were unconvinced. One man's voice rose to a higher pitch, with a trace of anger. "Who the hell is the Taxi Alliance?" he asked, and what assurance could we give him that the cops wouldn't turn nasty during the strike?

Javaid shot me a sharp look and responded: "The call is for a strike, not for a procession or a demonstration, brother. We stay at home on the thirteenth. We took the decision exactly for the reason you said, that we should not give Giuliani a chance to get us till we are a lot stronger."

The response came back quickly. The voice had lost its irritated edge. "I see, I see . . . I understand," The speaker paused, then returned to his question, "But what is this Taxi Alliance?"

Javaid began again: "It's a new union, brother . . . we are driver-led and driver-focused . . . and we are here to replace that useless old union. . . . You may not be a member now, but we hope you will be soon. And the best way to show your support is to put your weight behind the strike." He trailed off and waited. That driver fell silent, and another round of questions emerged.

A driver with a markedly Haitian accent asked in English what would happen to his cab lease if he were to take action. Immediately different strategies were suggested. Another Haitian driver asked him who his broker was before giving his suggestion. "I am going to tell my broker that he is not getting a penny in lease for the days of strike." A moment of static followed this suggestion before the sardar with the raspy voice we had first heard asked, this time in English, "And what if he take my car then, man?"

Ilyas moved into the silence the question left in its wake. "Nobody knows all the answers, brother . . . but if anybody has any trouble, the Alliance will give you legal support," he said, starting out in English but quickly switching to Punjabi. Someone else joined in, translating Ilyas's answer and then asking for the Alliance number.

Javaid turned to me and said, "We must listen to the other channels also." I nodded and he went back on the air. *"Ilyas saab,"* he announced, waiting for Ilyas to answer before telling him that he was getting off.

We surfed all the channels, staying on each long enough to get a sense of what was happening. Most of the other channels were also abuzz with talk of the strike. Some of them were small groups of ten, maybe twenty, drivers who knew each other. There were others, like the three Bengali channels and the one Spanish channel, that were run by organized memberships such as the Bengal Cabbie Society, the Shapla Welfare Society, the Bengal Yellow Society, and Los Pantheros, each a driver-welfare organization with its own channel. On our second run-through, we announced the strike and the Alliance coordinates on the six channels where we heard no activity, just in case there were some silent listeners.

Now Javaid was running late for his shift change. He cursed under his breath. Drawn into the back and forth, we had lost track of time, but as he swung into the Mobil station on Second

Avenue to hand over his cab, Javaid was smiling. Fewer than a thousand yellow taxis had CBs, but they formed a critical backbone in driver communications. Later that evening the smaller cell-phone networks—groups of five to ten drivers who spoke with each other through the shift, exchanging information about what was happening around the city—would all be talking about the strike.

THE SAFETY CHARADE

On May 2, 1998, the previous night, the Alliance's organizing committee (OC) held an emergency meeting at its West Twenty-seventh Street office. The meeting had been called in response to new rules, purportedly designed to improve taxi safety, that had been announced earlier in the week by the TLC. Sixteen members of the OC sat around the table and considered these proposals, which included higher fines, higher liability insurance requirements, and mandatory drug testing.

The new system also included a different way of attaching penalty points to the drivers' licenses. The rules sought suspension or revocation of a driver's hack license if he accumulated more than six points on either his regular license or his hack license in an eighteen-month period. This is in contrast to laws covering a driver of a private car, who can accumulate eleven points on his or her license before facing temporary suspension, and fourteen before revocation. While an ordinary private-car driver spends about two to three hours per day behind the wheel on average, a yellow cab driver clocks twelve driving hours per day; probability alone would dictate that a yellow cab driver stands a higher chance of accumulating points on his license.

"The rules make no sense," Ilyas said, his face pensive and creased with worry. "It would be impossible to survive these rules if they actually implement them. Six points in eighteen months . . .

that's two or maybe three red lights, gridlock, unsafe drop-off, or any such stupid ticket. I spend twelve hours a day on the street and if I get one of these tickets every six months, I am dead. If I were to get just DMV tickets, I stand a chance. I can go to DMV court and explain that I didn't cut a light . . . but I'm sure they'll give out TLC tickets for everything and we all know that in TLC court we are guilty even before the hearing starts. . . ."

Ilyas trailed off, lost in thought. The meeting fell into silence. It was true. Every driver in the industry knew that the TLC court system was rigged against the driver. In eight years of organizing in the industry, I have not met a single driver who felt otherwise. The TLC is the second highest revenue earner for the city, following just behind the Parking Violations Bureau. Drivers understand that, given this fact, they are better off paying a fine than trying to dispute a ticket in the TLC courts, even when the drivers are entirely convinced of their innocence.

The proposals, those at the meeting agreed, were punitive, and had little to do with safety.

"How does increasing the fine by 300 percent increase safety?" Javaid asked. "It increases fear for sure! It increases pressure . . . and it increases the city budget . . . but safety? I want to know who wrote these rules. I can say that they have never driven a yellow cab on the streets of NYC . . . not even for a day."

As angry as he was, Javaid was the last person on the OC to agree to the strike. In the end he was convinced not because of the specific problems with each new rule but because of the way the rules were being introduced. The TLC had not made any attempt to consult drivers, the people whose working lives were about to alter dramatically.

"Who, may I ask, knows more about safety and driving than a driver?" Bhairavi demanded of the press a day before the strike. "Who is most interested in driving being a safe occupation? Who is the most affected by these rules? The answer to all these questions is 'the yellow-cab driver.' And yet the mayor and the TLC chair, who have never sat behind the wheel of a yellow cab, make decisions without as much as a word with the drivers."

Although the new rules were being sold to the New York public as a "safety reform," they were based on little more than a patchwork of ill-informed assumptions about taxi driving, including racist stereotypes about immigrant taxi drivers as well as deliberately obfuscated statistics. Asif Shah, normally silent, summed it up: "I got a ticket for an unclean taxi cab in the past . . . and guess what was on the backseat that made my taxi unclean? A chewing gum wrapper. Not even chewing gum, just the wrapper some passenger left on the seat. Now they have doubled the fine for an unclean cab and they are telling the public that a chewing gum wrapper in the backseat is somehow harmful to their lives. Let's face it . . . this is about harassment, this is about making money. . . . What do they want me to do . . . get out of the cab after I drop each passenger and check the backseat for chewing gum wrappers? What is more dangerous—a wrapper, or me getting in and out of the taxi each time I do a drop-off?"

Javaid, too, was fuming. He lit up another cigarette and exploded the moment Asif stopped talking: "Now tell me, how the hell am I posing any danger to a nonexistent passenger if I am parked safely at a taxi stand and smoking a cigarette to cool my nerves after dealing with a pathetic racist passenger who has just gotten out of my cab? Why have they doubled the fine for smoking in my own cab? And what if I have a passenger who is smoking in my cab . . . am I responsible for that too? And look at this . . . the fine has been doubled for having three receipts hanging off the meter. Three receipts!! Three pieces of paper! Is that some kind of a weapon that an angry immigrant driver will use to stab a bloody passenger? . . . These guys are mad. . . . I am telling you . . . these rules have nothing to do with safety."

His hands swept over the papers that lay across the table. Even the rules that could be construed as safety-related were clearly designed to punish drivers more than to increase taxicab safety.

"Like the 'unsafe passenger drop-off,'" Ilyas said, smirking. "Now I know that I should drop a passenger off close to the curb and not in the middle of the street. But you tell me, what am I to do if a passenger throws the money into the front seat and jumps out of the cab when I am waiting at a light? The same TLC says I am not allowed to lock my doors, so I cannot stop passengers from jumping out of the cab whenever they want to. Will they fine the passenger? Of course not."

A cursory analysis of the data the TLC had at its disposal would have revealed that the number of accidents involving yellow cabs had steadily decreased over the previous five years (1994–98). But the TLC worked hard to misrepresent such data. That effort was led by the same TLC chair—Diane McGrath McKechnie—who, under Giuliani's instructions, cut the entire research division of the TLC lest it produce information the mayor didn't like.

By 1:00 A.M., the fifth hour of the OC meeting, the anger around the table was palpable. Bhairavi had been silent for the last half-hour, listening intently as different individuals shared fine-tuned assessments of the daily driving experience. Now she spoke. "We need to respond," she said. "What do you think we should do?" She stopped, wanting to say a bit more, but looking around the table, inviting ideas.

Saeed was the first to respond. He had walked into the meeting that evening convinced from his many conversations with drivers that the only effective response to the rules was a strike. "What is there to think about in this?" he asked. "Let's go on strike. Every driver I have spoken to in the last two days agrees that a strong response is important."

A silence fell across the table. In a matter of a few moments Bhairavi and Saeed had taken the whole meeting forward, moving from anger and analysis to the idea of action.

It was Ilyas who broke the silence. "Yes," he agreed. "We have to respond. Even if we fail, we must respond . . . because not to respond means to accept the disrespect."

As the strike idea caught fire, it brought another question to the fore: How would we mobilize? Nothing so momentous had happened in the industry in decades. The Alliance's membership stood at approximately six hundred, a significant but nevertheless very small fraction (less than 3 percent) of the total driver population. "How can we reach out and mobilize?" we asked each other, and spent the next two hours working out the initial logistics.

After much discussion, May 13 emerged as the best date for the strike. Strategies were assessed and responsibilities divided up. The first five thousand flyers would be ready by noon the next day.

THE STRIKE THAT WAS NOT TO BE

By May 6, 1998, we had reached out to many small driver-welfare organizations with whom the Alliance had a history of association. All of them endorsed the strike call. At an assessment meeting that afternoon, we determined that while nothing was certain, we were most likely headed toward a successful strike. Mamnun ul Huq, an Alliance organizer and key member of the Bengal Cabbie Society, was particularly confident. Moiuddin Ahmed, who was much older than the others and a longtime Alliance organizer, couldn't attend the meeting but sent his brother, Jasim, in his place.

Jasim didn't share Mamnun's optimism. "Everybody agrees,"

he said, "but until I see them talking to one another and pushing one another, I cannot be sure."

Asif Shah was far more concerned about what the city would do to break the strike. "Whether or not the drivers are joining in, that is no longer the point," he maintained. "We have already committed to the strike. The question now is how will the city respond?"

As the evening drew to a close, the committee drew up elaborate outreach maps and assigned tasks for the next four days. Saeed was to continue with intensive contact at LaGuardia as well as to reach out to the large group of West African drivers who ate lunch all along Central Park West. Bhairavi, Rizwan, and I would focus on the southern Manhattan shift-change locations where day drivers handed their cars over to their night-shift partners. Asif would do most of his work at the Lexington Avenue restaurants. Javaid and Jasim were to focus on the Manhattan garages. Mamnun would continue with late-night outreach in all the Bangladeshi restaurants; he was also to contact all the driver welfare societies, and to conduct early morning sweeps of the large garages in Manhattan, including Susan Maintenance, Ann Service, Andy's, and Doc's. Ilyas was in charge of Long Island City and the Bronx. When Manjit returned from India, he would take on much of the work in the Richmond Hill restaurants. Parnell was to visit the Haitian restaurants on the West Side and Harlem.

The map was complicated and never complete. Every member of the OC was stretched to the maximum and beyond. Many organizers were in debt because they were giving up driving time for meetings and outreach. But the commitment was firm and the decision was made. There was no turning back.

On the evening of May 7, another five thousand flyers went out. I drove with Ilyas to Glenty's, a garage in the Bronx, to speak with the drivers there because the Bronx garages had received little attention. Though the lease manager at the garage blocked our entry, drivers came out onto the street, promising that everyone would be informed of the strike and persuaded to participate. Gamal, an Egyptian driver, was vehement and clear: "You know how they will stop us . . . by telling me that the Pakistanis are not cooperating and by telling the Pakistanis that the Bangladeshis are going to drive. . . . We have to tell each other that we are going to strike . . . give each other confidence. That is the only way."

By now the Alliance office was abuzz with activity as drivers came off the streets and signed up to work for the strike. Drivers had taken the original flyer and added to it. One had translated part of the flyer into Bengali, incorporated a few additional slogans into it, and made a thousand new photocopies. Other drivers were volunteering to make several hundred copies daily of each new flyer the Alliance put out. The pace of events had intensified.

The TLC's first response to the strike call was to ignore it, evidently hoping it would just go away. But then rumors started circulating that the TLC had asked the largest fleet owners in the city to mobilize against the action. Many garage owners repeatedly told drivers not to "waste everybody's time and money." On May 5, one garage owner told an Alliance organizer to "use your money to hire a good lawyer who can sue the city. Don't piss in the wind with all this strike talk." The organizer was undaunted. "Just stand out of the way when I do piss in the wind," he said, "if you know what's good for you."

On May 6, the Alliance met with representatives of Local 3036 (later to merge with Local 74), the AFL-CIO union in the industry. The local had a miniscule membership, but it did have some valuable infrastructure. The organizers called on the local to endorse the strike and asked it to put, as an act of solidarity, its name on the strike bill as one of the sponsoring organizations. The local refused. Larry Goldberg, one of its officers, was skeptical. "Do you really think this strike is going to happen?" he asked. His question showed how out of touch he and his organization were with the taxi drivers in the city. He was evidently not aware that the taxi industry and driver community had progressed past the point where Local 3036 had abandoned them in the mid-1980s.

The last round of ten thousand flyers was circulated on May 11, announcing the location of the strike headquarters at Jinnah Hall, as the basement of the Kashmir restaurant on Eighth Avenue between Thirty-ninth and Fortieth Streets was sometimes called. By this time, most drivers on the street were refusing flyers because they had them already, indicating their support with a cheery thumbs-up.

At a little after midnight on the May 11, Mamnun and I did a run up Eighth Avenue toward my home. We slowly worked our way uptown, stopping at every light with our windows rolled down, handing out flyers to the cabs beside us. "The thirteenth?" a Haitian driver asked me. "You guys all set?" I nodded. "I am too!" he yelled as his car pulled out. The drivers were beginning to give one another confidence, the way Gamal had said they would.

Passengers, too, had started to hear about the strike and to ask questions. The studied indifference of the mayor's office and the TLC was not doing much to boost public confidence in the face of a growing wave of press coverage of the strike. While many passengers were irritated, if not downright hostile, about the potential inconvenience, some wanted to know why the strike was being organized and how they could help. For the first time in decades, drivers and passengers had conversations about more than just the weather or the news.

Ilyas came in laughing one evening. "You have no idea how badly informed our passengers are. We really need to do something," he said. "I just dropped somebody off at a restaurant on Bleecker who had no idea that we leased the taxi, that we paid rent on it, that we didn't own it, that we hardly make any money.

He kept talking to me as if I made a lot of money, and for a long time, we kept misunderstanding each other. I was saying that it was a bad job and he thought I was talking about crime for some reason, and not the money or the long hours."

Asif and Jasim joined the conversation. Jasim had just explained to a passenger that drivers always prefer to take the quickest route, because they make more money that way. "You know, American culture is all about ripping people off. If you can find a way, you rob somebody. That's the rule. Nobody gives a shit if somebody is dying; you see if you can make some money off that situation. . . . and that's what the passengers think about us. So every time this passenger sat in a cab he thought the driver was going to take him on a long ride through the five boroughs!"

Jasim was indignant at the passenger's ignorance. Drivers make most of their money on ten-to twenty-block runs, which allow them to get a high turnover of $2.00 minimum fares. It's in a driver's interest to get a passenger to his or her destination as quickly as possible so that he can pick up a new fare. On longer runs, especially if the driver hits traffic, there is less money to be made. " 'Why would I take someone around the same block again and again, sir?' " Jasim recounted. " 'I make more money if I drop you off quickly,' I told him," Jasim ended his story triumphantly. "And guess what he said! 'I don't know, man . . . you tell me . . . this is America!' "

On May 11, Mayor Giuliani denounced the strike as an effort by a small group of drivers to ensure they could drive around the city at reckless speeds without losing their driving privileges. On May 12, he predicted that at most two hundred drivers would strike. "A set of bad apples," he called them. Police Commissioner Howard Safir joined the mayor in heaping scorn on the drivers. He called those planning to strike or demonstrate "taxi terrorists."

As popular support surged, many of the garage owners who

had earlier dismissed the strike started changing their tune. Some who had initially barred the distribution of strike flyers in their garages began encouraging drivers to strike. Some, once they saw the strike as inevitable, even went so far as to announce that no cars would leave their garages on May 13, either because they feared violence and potential damage to their cars, or because they were themselves against the new rules.

Only city officials continued to pretend nothing was happening. "What strike?" the mayor asked on the May 12. "We really don't think this will have any significant impact on the city," Diane McGrath McKechnie, the TLC chairwoman, told the *New York Times* the same day. "In the event that it is larger than we expect, the Police Department is geared up, the Transit Authority is geared up, and we're ready."

We were ready, too. Things were running at fever pitch at the Alliance office. Venantius Pinto, a local South Asian artist, painted posters with the able assistance of other brush-wielding volunteers. Press packets rolled off our borrowed printer, and we made do with a temperamental photocopier that refused to work if the humidity level was high. At this point, our office consisted of one desk and two chairs squeezed in the middle of the already-crowded office of the Brecht Forum, the educational non-profit organization with which we had shared space since early 1998.

By 6:00 P.M. on May 12 it seemed as if everyone except Rudy Giuliani and Diane McGrath McKechnie understood that there would be a strike in the city the next morning. Members of the mainstream press streamed in and out of the office. Television crews and reporters arrived with only one question: "How big will this one be?" Alliance organizers were confident something major was in the works, but last-minute organizational matters needed to be addressed that were more pressing than the size of the strike.

"There should be no violence against any drivers." This was

Bhairavi's opening line at the Alliance late-night meeting on May 12. She continued: "And you can be sure that the cops will do everything to provoke violence. When Giuliani realizes that he has egg on his face, he will encourage the cops, so we need to be careful. We know that we can have a good and peaceful strike tomorrow, but given the tension that the cops are bound to create, our single most important concern will be those few drivers who may try and come in to work. There will be hundreds of people looking for cabs and the trouble that can start will surely be exploited by the cops. Cabs may be confiscated, drivers harassed, arrested, and beaten up. . . . Our task is to protect the drivers who do not join the strike, whatever their reasons may be."

Some drivers had talked about giving nonparticipating drivers *chakka jams* (flat tires in the middle of the road so as to immobilize traffic), but once again, Bhairavi's clarity was remarkable, and she turned a mood of antagonism into one of concern and solidarity. We spent the next hour chalking out a two-tiered strategy. At 5:00 A.M., Alliance teams would fan out along the bridges connecting Queens and Brooklyn to Manhattan to talk to the drivers coming to work, if any did. Our task was to convince them to turn around by pointing out that they would be sitting targets for cops and angry passengers. Bhairavi, Ilyas, and Mamnun would work the lights on Tillary Street just before the bridge on the Brooklyn side. Javaid, Taara, and Narges were to take on the Fifty-ninth Street Bridge. I lived too far uptown to get to any of these points easily, so my job was to keep track of the media and to do as many interviews as I could on morning radio shows. At 7:00 A.M., all of us were to meet at Jinnah Hall. Another team of volunteers would head for the airports and the train and bus stations to leaflet stranded passengers, explaining to them the conditions that forced the strike and arguing that their ire should be directed at the mayor and the TLC rather than the drivers. After a final update, the passenger information flyer was sent to the moody photo-copier.

Many drivers were eager to volunteer for the novel and important task of passenger education. "How often do you get a chance to tell passengers what driving means?" Rizwan asked. "It's like this: when a passenger gets into your cab, it's a different situation. The first thing they do is run a glance over the hack license and rate card. Immediately they have so much power over you. They know your name, your religion, your face . . . and generally the first question they ask is 'Where are you from?' As if it is their right to know that. It would be different if they said, 'Hey, my name is Joe Smith and I work at so and so place . . . and live in Chelsea,' and then asked me what my name was or where I was from. But that doesn't happen. My normal answer is always 'You tell me where you are from and then I will,' or if I am in a bad mood, 'None of your business.' Either way I know I am taking a risk by irritating them . . . but what can I do? I really feel there should be some equality between driver and passenger if we are to have an honest conversation."

Everyone around the table echoed Rizwan's point of view. The drivers were eager to not just educate the passengers, but to talk to them as equals.

At 2:00 A.M., after one last cheer, the OC headed out of the office together to catch up on some much-needed sleep. Three hours later, I awoke to two alarm clocks going off simultaneously, and took a moment before rising to imagine what was happening outside.

Just after five, I called Mamnun's cell phone. Bhairavi answered. From the calm, triumphant tone of her voice alone, I knew that the strike was on.

"We are in good shape," she said. She told me that some television crews were headed for the bridge.

I tried to get my television to cooperate, but to no avail, so I flipped across frequencies on the radio to get an idea of the media coverage before going on the air myself. Then, from 5:30 to 6:30, I talked to one station after another, insisting as politely as possible that the mayor's rhetoric equating immigrant drivers to a "public safety" threat was empty, racist, and manipulative. Who could care more about safety than the worker who drives twelve hours a day in order to put bread on the table for his family?

That such obvious truths needed repetition was depressing, and my mood was low when I got into the car with Raju Rajan, the volunteer from the Forum of Indian Leftists (FOIL) who was to drive me downtown. Already, by 7:00 A.M., the day was brutally humid. But as we drove away, I heard the voice of an old woman on the car radio denounce Giuliani and declare her complete agreement with the Taxi Workers Alliance. I was elated. As we flew down Riverside Drive, each empty block vindicated our optimism. From Washington Heights all the way to Fortieth Street, I saw just one yellow cab, and that was a 6Y medallion—an undercover cop cab.

And so it came to be that more than 24,000 New York city yellow cab drivers—more than 98 percent of the active workforce of the city's yellow cab industry—struck from 5:00 A.M. on May 13, 1998, to 5:00 A.M. on May 14. It was the single largest worker mobilization the city had seen in more than two decades. The mayor whom nobody dared oppose was effectively challenged, and the tide had begun to turn.

A sea of journalists passed through Jinnah Hall, and the OC held two press conferences during the day. Just outside, the cops had set up a pen to contain the strike supporters. Drivers came in large numbers, mostly in groups of friends or neighbors, between 9:00 A.M. and 7:00 P.M., to take turns standing in protest outside, chanting slogans and making speeches to stranded passengers and

anyone else who would listen. We discovered many future organizers that day. Kevin Fitzpatrick stood in the pen for hours, speaking in detail about the history of the taxi industry; Mohammed
Kazem stayed the whole day and expressed his determination to
work with us in the future; Shagur, Ahmed, and Wadud, all of
whom would remain involved in the Alliance in the months to
come, walked through the door into Jinnah Hall that day for the
first time.

The atmosphere at strike headquarters was electric as the media
tried to fathom how immigrants of so many different ethnicities
had united in the action. Many reporters found it difficult to understand how just one week after India's nuclear test, followed by
Pakistan's ominous promise to respond in kind, Indian and Pakistani drivers could be brothers on the streets of New York.

"Why?" Ilyas asked a reporter, frowning irritably. "Is it that
you don't expect us to get along? Do all Americans go around
with a desire to beat up Russians? Or is it that because we are from
some other part of the world we are not capable of thinking. . . ."
He stopped, waiting for a moment to swallow his aggravation.
"Listen, man," he said at last, "when a New York cop stops me on
the streets, he isn't asking me if I am Indian or Pakistani. For him,
we are all the same."

FIFTY WAYS TO BREAK A STRIKE:
THE MAYOR AND THE TAXI BOSSES

Even as 24,000 drivers stood together to tell him how much they
were hurting and wanted a dialogue, New York's mayor proceeded
to move ahead with his plans for taxi industry "reform." Giuliani
denounced the strike as "a demonstration for the purpose of being
able to drive recklessly," telling reporters at city hall, "We've gotten
a surprisingly large number of calls saying this was one of the more

pleasant days in a long time. If they would like to stay at home forever, they can stay at home forever. The city will function very well
without them. It functioned very well today without them."

In the days that followed, the driver community was abuzz.
The mayor had not backed down. What was next? The Alliance
called an open meeting for drivers on May 16 at 2:00 A.M., the tail
end of the night shift, to plan a future course of action. More
than 800 drivers came through the Alliance office doors that
night, making Twenty-seventh Street a sea of yellow as a rolling
series of twenty-minute meetings drew 100 to 150 drivers at a
time to the tenth floor. As the night progressed, the crowd
expanded, overflowing the Alliance's office space. Organizers
moved the meeting onto the street, where Bhairavi climbed onto
the roof of a cab in order to address the last meeting of 200-odd
drivers. By the night's end, a consensus had emerged: a second
strike was to be called for May 21.

One significant obstacle the Alliance had encountered while organizing for May 13 was opposition from an owner-driver–led
organization called the United Yellow Cab Association, or United.
This group of primarily Sikh drivers who owned their own medallions had, with the sponsorship of a Greek brokerage and garage
owner named Gus of Mystic Brokerage, for a brief period openly
mobilized against the strike. For Gus and many other garage
owners, the emergence of a driver-led organization was an unwelcome development. In response, these owners did something they
had done in the past: they set up an in-house "union" with owner-
drivers as its apparent leaders. When it became plainly apparent
that the May 13 strike was going ahead and there was nothing
United could do about it, the "union's" leadership called the
Alliance office and announced United's support. In the hope of
continued cooperation, we let them know about the second strike
we were planning for May 21.

United's response was unexpected and unwelcome. The "union" announced that it had decided convene a taxicab procession across the Queensboro Bridge the same day as our strike. We thought this was a bad idea. A procession would only give Giuliani a chance to mobilize his forces against us, bringing drivers under a greater threat of violence. We met with United representatives at Gus's Brooklyn office and attempted to get our point across, but they were adamant. Santok Singh, one of their officers, told us, "You did the strike, now allow us to do what we want."

It was only as the meeting proceeded that we realized what was really happening. The first clue was the presence of nondrivers like Gus, who walked in and out of the meeting as if he owned the place (which of course he did), and Ron Sherman, the president of the Metropolitan Taxi Board of Trade, the garage owners' association. Sherman was sprawled in a chair in Gus's meeting room when we arrived, all smiles, and clearly chummy with the United people. He proceeded to try everything short of bribery to convince us not to go on strike. As Bhairavi said later that evening on our way back to the office, "His pockets must have been burning each time we mentioned the word strike."

The United leadership's proposals were a mess of contradictions. They alternately insisted on marching across the bridge, and then suggested that they could strike some kind of a deal with the mayor. Each time the discussion reached an impasse, one or more officers would pop out of the room, have a quick, hushed conversation with Gus, and return with a new, equally unpalatable offer. It wasn't exactly clear what they were up to. Occasionally the United representatives would cede the floor to Farooq Bhatti, president and probably sole member of Pak Brothers Yellow Cab Association, whose primary work in the industry seemed to be that of a tout for a few DMV lawyers. He repeatedly tried to convince us to relinquish all control over May 21 and work under the leadership of United in a cab-based procession across the bridge.

Again we outlined our objections. Bhairavi was steadfast. "A procession across the bridge would be a gift to Giuliani in a public relations war. What is crucial at this moment is to strike the city with the same vehemence as we did on May 13—bring the city to a standstill. Each successful day of strike will expose Giuliani more, and the day will come when we can take a procession out and he will be powerless against it. Already just with one strike, public perception has begun to shift in favor of drivers, especially since Giuliani was so way off in his understanding of the mobilization. If we go ahead with a procession across the bridge, every car that appears on the streets would be subject to intense harassment if it refused to pick up passengers. And moreover, any effort that involves picking up the cars in the morning instead of leaving them parked and dead in the garages would involve garage owners."

After seven hours of discussion, the United leadership came clean with a piece of information it had been withholding all day: "We're trying to make a deal with the mayor through a contact," one of United's leaders informed us. "Will the Alliance agree to go along with it?"

Suddenly the real situation became clear. The presence of Ron Sherman that morning at the meeting, the hushed conversations with Gus outside the meeting room, and now the offer of an unspecified deal with the mayor—everything added up. Giuliani had used one of his major South Asian supporters, a businessman by the name of Shafqat Chaudhury, who ran a big black-car operation called Elite Limousine, to negotiate with the owners on how to end the strike and break the unity among drivers. Chaudhury had roped in a range of cronies to help, primarily United. We rejected the idea of any deal that had not been approved by the drivers themselves and told the United representatives so, in no uncertain terms. The meeting ended then and there. It was clear that the mayor's office was moving to crush the mobilization.

On May 21, the Giuliani administration opened up a widespread, military-style operation. Riot police and armored vehicles blocked the Queensboro Bridge, preventing all taxis without passengers from entering Manhattan from Brooklyn or Queens in order to join the United procession. The Alliance refused to call off the strike and remained silent on the subject of the procession. The United owner group was forced to join the strike. More than twenty thousand drivers observed the strike call. On the bridge, the mayor's armed forces broke up the taxicab procession, finally allowing drivers to march on foot after at least four of them had been harassed and arrested. A driver who had joined the march said, "If I wasn't a driver and didn't know what was happening, I would have thought that Giuliani was going after the KGB, not ordinary immigrant drivers. You should seen the number of cops in riot gear there!"

In the end, May 21 had two consequences. First, it became obvious to the mayor and the ownership that the Alliance would not budge from its position on renegotiating the "reform" package. After all, the second strike the Alliance had called came through, and driver participation remained high. Second, the confusion that the mayor and the ownership had hoped to seed in their discussions with United had begun to take root. The mayor's brutal response to the procession demoralized the drivers. As one driver said at the end of the day, "After I saw what happened on the bridge, I agreed that this mayor was indeed a fascist."

In the course of the two strikes, the city administration had justified its violent attitude toward an immigrant labor force by conjuring racist stereotypes with epithets like "taxi terrorist." Giuliani depicted immigrant drivers as uncaring, brutal men who would not hesitate to block the passage of ambulances carrying dying old women. It was a calculated strategy that Giuliani knew he could sell to the "tough on crime" white middle class. Unfortunately for Giuliani, the drivers involved in the action showed deep-seated commitment to peaceful protest. The most violent action on either strike day occurred when some drivers threw an egg at a scab taxi, which turned out to be driven by undercover cops who immediately arrested the egg throwers and confiscated their hack licenses.

In those fifteen days of May 1998, Giuliani was revealed as a virulently antiworker mayor—one more ready than any public official in recent New York history to stoop to anything to break the backs of the workers who kept "his" city running. The pro-immigrant rhetoric of his election campaign was quickly belied as his administration used every trick in the book to fracture the remarkable unity displayed by an immigrant workforce. Citing a radio advertisement sponsored by garage owners and brokers that aired the day before the second strike, the administration maintained that drivers made $150 a day, conveniently making no mention of the crushing cost of cab leases.

A range of police operations was initiated just before the second strike. Numerous fake flyers made the rounds, each claiming to represent drivers, including a mysterious one from an organization named PBA that urged drivers not to strike. The only PBA we knew of was the Police Benevolent Association.

On May 28, 1998, fifteen days after the first strike, Giuliani pushed a vote through the TLC to implement the seventeen new rules. It was the beginning of the end of the liberal façade he had maintained through his first term as mayor. For the next three years, the mayor's public ratings plummeted. They did not rebound until his remarkable display of managerial skill and statesmanship in the wake of the World Trade Center tragedy.

How did a largely immigrant workforce achieve such unity, defying all the conventional wisdom about organizing? And how could a popularly elected mayor afford to ignore the united call of 24,000 New Yorkers, implementing a reform package they were utterly opposed to? The answers lie in the complexities of the taxi industry, the lives of the workers, and the politics of the larger transformation of urban spaces like New York.

2

HORSE HIRING:
ABOLITION AND RETURN

THE UNITED CALL of 24,000 drivers on May 13, 1998, heralded a new beginning. After years of trying, drivers had achieved a unity nobody imagined possible. New York's taxi drivers come from more than eighty ethnicities and speak as many languages. For decades, both corporate managers and the mainstream labor movement accepted the conventional wisdom that to bring together such a diverse and isolated workforce was impossible. When I began organizing in the taxi industry, I knew almost from the first day that this assumption would be proven wrong. True, the drivers around me were acutely aware that lines of ethnicity, language, religion, and nation divided them. But they also told the same stories of harassment, abuse, and exploitation by the TLC, garages, brokers, and the numerous agencies that have been created around the industry.

"They treat us worse than animals," Agha Saleem, a driver organizer, comrade, and friend, told me by way of introduction to the drivers' situation. His was a sentiment I heard expressed again and again. As one driver said during a huge demonstration in 1994 in response to a spate of murders of cabdrivers, "When a driver is murdered nobody cares, nobody even wants to know. For the last three or four days now, there has been a story on television about a dog in New Jersey that is going to be put to sleep. There is a whole controversy around it. Here, a driver has been murdered and we don't even get a few seconds on TV."

Within a few weeks of talking to Saleem, I had met a host of drivers and heard their stories, each one worse than the last. Man-jit told me police officers had roughed him up because he had dared to challenge them. "This ain't India," they taunted repeat-edly as they searched him, pinning him against his car. Mansoor told me that he burned his foot on an overheated gas pedal, lost fifteen days nursing the injury, and then got thrown out of his garage when he demanded workers' compensation. Instead of helping him negotiate, Local 3036 at his garage had told him to speak directly with the garage manager. Moiuddin told me of a cop who gave him three tickets for no reason. The TLC and its court system are a sham, he said: "You tell me, have you ever heard of a ticket for a torn map in the back cabin of a cab? The police, garages, and the TLC are all hand in glove."

I learned about the industry from all of the drivers I worked with over the course of eight years, and from Bhairavi, whose knowledge of the industry is today unparalleled. Kurshid, Tahir, Kasif, and Rizwan, who gradually became my closest friends, gave me eye-opening tours of the city from the point of view of its taxi drivers. They showed me where cops lie in wait for them, where drivers congregate at the end of their shift, where one could expect a passenger late in the night; they demonstrated the art of spotting an undercover TLC inspector, the "shorty" system at the airports, and the best routes to the bridges in and out of Manhattan.[1]

"Twenty cars can be speeding here as they come out," Kurshid would say, speaking of the First Avenue tunnel, "but if there is one yellow cab amongst them, then that will be the only one that is pulled over." Bhairavi pointed to the unique relationship between drivers and cops: "Which other workforce in the whole world has the police force as its direct, moment-to-moment supervisor?"

"Druggies," Kurshid replied, laughing. "And at least they can pay them off. We can't even do that."

As I continued attending Alliance meetings and became an active member of the organization, I heard more stories. Every new driver I met had more than one to tell me about his garage, brokers, the police, the TLC, the locals 3036 and later 74, and customers. Most of these were angry stories, replete with frustration and fury over the indignities that drivers face in dealing with the ownership and the city. Occasionally I would hear a story about a customer who responded with respect and warmth toward a driver.

It is less common to hear drivers talk about why they're in the United States and how they got here, ten thousand miles from home, leaving wives, fathers, mothers, and children behind in the Punjab or Bangladesh, Senegal or Haiti. That is a conversation that takes place elsewhere. It begins in whispers, as the driver tests the listener and negotiates the pain in the story's telling. But as I began to hear these stories, the connections became visible.

The stories of anger and pain are intertwined. Only together do they answer otherwise bewildering questions: Why do drivers endure the indignities and sweatshop-like conditions of this industry? How did the taxi industry come to be structured the way it is? Why does the city respond to drivers the way it does?

An array of forces, large and small, organizes and runs the lives of the more than 24,000 active yellow-cab drivers, most of whom work ten to twelve hours a day, six or sometimes even seven days a week. A superficial approach to the story of the strikes would lead one to believe that a racist mayor and his police department were the industry's primary villains, but they are just the tail end of a chain of exploitation and oppression that extends from the garages, brokers, and the TLC to a whole host of corporations that surround the industry, including banks, taxi equipment manufacturers, testing agencies, auto companies, credit unions, and insurance firms.

LIKE A HANGMAN'S NOOSE

In late 1996, after I'd been working for several months as a volunteer organizer in the taxi industry, I started joining Kurshid in the front seat of his cab during his shifts. Every other day, we would meet a little after 4:00 P.M. at a deli at the corner of Thirty-fourth Street and Eighth Avenue. We'd grab a cup of tea and then walk over to the garage at Thirty-eighth Street and Eleventh Avenue, where Kurshid would pick up his car. It was a simple enough routine: Kurshid walked into a small cubicle at one end of the garage, dropped off his money, and picked up the keys to a taxicab. The cost of a daily lease was about $110, and Kurshid would have to pay an additional $20 toward gas. Before earning a single penny for himself, he, like almost every other driver in the industry who leases his cab, had to earn the money he had already paid out in lease and gas. "Let's go, brother," Kurshid would say to me every time he stepped out of that cubicle. There would be a particular urgency in his voice at that moment. Within minutes, we would be on the road, and after saying a small, hesitant prayer, Kurshid would begin trying to earn his living.

The first five to seven hours of a shift, during which Kurshid would collect fare after fare with the knowledge that he still hadn't earned a single penny for himself, were particularly brutal. "This one's for my boss's lunch tomorrow," Kurshid would say, after dropping off a $10 fare. "What kind of a life is this, my brother?" he would ask, hesitating before continuing. "You know, in every other profession, the fact that you are making money for somebody else is hidden so that you maintain some dignity saying that you are earning a living for yourself. In the taxi industry it is naked . . . no pretense . . . you are making money for somebody else six, seven, eight hours a day."

Kurshid's shift ran from 5:00 P.M. to 5:00 A.M. Each day,

circumstances beyond his control would determine whether or not he could earn his living. Would his usual car be available at the garage? Would the driver who drives the same car from 5:00 A.M. to 5:00 P.M. return on time? What kinds of problems would he run into that day? Would there be anything wrong with the car?

"Did you notice?" he asked me one day after picking up a brand new car that the garage had acquired, "A zero meter car, my brother," he said, using a common expression referring to a new taxicab. "At least this garage has decent cars. . . . That's the only reason I drive for him [the garage owner]."

He flung the door of the cab open for me, like it was his own brand new car. I wondered for a moment why he was so happy. Then he said, "At the last garage, my God, the cars were terrible. . . . I drove one for three months with a bad transmission . . . you know, the cabs with a constant high-pitched hum . . . oh, man . . . it drives you crazy. . . . Can you imagine, sitting with that wretched hum ringing in your ears for twelve hours? . . . You go mad, man, you go mad." A car with a bad transmission or faulty suspension is a minor irritant for a passenger. For a driver, it can constitute horrible working conditions.

During the months I spent driving with Kurshid, I learned through experience about an industry I had until then understood only in theory. Kurshid thought I was crazy to want to spend time in a cab, but I think he appreciated it. For those few months he had a companion for at least part of his shift. I couldn't drive with him for more than a few hours, because after rush hour, when the crowds thinned out on the streets, passengers became more discerning. They preferred a cab with only a driver in it, without another guy sitting in the front seat. But until 7:00 P.M., they were happy to get into any cab at all.

Those first five to seven working hours are a time of constant stress. "When you start at minus a hundred and thirty or one-forty, you cannot think of anything else, my friend," Kurshid explained to me. "Every moment you are worried. . . . Will something that will screw up the shift happen?" A "bad ride" in the early hours of a shift can leave a driver very rattled.

Once I asked Kurshid how he felt when he started a shift. His response was vivid and angry: "It's sickening, you know, but I begin each day hoping I will make some money, right? I say, I'll make $100 for myself, maybe $150 . . . that's what gets me to drive for these assholes, right? And . . . if in my first hour of driving I get a passenger who takes me up to the Bronx someplace, I know I am screwed. I will spend a half-hour or 45 minutes going up for a $15 ride and the same amount of time coming back . . . all this if I am lucky and I don't get traffic on the highway or the bridge. If I do, it's worse. . . . Sometimes it may take me two hours to get back, and all that for $15. I know immediately that I am not going to make my $100 now that I have only $15 to show for my first two odd hours. Naturally I am pissed. . . . Somehow I have to continue to drive knowing I won't make any money. . . . Somehow I have to drive knowing that all I will do today is make money mostly for my boss."

And yet there is a myth, especially among members of New York's cab-riding middle class, that taxi drivers make a lot of money. When one finds oneself constantly paying money to someone, one assumes that person must be raking it in. In fact, the extent of drivers' income instability is difficult to fathom unless one understands precisely how a driver's day typically unfolds.

I learned this firsthand on a day I was riding with Rizwan and he had to take a passenger to downtown Brooklyn during rush hour. Our start had been delayed because Rizwan was working two jobs and had emerged from his day job a little late. Still, by 6:15 P.M., he was catching up, having managed to do two fares, including one for $13 from Worth Street downtown up to East Seventy-first Street. Then disaster struck. Some commotion at the United Nations had caused a major backup on Park Avenue going south, and Rizwan was already cursing the traffic when he was hailed by a young white man at Sixty-first and Park. "Court Street, Brooklyn," he said. I saw Rizwan tense up and his face drop. "How do you want me to go?" he asked, a customary question for long rides. "FDR," the man instructed.

The FDR Drive was a mess, but not quite a parking lot yet, since the traffic was still moving in fits and starts. Past Thirty-fourth Street, we slowed to a crawl. Several minutes would go by before we could move a few feet on the expressway. At Twenty-third Street Rizwan convinced the passenger that it made more sense to go local rather than stay stuck on the FDR. As we neared downtown—by now we were already close to half an hour into the ride—Rizwan asked him another TLC-required question: "Bridge or tunnel?" "Bridge," the passenger replied, and Rizwan looked almost desperate. We tried to restart our usual stream of conversation, but we were too distracted by the fact that we'd barely made it onto the bridge in well over half an hour. Twenty minutes later we had inched halfway across the bridge. Another ten minutes went by, and just when it looked like things couldn't possibly get any worse, the passenger decided to walk the rest of the bridge. He dropped $15 onto the front seat and jumped out of the cab.

"Asshole!" Rizwan cursed. "Why the hell do they do that?" Now he was stuck in traffic and his meter wasn't even ticking. He was in a taxi driver's nightmare: terrible traffic, and a passenger who insists on a route that leads into worse traffic, only to leave the cab high and dry in gridlock without even the possibility of a passenger.

Luckily, the traffic started to move less than a minute after the

passenger left. The man came running back to the cab, but Rizwan's
anger got the better of him. "Fuck you," he yelled, snapping his
doors shut and switching on his off-duty light. "Walk, asshole,
walk," he said, laughing as he sped into downtown Brooklyn.

I still vividly remember the precise moment I realized the extent of
the lease's power over a driver's daily existence. It was a damp and
chilly Monday night, and I called Kurshid on his cell phone after returning to the city from New Jersey. "It's slow my friend, very slow
tonight," he said. "And I just got two tickets for no bloody reason."
I let a moment pass. I could think of nothing to say to ease his
mind. "Well, I am off to eat," I said, an announcement he was pre-
sumably waiting for. "Let's go," he said, "Where to?" We chose
Chatkaara, the Punjabi haven on the East Side, and a few minutes
later were busy working our way through hot rotis and meat.

It was wet and cold outside, which for cabbies means a brief
burst of activity as New Yorkers hurry to get out of the rain after
work or an early dinner, but after an hour or two, by around
11:00 P.M., on a cold damp night, only hookers are on the streets
and business comes to a standstill. On Lexington Avenue, outside
of Chatkaara, a veritable parade of prostitutes looked, like cabdrivers, for nonexistent customers. Kurshid had dropped off his
last passenger at 9:30. He fruitlessly cruised around for a fare for
half an hour before being pulled over by a cop at Seventh Avenue
and Thirty-sixth Street. One of his taillights had blown. "Every
other motorist gets a notice for a blown light, except a taxi
driver . . . we get a bloody ticket!" Kurshid exclaimed angrily.
"How are we to know when a light goes dead . . . unless of course
I check my lights after every passenger, or if I am God!" I listened
quietly as a host of other drivers joined our conversation, each
contributing his own story about a cop who gave multiple tickets
for nothing. There was a driver in the restaurant who had gotten

six tickets at one time a few months ago—three DMV tickets and three TLC tickets—because he tried to argue with the cop.

Kurshid snorted, exasperated. "You know what the asshole did?" he continued. "He took a piece of paper and wiped it across my roof and then held it up against my face—then wrote a second ticket for a dirty cab. Can you believe it? What am I supposed to do, pick up a car at the garage and then take it for a wash?" Kurshid had been slapped with tickets, which, if issued at all, should have gone to the garage and not to Kurshid.

"They know we don't have the time to go and fight these tickets, because then who will pay the lease? If I have to go to court during the day, it means I don't sleep and that I don't drive that night . . . so they are assured of the money." Kurshid said in summary.

The beat of the rain increased, forcing a group of drivers who were just exiting the restaurant back inside because their cars were parked some distance away. "There," said Kurshid, "goes the rest of the shift. *Ab tho saala koi sharaabi bhi nahi milegaa.*" With the rain pouring down, even the drunks would be indoors now.

The weather, of course, greatly affects the business of taxi driving. Rain produces a flurry of passengers, but then they vanish. Like bitter cold, it forces people indoors early. Snow is another killer. Rizwan and I have endured many snowstorms together, driving around the city in the melancholy light of a night snowfall, slipping and sliding, getting struck behind salt trucks, all in hope of finding that odd passenger trying to get home. The lease had to be recovered, after all; a driver doesn't want to end the shift having lost money.

The rain stopped abruptly and the drivers rushed off to make what they could of their shift. Kurshid and I quickly finished our food and, as usual, simultaneously reached for our wallets. There was always a tussle of sorts over who would pay. As I watched Kurshid pull out money, I asked, without considering what the question actually meant, "Whose money is it? Yours or the boss's?" Kurshid did not break his stride. He got to the counter first and dropped the money by the till. "That," he said, pointing to the money on the counter, "was ours. The rest," he said, patting his trouser pockets, "is still his."

It was past midnight by then. Kurshid was into the eighth hour of his shift, and he had only made enough for the lease and dinner. He would be lucky if he went home that night with $20 after gas. The power of the lease sunk into me at that moment. Here was a worker who had spent the better part of seven hours laboring and had made nothing. Yet he had bought me dinner, and he still had a smile on his face. What, I remember wondering, did he do to ward off depression and anger?

As we turned off Lexington, squinting against the glare of lights off the wet road, Kurshid tried to rekindle his motivation. *"Aare yaar, abhi ek lamba savaari mile na! Yahin utaar doonga tere ko."* Kurshid was willing to eject me from the cab if he were to chance on a "long fare." At this point, only a long ride, maybe to Long Island or some place in Jersey, could convert a wasted rainy night into a reasonable expenditure of his time. But fifteen minutes later we hadn't even found a passenger, let alone a long fare. As Kurshid dropped me off at the Port Authority bus terminal and joined the long line of cabs waiting for the next bus to deliver a handful of passengers, he turned to me and said, *"Yeh lease saala kambhakt phansi ke tarah baitha hai*—The lease sits around my neck like a hangman's noose."

KILLING ONE BIRD WITH TWO STONES: THE MEDALLION AND THE LEASE

The lease makes taxi driving, as Bhairavi put it aptly, "one of the few professions in the world where not only are you not guaranteed an income, but you might end a long twelve-hour workday losing the money you started with." Who put this burden on the driver's shoulders? How could such a primitive practice, and one so disrespectful of human labor, survive in a city that claims to be one of the most modern and civilized in the world?

This story is best begun with a close look at the enigmatic object that lies at its center: not the taxicab itself, but a small ten-square-inch shield of sheet metal, embossed with the city seal, attached to the hood of each cab and bearing a number. This is the New York City yellow-cab medallion. The string of four-characters on top of each cab—the 5Y11 or the 2G33, dimly lit or unlit depending on whether the cab is available—is the medallion number of the taxi. The medallion is essentially a license or a permit issued by the city that allows the person who controls the medallion to put a cab on the street. It has thus become a valuable commodity sold at an astronomically high price.

12,187 medallions have been issued in the city.[2] In the months immediately preceding the historic May 1998 strikes, the price of a medallion on the open market had reached an all-time high of $300,000. Immediately after the strike the value went down to close to $200,000, but by late 2003 it had recovered to approximately $260,000. The medallion is an expensive piece of private property, a financial instrument that is used today to deny workers a decent living, though at its inception, it was intended to regulate the industry and ensure some protection to the workers.

The medallion's history begins in dark times.[3] In Depression-era New York City, thanks to the industry's completely unregulated nature, taxi driving was a readily available job for poor, displaced, unemployed people. Anybody with capital could put a cab out on the streets, provided he could find people to drive it. To some extent, it is from the taxi-driving workforce of this period that the image of the philosopher-driver derives. Engineers, doctors, professors, and artists drove taxis. With more and more people unemployed and seeking work under any circumstance, taxi owners could set whatever terms they pleased.

The prevalent practice of the times was what Mayor Fiorello La Guardia called "horse hiring," in which a driver paid a fixed amount to the owner and earned whatever he could over and above this amount through fares. The emergence of horse hiring in the city's taxi industry had been gradual, accelerating after 1921.[4] As Kevin, who has driven taxis on the city's streets for more than 30 years, said the first time he explained the history to me: "Sounds familiar, doesn't it? Well, that's what horse hiring was: leasing. The only difference between what we had then and what we have now is that in the 1930s, it was entirely unregulated and controlled by the mob. Now we have a claim that the leases are regulated, and instead of the mob we have a set of drunkards and gamblers controlling the industry."

The taxi industry of the early twentieth century was controlled by car manufacturers who financed or ran their own fleets, as well as by a range of mobsters, including Ciro Terranova, Gurrah, Lepke, and the underlings of Lucky Luciano, who was a well-known mob boss of the era. Starting with Prohibition in the 1920s, the mob influence on the industry mounted. Drivers had secured a daily wage rate of $2.53 under the Chauffeurs and Helpers Union in 1911, but by the 1930s, when mobsters such as Samuel Smith took over the union, little or no protection remained. Alongside horse hiring, by 1934 or 1935 the industry was plagued by extensive loan sharking operations that drew on the funds it generated.

The taxi business served as an excellent front for the mob because payment was all in cash, and it provided fine cover for transporting bootleg liquor in the 1920s. (The industry during this time is well depicted in the Jim Cagney/Humphrey Bogart film, *The Roaring Twenties,* in which Cagney plays a bootlegger who also runs a taxi fleet.) By the time of the Depression, as the ranks of the unemployed swelled and increasing numbers of cabs crowded the streets, drivers were forced to reduce their rates to compete with one another.

To the merchants of despair—the cab owners—whether or not drivers got fares hardly mattered, so long as they were paid up front. But for the drivers, conditions got so bad that in February 1934, more than twelve thousand drivers went on strike against the imposition of a new five-cent tax. By 1936 the situation had reached a breaking point, and Mayor La Guardia called for an end to "horse hiring." As Kevin put it: "During the Depression, I have heard that a driver could drive a whole day and not pick up a single fare . . . that's how many cabs there were on the streets. Maybe if you were lucky you would pick [up] five fares. . . . At the end of the day it was not uncommon for a driver to go to bed with just a few pints of water in his stomach."

To end horse hiring and wrest the industry from mafia control, La Guardia came up with a unique scheme in 1937 called the Haas Act, named after the chief architect of the new system, a member of his administration. There were two key components to the Haas Act. First, it required that owners obtain a permit before putting a taxicab on the streets. The permit took the form of a numbered medallion and could be issued only by the city. This allowed the city government to keep track of the number of cabs on the streets and to regulate their volume accordingly. Second, the Haas Act introduced an employer-employee relationship into the taxi industry. In place of horse hiring, the new plan insisted that taxicab corporations employ drivers.

The Haas Act of 1937 called for medallions to be issued at an initial price of $5 each. It also divided the potential market into two discrete segments—fleet medallions and private owner-driver medallions. A fleet medallion would be operated by a taxicab corporation or garage, which then had to employ drivers to drive the cabs. The private owner-driver medallion was to be driven only by the "owner" of the medallion and could not be run by a fleet. In other words, the fleet medallions were set up for those with enough capital to buy and operate large numbers of cars, employing drivers who would in turn receive all the protections available to employees in the American economy at that time. The private owner-driver medallion, meanwhile, could be purchased by an individual who had at least enough capital to buy a car.

In 1937, fleets operated 60 percent of the medallions, while individuals owned 40 percent. Self-employment was now within the reach of waves of new of immigrants, if they could only achieve enough stability to raise the capital required for a used car. At the same time, it was difficult to regulate how long these drivers could stay on the streets each day. But economic logic dictated that in order to maximize their profits, the fleets would strive to make sure that their medallions were on the streets at all times. That in turn would ensure the continuous availability of taxicabs.

The La Guardia administration introduced the medallion both as a means of disrupting the mob- and manufacturer-dominated monopoly over the taxi business, and as a way of ensuring that those who sought to make a living driving—in most cases new immigrants with no other support structure in their new country— could do so with some protection. And indeed, the Haas Act gave the working driver a few years of relief. Many of the owner-drivers from the 1940s and early 1950s say that the taxi industry allowed them to create lives in New York City as new immigrants of modest means. Take Neville Cooper, for example. Cooper is today a frail old man, his gray beard a brilliant contrast to his weather-beaten black face and mischievous eyes. He runs a small car service based in Brooklyn, a business in which he invested when he felt he could no longer drive for a living. "I don't know any other business but taxis," he told me as we rode the subway together to the Bronx. "Ever since I came into my own as a young boy trying to make a living, I drove cabs. That was . . . 1943 . . . 44. . . . And you could actually make a decent living doing it, once you got good at it. Those days I didn't need to come into Manhattan at all. . . . I could drive all day in the Bronx and never cross the river."

For the employee-drivers, too, the medallion system first came as a relief, compared to the practice of horse hiring. The employee-employer structure that the Haas Act introduced evolved into a commission system by which the driver and the fleet owner split the meter by a preagreed ratio. Under the commission system no driver would under any circumstances go home without money in his pocket. As Kevin recalls: "By the time I began driving, in the 1960s, yellow cabs were mostly in Manhattan. But it was not uncommon to spend a good part of the day in one of the outer boroughs . . . and what is more, it wasn't easy, but I'll tell you this much: you could make a half-decent living. You see, however bad a day [I] had out on the street, I knew I would have some money in my pocket at the end of the day. The taxi driver of the 1930s and the 1990s could go home with not a penny in his pocket."

Nonetheless, the reforms of 1937 did not create a perfect system. The medallion had developed a market of its own, and the Haas Act did not go far enough toward defining the medallion purely as a permit that could not, for instance, be traded in an open market. By the 1950s, the medallion was treated increasingly as private property. The corporations who controlled medallions could profit not only by putting drivers to work but also by trading medallions on the open market. The best testament to the medallion's emergence as private property was that it increased sharply in value—from $100 in the early 1940s to $4,000–$5,000 by the mid-1950s.[5] The owner-driver medallion was an even hotter property, for it allowed a driver to work as much as he pleased and to pass the medallion on to his children as an assured source of income. Furthermore, as there were fewer owner-driver medallions, they were in greater demand, especially during the boom of the 1950s.

To understand why the New York City taxi industry is what it is today, it is critical to understand how a permit like the medallion became private property. I spoke with Mohammed Awan, a taxi driver in nearby Trenton, New Jersey, who owns his taxi permit. The practice of leasing is the norm in Trenton too, with one crucial difference: the permit in Trenton is not private property. Awan explained: "*Dekho. . . . Ye* city *ki permit hai . . . iski aur koi value nahi*—This a city permit and it has no other value. Yes, it is possible to transfer this permit to somebody else but it is difficult, and the city will not acknowledge it as a sale. As far as the city is concerned, it cannot be sold. Recently, there was a case . . . Eduardo . . . he was a driver here . . . he died, heart attack right here in the train station line. . . . His son tried to get his father's permit transferred to his name, tried to sell it, but it didn't happen . . . it just went back to the city. . . . Now the city will decide whether to issue it again."

I investigated further with Mallik, who runs a small fleet of eight taxis in the same city. His rendition was a little more complex but the conclusions were the same: "No . . . it's not easy to sell a permit. As a matter of fact, you are not supposed to sell it. There is a small black market and so sometimes people do manage to transfer ownership and collect some money—maybe $10,000 or a little more—illegally, but it is difficult."

From the example of nearby Trenton, we can see that while there is pressure for a permit that's in short supply to transform itself into private property, a city government can easily prevent that by making the permit nontransferable. In London, where the equivalent of the yellow taxi is the black cab, the taxi license is just that: a license, not a commodity subject to market valuation. But because the procurement and sale of medallions in market auctions is not prohibited in New York City, what was initially simply a permit to put a taxi on the streets has been transformed into private property. Accordingly, the value of the medallion has risen. By the mid-1970s, fleet medallions were selling at $12,000 to $14,000, while private-owner medallions were nearly double that, going for close to $28,000.

Because the medallion is also a permit that the city issues based on traffic demand, it is a commodity whose supply is artificially curtailed. As a result, there is a significant upward pressure on its value. As the cost of the medallion rises, so too does the cost of a lease, as the medallion owner pushes to ensure a minimum rate of return on the medallion investment. The fact that this permit has been converted into private property, then, largely explains why the leasing structure of the New York City taxi industry is so exploitative—and how leasing became nothing more than horse hiring under a more acceptable name.

3

THE AGE OF GREED, OR
WHAT'S NEOLIBERALISM GOT TO DO
WITH IT?

THE HAAS ACT was certainly not perfect, but given that the industry had been overrun by the mob and the car manufacturers
for most of the previous two decades, the legislation provided drivers with welcome opportunities to better their lives. In its immediate wake, the Haas Act created a space for active labor organizing.
Within months of the legislation's passage in 1937, the Transport
Workers Union (TWU) secured the industry's first collective bargaining agreement in several decades. It assured drivers $28 a week
in wages and 40 percent of all bookings above $45. This meant
that, unlike in the 1930s, the driver was almost guaranteed to take
something home. The fleet owners didn't always respect the split;
they sometimes harassed and cheated employee drivers out of their
commissions. Still, drivers had a new law that gave them some relief
and a responsive union that had secured a contract.

The fleet owners responded to this new situation in the way they
knew best. Within a year of the TWU's new contract, many fleets
began to encourage in-house unions, bringing in racketeers to dis-
rupt the TWU efforts. The 1940s and 1950s saw the collapse of the
TWU in the taxi industry and the emergence of another round of
taxi industry racketeers closely connected to the underworld—
wholesome characters like Johnny Dio, Jimmy Doyle, and Tony
Ducks (Anthony Corallo). By the mid-1950s, despite the endurance
of some Haas Act protections, including the employee-employer
relationship between fleets and drivers and the commission rate

structure, taxi drivers' working conditions were deteriorating. It was time for a new round of organizing.

ORGANIZED COLLUSION

The next successful wave of taxi industry organizing came in the early to mid-1960s. Harry Van Arsdale, the president of the Electrical Workers Union, came into the taxi industry with the full support of the New York City Central Labor Council and Mayor Robert F. Wagner. In 1964, for the first time in two decades, drivers won some collective bargaining victories. These triumphs were short-lived, however, and in hindsight that's hardly surprising. Any organizing that came with the full blessing of city hall was bound to be suspect, as it was clearly a reflection of some temporary gains struck in backroom meetings. Mayor Wagner could not have been free of industry influence. In many ways, the Taxi Rank and File Coalition, which emerged in opposition to Van Arsdale during this period, showed a perfect awareness of these contradictions. In delivering a labor organization open to backroom deals, Van Arsdale laid critical groundwork for future collusion between the city administration, taxicab ownership, and the union.

Between 1964 and 1968, Local 3036, led by Van Arsdale and backed by the mayoral administrations of Wagner and John Lindsay, nonetheless won some significant victories for the drivers. The last of these "successful" contracts, negotiated in December 1967, gave drivers an average of 48 percent of the meter with the additional provision that older drivers would get 49 percent. The 1 percent differential between older and younger drivers deliberately divided the driver labor pool—a strategy to which the union acceded. What's more, the very city administration that had backed Van Arsdale in negotiating the 1967 contract supported the owners as they began to undo it.

The owners forced the city, in all probability as a favor in return for the 1967 contract, to agree to a "temporary licensing program" run by the Metropolitan Taxi Board of Trade (MTBOT)—the fleet owners' association. This program licensed new drivers by the droves, effectively creating a new workforce at the beck and call of owners. Two years after the MTBOT gained control over hack licenses, it had granted forty thousand to new drivers. By 1971 the city had over ninety thousand authorized taxi drivers—more even than at the peak of the Depression. Van Arsdale's 1967 contract had appeared to be favorable to drivers, but he had also allowed for a rapid increase in the driver workforce under the full control of the ownership. The next contract, settled in 1971, would reflect the dire consequences of this reorganization. As Kevin explained to me, "The next thing they did was to eliminate one of [the drivers'] other victories—pension and health—when they agreed to let 10 cents come out of the meter on each drop to pay for the benefits. In other words, we were back to square one—we were paying for our own benefits again." Perhaps most important, the 1971 contract deepened the division between old and new drivers to which Van Arsdale had conceded in 1967. This time, the contract gave part-time or new drivers 42 percent of the meter, while the old driver retained his 49 percent.

No union that understood both the taxi industry and the fundamentals of labor organizing could have agreed to differential commission rates based on the length of a driver's service. In an industry that relies significantly on a transient workforce, differential rates are a dangerous thing. Those left out in the cold—new, occasional, or part-time drivers badly served by the contract—feel no commitment to the union and have every reason to serve as a ready-made scab workforce. It is therefore unthinkable that the idea of differential rates came from within the labor organization. It was an imperative drawn from elsewhere.

The corruption was equally evident in the 10-cent-per-meter-drop bound for the pension fund. Either the ownership or the union bosses—or both—made millions on this. With the sharp increase in part-timers created by the MTBOT licensing program, large numbers of drivers paid out 10 cents on the drop but never collected any benefits.

As the Rank and File Coalition continued to organize against the Van Arsdale sell-out, driver opposition to these new stipulations mounted. A compromised Van Arsdale went into binding arbitration and came out with 43 percent instead of 42 percent commissions for new and part-time drivers. That was not even enough to save face. As Leo Lazarus of the Rank and File Coalition said: "Harry Van Arsdale had said that 42 percent was in opposition to everything that we stood for. Not even 48 percent was good enough. However, when we went to binding arbitration, it went from 42 percent to 43 percent. Harry Van Arsdale is the best organizer the fleet owners ever had."[1]

Van Arsdale signed off on 43 percent. In return, he got the same contract to include an automatic dues check-off. In other words, the local no longer had to go to the drivers for their dues; instead, the owners would deduct the dues from the drivers' commissions and hand the money over to the union bosses. This was a perfect arrangement for everyone but the drivers. The union bosses would get their dues even if they alienated the union's membership.[2]

Having thus built an infrastructure for collusion, Van Arsdale handed it over to Ben Goldberg, who brought the union to a new low before handing it over to his son, Larry Goldberg. More about these two later.

THE RETURN OF HORSE HIRING

Under these conditions, two phenomena were to sweep the industry: privatization and extreme corruption. First, following the logic of commodities, the market for medallions rapidly reorganized. Second, following the logic of corruption and greed, the practice of horse hiring returned under another name—leasing. It would be a mistake to analyze these two practices separately, as they occurred almost simultaneously and reinforced each other.

The context is also significant. In 1971, the Taxi and Limousine Commission was created as a mayoral commission that would administer the taxi industry. The TLC wrested control of taxi industry regulation away from the police department. Some older drivers suspect that Mayor Lindsay created the TLC as a payoff to the Queens Democratic machine. "I can't prove anything, but you put two and two together," Kevin told me at a pizza shop in the old garment district, his face flushed with anger. "Before the TLC existed, the police department administered taxi medallions. Drivers often joked that the cops assigned to taxi administration were the ones who couldn't be trusted with guns—those who had alcohol problems or internal inquiries against them, or who were just too old to walk the streets. Within its first few years of operation, the TLC opened a discussion on leasing . . . it promoted leasing. Given the history of collusion between City Hall, the ownership, and the union bosses, this was hardly surprising. In 1979, the union leadership agreed to the arrangement to make leasing official. I can't think of a better example of near-perfect collusion between the government, the ownership, and a corrupt and corporatized union leadership that left working stiffs out in the cold."

It may not be possible to prove that the TLC's creation set off the chain of events that transformed industry arrangements from commission to leasing over the course of the 1970s. But there is considerable evidence that the TLC actively colluded in that process. In the 1950s and 1960s, New York grew rapidly, and its taxi industry strained to keep pace. By the early 1960s, illegal leasing operations had sprouted up all over the city, particularly in the outer boroughs, because increasing demand for taxis in lower Manhattan had made yellow cabs scarce in both upper Manhattan and in the outer boroughs. Many older drivers recall that their bosses would regularly take yellow cabs off their fleets in order to run parallel operations in the outer boroughs. There, they would lease the cars as gypsy cabs, earning greater profits with them than they could using employee drivers who were entitled to commissions. The TLC did little to control this practice, nor did it address the shortage of yellow cabs. Instead it argued that permitting leasing would bring a new stability to the taxi industry—echoing owners' claims. As it turned out, the move toward leasing was a national phenomenon. In 1974, the National Labor Relations Board under President Richard Nixon ruled that leasing was legal.

When the TLC did push leasing through in 1979, it did so not as a replacement for the commission system but as a complement to it. In other words, the TLC presented leasing as an option drivers would have. However, given that one option (leasing) presented owners with such obvious advantages over the other (commission), drivers did not wind up being the ones to make the choice. The TLC could have instituted rules or offered incentives to ensure the survival of the commission system, but it failed to do so, and, as a result, leasing all but took over the industry by the mid-1980s. Commission garages vanished.

The TLC had effectively employed a tactic that is now common in politics: an unfair practice is brought into being in the face of bitter resistance—not on the grounds that the practice is better than the ones already in place but under the guise that it offers "choice." Fundamental differences in power among groups are ignored or presumed irrelevant. In the case of the taxi industry, the ownership was clamoring for a new system (leasing) to which the drivers were fundamentally opposed. A seemingly liberal resolution to this impasse was to give each group what it desired—a choice.

But what goes unsaid is that power differentials affect whose choices actually shape final outcomes and whose don't. In the end, that resolution, without explicitly saying so, allows the more powerful group to impose its choice on those less powerful. In this case, it allowed the taxi ownership to eliminate commission within four or five years.

The only force that could potentially have stopped this from happening was the drivers' union, Local 3036, but that union was squarely in the pockets of the owners. This was the full effect of the politics of collusion that Van Arsdale had initiated. In fact, Local 3036 bosses worked hard to ensure that leasing was legalized. I was able to reconstruct this history through the memories of Kevin and Steve.

"Isn't it an irony," Kevin asked me once, "that leasing was brought in on the threat of some old drivers losing their pension? Scare one set of workers about losing their union benefits to create a system that robs every future worker of exactly the same."

Kevin was referring to the way the leadership of Local 3036 managed to fix the vote on leasing. For years the rank-and-file movement in the taxi industry had, with next to no money, fought a corrupt local leadership awash in resources. As a small insurgency, the movement tried everything: newsletters and leaflets, litigation and direct organizing. Its newsletter, *Hotseat*, commented, "In the past the union has been able to manipulate us because we were disorganized. In the strike three years ago, [the union bosses] were able to call off the strike without getting what we wanted. . . ."[3] These rank-and-file reformers launched a spirited battle against their union bosses, but court battles and on-the-ground campaigning took a toll. By 1979, although Local 3036 had lost nearly all of its credibility with drivers, the dissident movement within the taxi workforce was drained of resources.

The fleets began leasing cabs as soon as they could in 1979, but for the practice to be fully legitimized, the union membership needed to ratify it. One evening at the Alliance office, Steve Seltzer, probably the only rank-and-file organizer from this period who stills remains active in taxi industry politics, told me the story: "The rank and file was stretched. It had fought this battle for a long time. The first time a vote was taken, drivers voted against leasing and affirmed commission. So the bosses got wise the next time. . . ."

The next time around, the union leadership turned the tables on the rank and file. The vote was to be at Madison Square Garden. On the same afternoon, union bosses organized a pensioners' dinner at the Pennsylvania Hotel across the street, where they riled up the attendees by telling them they would lose all their retirement benefits unless they went along with leasing. Then the bosses trotted the pensioners over to Madison Square Garden for the vote. Leo, another old timer, recalled that even "apart from the pensioners, the union leadership had gone out of its way to bring in as many sympathetic drivers as is possible—guys who were in large part occasional drivers." So the well-fed pensioners and the bused-in hacks voted in leasing, and the working driver lost all he had struggled for over more than three decades.

MEDALLION BROKERS: THE NEW "FINANCE" CAPITALISTS

Owners sought other structural changes in the taxi industry in the 1970s as well, and like leasing, these changes would come to shape the industry for decades to come.

As early as the 1950s, fleet owners understood the value of their medallions as private property. They also understood that they were potentially liable for them, and so they set up a racket to limit liability. They divided their medallions into groups of two and then registered them under different company names. In other words, if a fleet had two hundred medallions, it would typically set up one hundred corporations, with imaginative names such as Bob and Company or John and Company, each one of which would "own" two medallions. This sleight of hand ensured that if any one of the fleet owner's medallions got into an accident or any other situation incurring heavy liabilities, the liability would be limited to the two medallions in its registered "mini-fleet." The larger fleet's remaining medallions would be safe. This was a brilliant, if dishonest, business practice, and it became a fixture of the industry. The TLC was surely aware that it was happening and upon its formation should have reined in the dirty players immediately. Instead, it went to bed with them, allowing the greediest and most unscrupulous owners in the industry not only to function but to flourish.

In 1973, an insurance broker known as Haber (of Cobert and Haber) came up with yet another dirty trick—one on a much larger scale than the old mini-fleet trick but in the same spirit. Since the two types of medallions—fleet and individual—were nontransferable, meaning that no fleet medallion could be converted into a private owner medallion or vice versa, the two markets had always remained separate. Haber changed this. He found two individuals who were separately looking to invest in individual medallions, brought them together, and got them to incorporate as a fleet. Then he sold them two fleet medallions—each valued at approximately half the amount ($14,000) of an individual medallion—at the individual medallion rate. Overnight he made a killing, gaining profit margins of close to 100 percent.

Now the value of the fleet medallion doubled from $14,000 to $28,000. Never again would an individual medallion cost more than a fleet medallion.

"The medallion," Kurshid told me during my early days at the Alliance, when I was still trying to understand how a permit could assume such importance, "is what will keep me a driver and nothing more all my life." Indeed, the changes that took root in the 1970s created an industry in which control over the medallion meant superprofits. With leasing, there was no longer any limit to the profit owners could make. From the time the medallion was normalized as private property in the 1950s until the mid-1970s, its value rose by approximately 300 percent, from $5,000 to $14,000 in twenty-five years. The reinstitution of horse hiring and the increased blurring of the difference between individual and fleet medallions together propelled medallion values exponentially upward—from $14,000 in the mid-1970s to approximately $300,000 by 1998. That is about a 2,000 percent increase in a twenty-five-year period.[4]

Alongside the old fleet owners, a new class of capitalist had emerged, created by Haber: brokers, who were now positioned as middlemen. With the accelerated creation of mini-fleets and the subsequent fragmentation of the ownership structure, brokers emerged as all-powerful just by knowing the industry. They knew who owned medallions, what the owners wished to do with their medallions, who was willing to sell medallions, and who was ready to buy them. As new capitalists who engineered the industry's deals, they also became the medallions' chief managers.

Meanwhile, not only did commission garages transform into leasing operations, but a large number of small fleets as well as private owner-drivers (most of whom were European Americans) pulled out of the industry. Brokerages such as Haber's emerged as powerful institutions that managed the medallions of these absentee owners. Some of the absentee owners were aging owner-drivers who wished to retire but hoped to continue to profit from the skyrocketing value of their medallions. Others had acquired their medallions under the Haber innovation but no longer needed to drive.

Brokers were further empowered when a significant number of small fleets went under, bringing a large number of medallions onto the market. It is unclear what caused the rash of failed fleets, especially during a period when medallion values were rapidly rising. Kevin, as usual, had a theory: "You see, the taxi business was never able to shake off its Prohibition-era legacy. Many of the mob bosses, associates of the early racketeers who were already involved with the pre-medallion fleets, were the ones to grab medallions up front in 1937. A large number of mob torpedoes landed with ownership in the industry. And the taxi business was not all that they were involved in. They ran every conceivable racket—from gambling to prostitution. And I am sure they all were carried away by the new turn in the industry. . . . They all thought they were going to turn [into] multimillionaires overnight with rising medallion values. Only they can tell you what kinds of deals they put their medallions into but clearly they did. . . . This was the trend even in the 1960s . . . but it just got worse in the 1970s . . . and when things didn't square up they went belly up. . . ."

The 1970s thus saw some drastic changes in the industry's ownership structure, largely resulting in greater fragmentation of medallion ownership. Whereas once only fleets and private owners owned taxicabs, now there were new institutions: brokerages. Brokers consolidated medallions from multiple sources. A broker might control one set of private medallions owned by retired drivers now residing in Florida, another from a set of mini-fleets that emerged in the 1970s, and yet another from a struggling fleet seeking to offload some of its medallions into a steady income stream to minimize risks. A broker does not necessarily own any of the medallions that he controls. He merely brings their management under one roof.

ILLUSORY INDEPENDENCE

The structural changes to the taxi industry over the last thirty-five years have been dramatic, but an even bigger and more visible change has been the shift in the demographics of the driver population. Only in the mid- to late 1980s did the Third World immigrant emerge as the typical New York cabdriver. Prior to the advent of leasing, under the commission system, more than 50 percent of the drivers were European or African American. Only a few were Third World immigrants, and these were mostly Caribbean Americans. By the late 1980s, you could hardly find a white driver. Instead, the ubiquitous sight was the Sikh driver, who looked, talked, and thought about New York City and the United States in a distinct way.

The garage owners and the brokers, meanwhile, had grown from petty small businessmen into millionaire fat cats, and the TLC had authorized this feast of greed at the expense of the new working men and women—men and women who had now been turned into "independent contractors" with no protections and no benefits.

Rizwan put it succinctly and brutally during one of our conversations about why drivers should attempt to unionize in spite of being "independent contractors." "Independent contractor," he laughed. "How dare they call us independent contractors? All right, a plumber who I call to come and fix something in my apartment is an independent contractor. Sure he is. When he steps into my apartment to work, he is already making money for himself. And why is that so? Because he owns the tools he is using. Because he owns that small van in which he came up to my apartment. And because he has the skills to fix a leak. And what about me? I do the driving. I can own a car if I want, but I cannot put a cab on the street because somebody else owns something called a medallion. An independent contractor is someone who owns the business, has the skills of the trade. . . . What is this? The medallion is owned by somebody else and those who have the capacity to work don't own shit. . . . I tell you, this medallion it is root cause of all our problems."

The poorer you are, the less access you have to the means of production (the medallion) in the taxi industry. The changes in the industry in the 1970s were primarily set into motion by the conversion of that permit into property. In reality, only a small percentage of drivers—the owner-drivers who own and drive their own medallions—are true independent contractors. In 1937, Mayor La Guardia pushed for 40 percent of the medallions to be independent owner–operated; in today's taxi industry, owner-operators are estimated at only about 12 to 15 percent of the workforce (approximately 1,200 to 2,000 drivers), while the remaining 22,000 active drivers slave under the conditions of horse hiring imposed by the TLC, garages, and brokers.

The transformations of the 1970s had effectively brought a new labor paradigm into being. What we must still explore is the fundamental core of this new paradigm. What is it about the current working conditions in this industry that make it so unattractive to a vast majority of native-born Americans, while it simultaneously draws large numbers of Third World immigrants? "The noose around my neck," as Kurshid puts it, is the simplest answer. But the full implications of the leasing system under conditions of exorbitant medallion values are merely touched upon in this evocative phrase.

ABSORBING RISK:
LABOR IN THE NEW ECONOMY

Under the commission system, the employee-driver and the employer–medallion owner split the meter. It was impossible for a driver to go home empty-handed, no matter how bad business was on any particular day. Leasing, on the other hand, created a situation where drivers were no longer employees. Garages maintain cars with medallions on them and a driver walks in each day hoping he will get a car to drive. He is an "independent contractor" who pays a certain lease amount up front to the garage before beginning his shift. Under commission, employee and employer shared risk almost equally; leasing shifted the inherent risks of the taxi business almost completely onto the drivers.

On a day when the island of Manhattan was clogged beyond belief because Dubya was in town, or a bitterly cold night when New Yorkers scampered indoors by 8 or 9 o'clock, or a night when early rain showers and the threat of more kept folks at home, a driver might end his shift with a $120 in his pocket— maybe $110 on the meter and $10 in tips. In the old days, assuming a 55 percent to 45 percent split under commission, with the tips going only to the driver, he would go home with approximately $60 and the garage owner would do the same. At today's wage rates, this amounts to just below the minimum wage of $5.25/hour. Under leasing, the picture is far grimmer. Having paid $100 to the garage owner and $20 for gas, the driver goes home with nothing. He has just worked at an hourly rate of zero dollars for twelve grueling hours. The owner, on the other hand, has his $100. Small wonder that the most common exchange among taxi drivers on a bad night is, *"Aare yaar, abhi lease nahi bana,"* or, "Hey friend, I haven't covered the lease yet."

Of course, these figures of $110 or $120 are merely for purpose of illustration. In reality, the picture is more complicated. For one, the daily lease rate varies from shift to shift and is not a fixed $100. Working a lucrative shift is more costly to the driver than working a low-end shift. For instance, at December 2003 rates, a Monday night shift in many garages was $95, whereas a Friday or Saturday night shift hovered around $120. A Sunday day shift ran at around $90, while a Monday day shift cost close to $100. Further, a driver could lease a taxi for a whole week instead of daily, for around $600,[5] bringing down his average daily costs from approximately $100 to around $87.

In all of these situations, the one point of consistency is the movement of risk onto the shoulders of the driver. What varies is merely the specific amounts exchanged and the driver's own outlay. Why is the weekly lease rate a little cheaper than the daily lease rate? The answer is entirely based on how much risk a driver takes on. For instance, if a driver falls ill one day during a week for which he has already paid his lease, he loses that fraction of the money he has already paid up—i.e, approximately $87. The driver is not only unable to earn because he is not working, but he is actually losing the $87 that he has already invested. The garage owner, on the other hand, is sitting pretty, having already pocketed his money for the whole week.

In another case, if the weatherman says one day that a snowstorm is approaching New York, a daily driver may choose not to go to work rather than risk dangerous driving conditions and no business. A weekly driver, however, in paying the garage owner his $600 for the week, has already absorbed the risk. In other words, this movement of risk away from the owner to the drivers is the principle behind leasing.

The logic of leasing set into motion an insistent recalibration of the rules of driving that has put drivers at greater and greater risk over the decades since it first began in the 1970s. One of the most visible examples of this is the brokerages.

Brokerages take the logic of leasing to its brutal, exploitative end. The broker often strikes lucrative deals for himself with retired small medallion owners who are willing to accept rents as low as $300 for a whole week. The broker then leases out the medallion to a driver. However, unlike a fleet-owner's medallion, the broker's medallion is not connected to a car that he owns. Instead, when a broker begins a lease agreement with a driver, he also "sells" the driver a car. This means that the broker has deals worked out with car dealerships. Thus a driver entering into an agreement with a broker enters a contract in two parts: the first covers the lease for the medallion and the second covers the weekly payments for the car. In such agreements the length of the lease on the medallion is rarely specified, but the car payments are often projected over a period of 104 to 130 weeks (two to two-and-a-half years). Drivers operating under such an agreement are referred to within the industry as driver-owned vehicles (DOV) operators.

At the end of the car payment period, the car is to be transferred to the driver. From that point on, it would seem that the driver would have to pay only medallion lease charges. Overall, then, the driver should stand to gain: he pays the broker $650 to $680 for the medallion lease and approximately $300–$350 in car payments, for a total of anywhere between $950 and $1,050 a week for both the day and night shifts. This is significantly less than a driver pays to lease a cab for a week from a garage, where both shifts over a weeklong period would cost $1,200.

But the gain is deceptive, because the driver who leases from a broker assumes the risk of equipment failure, which is normally borne by the fleet. If a fleet cab has a transmission problem, the fleet pays to fix it, but the driver who is paying for "his" car will bear the risk and the expenses. Inasmuch as the broker pays the medallion owner—who is probably sunning himself at a Florida retirement community—$300 a week and another $100 in insurance a week, and then collects $650 on the medallion lease from the driver, he pockets $250 with absolutely no risk. The broker doesn't even run the risk of having idle medallions, because once a driver is in a two- or two-and-a-half-year contract on the car, the medallion is assured of being in constant use for at least that time.

The reason the driver takes on these additional risks is that it seems at a glance that he is paying much less than a fleet driver would. In addition, at the end of the car payment term, the weekly payments are expected to come down to around $650 a week because the $300 a week that was meant for the car is no longer required. In other words, a driver in this arrangement would pay $300 a week less for the remaining life of the car—an additional two-and-a-half years.

At the outset, the problem with this seemingly favorable situation is that after two-and-a-half years of 24/7 operation on the street, the maintenance costs on cars go up tremendously. By the time a DOV driver has finished paying off his car, the car has already well above 100,000 miles on it. It is typically in the last two-and-a-half years that the car runs into major maintenance expenditures, yet many drivers assume this risk too, because the arithmetic seems too compelling. But it is often the case for drivers that the arithmetic doesn't quite work out.

We started hearing from some of those drivers in the months after the 1998 strike. During that time, the Taxi Workers' Alliance grew rapidly as more and more drivers knew and trusted the organization. Among those who sought us out were numerous drivers with cases against brokers. Consider the experiences of two drivers: Rizwan, whom we've already met, and Vivian, one of the few women drivers in the industry.[6]

It was 3:00 one morning in early October 1998. I had just fallen asleep when the phone rang. It was Rizwan. A little less than an hour earlier, he had dropped me off at home after we'd made rounds to some of the restaurants drivers frequent, dropping off Alliance flyers.

"Aare yaar, I have lost my car," he said, panicked. For a moment I thought somebody had stolen his car. "Where?" I asked. "I am at the broker's," he said, and I began to understand.

Rizwan leased from Tristar, a brokerage that has since changed owners and names because "Sam the Russian," as its owner was popularly known, bailed out of the industry once he'd made his millions. Rizwan began driving with Sam in 1996. Like all drivers who go to brokers, Rizwan was sold a car for a weekly car payment of $300 and a weekly medallion lease of $680, totaling $980 a week. His day-shift partner paid $475 a week to Rizwan, bringing Rizwan's weekly payment down to $505.[7] By October 1998, Rizwan had less than 20 weeks of car payments to go. He was looking forward to a couple of years during which he'd pay just $680 a week for both shifts. He'd continue to have a day-shift partner pay $450, which would reduce his weekly outlay to $230. He expected to build up his savings during those two years. Over his hundred or so weeks of car payments, he had already paid more than $30,000 for the car, not to mention the average of at least $100 a week he had put in for repairs and maintenance.

He paid his rent late every Wednesday night. This particular night, he had walked into the brokerage office a little past 2:00 A.M. Of course, Sam was not there, but Tristar's lease manager, a Pakistani like Rizwan, was on duty to take the money. Rizwan, as usual, opened the transaction with a greeting in Urdu: *"Haan ji janaab, kya haal hai.*" Then he continued with some idle banter while counting out his money: $980.

"That bastard," Rizwan told me later. "He didn't say anything till I had dropped the money on his counter. Then everything changed."

After securing the money carefully in the cash drawer, the lease manager made an unexpected announcement. "Sorry, boss," he said, "your car has lost its medallion."

"What do you mean?" Rizwan asked.

"The owner of the medallion has sold it. So we have to take the medallion off your car. Don't worry, we will get you another medallion for your cab."

"Wait a minute . . . what the hell do you mean? If you take the medallion off my car, I can't drive it." Suddenly Rizwan realized what the game was all about. "Bullshit! This is not going to happen. You can't take the medallion off the car. Ask Sam to call me in the morning."

Rizwan intended to take his car and drive out of there so that he could negotiate with Sam the next day. He knew that if the medallion came off the car, he was screwed. Even if Sam did as he promised and put a new medallion on the cab, the car would not pass a "hack up inspection." (Once a car is painted yellow and adorned with the fixtures of a yellow cab, it must undergo an extremely stringent inspection, and the only cars that pass are brand new.) Rizwan knew that Sam wanted to take control of his car, which he could then sell, perhaps for a paltry sum of $1,000 or $2,000. "Whatever it is, any sum he got off it would be profit for him," Rizwan reasoned later, telling me the story.

So Rizwan turned and rushed out of the office, but to no avail. In front of him, two of Sam's mechanics were already taking the medallion off. Rizwan screamed and tried to stop them. He had invested his labor into that car for two years, and he had just lost it all through no fault of his own.

Brokerages have perfected the art of farming out risk to the most vulnerable party. If Sam's story was true, the broker had effectively shifted the risk that his own agreement with a medallion owner might fail onto the driver. It would be Rizwan, not Sam, who would pay the price for the brokerage's losing the medallion. In fact, in a case like Rizwan's, the broker stands to gain when his agreement with an owner fails, because he inherits the car, for which one driver has already paid an exorbitant sum, and which the broker can then peddle for further profit.

What's more, when a driver first enters into an agreement with a broker, the broker is effectively guaranteed protection for five years. (The driver, of course, has no protection should the broker find himself a more lucrative deal somewhere along the way.) Several conditions make this so. First, if the driver defaults on a payment within the first two years, the broker repossesses the car on grounds of failure to pay. Once a driver has made a few payments toward the car, one missed payment could mean that he loses all the money he has already invested. As in Rizwan's case, it is not uncommon to see drivers lose their cars at almost the very end of their payment period. Brokers, of course, specialize in "creative accounting" that allows them to repossess cars that are nearly fully paid off. It's easy to see why this is to their advantage.

Vivian's case illustrates even more starkly the vulnerability of drivers who work with brokers, and the questionable accounting practices by which brokers make sure their arrangements redound only to their own profit. Vivian came to the Alliance office a few months after Rizwan's misadventure. Hers was the first complex broker case we had handled, and Bhairavi spent nights poring over her receipts. Vivian had entered into a three-part agreement with Kings Medallion Brokerage in Brooklyn. The first was for the medallion, the second for the car, and the third for a loan she had taken from the broker for the down payment on the car. The term of the down payment debt was 40 weeks, while the term for the car payments was 130 weeks. She paid a little over $1,000 a week for the first 40 weeks; for the following 90 weeks, she paid $980 a week. At the end of those 130 weeks, she would have paid off the car, which would leave her with only the $630-a-week medallion lease.

Vivian is a single mother who works twelve-hour days. She started out well, making her weekly payments according to the agreement. Within a few months, however, she ran into trouble because she lost her night-shift partner. For nearly three weeks, Vivian went crazy trying to find a replacement driver while driving fifteen to seventeen hours a day herself in order to meet her obligations to the brokerage. This would happen five times over two-and-a-half years. During the periods when she lacked a partner, she would sometimes fall a day or two behind in her payments, but she invariably caught up well before the week was out. In fact, Vivian had a nearly perfect payment record in spite of her terrible luck with driving partners.

Nonetheless, during one such crisis, when Vivian was actually a week ahead in her payments, the broker claimed that she was behind and repossessed her car. She had little time to do the accounting. For every minute she spent tallying her receipts, she lost precious time in recovering her repossessed car. She had no choice but to take the broker's word and work toward paying off the claimed amount in order to take possession of her car again. This pattern of abuse continued. In fact, it consisted not just of the broker's unfair accounting, but of verbal abuse the broker heaped on her, knowing that she was an isolated woman in the industry.

But Vivian persisted. She went to the TLC for help and was told instead to "get a lawyer" because the commission couldn't do anything for her. She also paid off her loan and, by her assessment, was in her last week of car payments when the broker told her she was six weeks behind. He repossessed her car again, this time for good. Vivian had paid the broker for a full 130 weeks, a total sum of over $130,000, which included a minimum of at least $35,000 for the car, only to be told that she had the lost the car based on inexplicable accounting that her broker conjured out of thin air.

Vivian's case dramatically underscores how fully risk has shifted to the driver. Every time she lost a partner, she—not the medallion owner or the broker—scrambled to replace him. If she failed to pay, her car would be repossessed. Under similar circumstances at a garage, the fleet owner would be the one scrambling. But the broker in such circumstances runs no risk at all. By shifting risk to the drivers, as well as engaging in a host of illegal accounting practices, brokers have created a whole new market for "paid up" cars. Having repossessed a car that is almost paid up, the broker then resells the car as a used car to another driver for, say, $3,000 flat plus the weekly medallion lease payment. The broker has then collected the interest from the first driver and pulled in an extra $3,000 in profit besides.

After investing hundreds of hours of hard labor, drivers are routinely left with nothing as brokers produce their "magic accounts" or "lost medallions" to set up conditions of superprofit for themselves. Vivian's case shows that the city is complicit in these practices. Given that drivers are considered independent contractors, their only protection comes from the industry's regulator: the TLC, which chooses not to regulate practices such as those that cost Vivian all her hard work and investment. Leasing exists for a reason: It is designed to ensure exploitation.

When broker cases started pouring into our office, we put a lot of rigorous work into figuring them out. We often spent hours going through paperwork in order to uncover specifically how a broker had defrauded a driver or how much a driver had ended up paying before losing his or her cab. Bhairavi spearheaded this effort, often in the company of drivers who were in broker agreements themselves. The members of the Alliance's organizing committee had been generally aware of broker practices, but prior to our effort, nobody had ever crunched the numbers and shown how systematically these practices worked to rip off the driver. When all of it was laid bare, there was often stunned silence as drivers quantified and concretized the meanings of their working lives in ways they hadn't before. After Rizwan's and Vivian's cases, the Alliance fought, and still fights, many brokerage cases. Vivian's was finally settled four years after it was filed. Rizwan's case still languishes in court because Sam has vanished.

WHAT'S NEOLIBERALISM GOT TO DO WITH IT?

One question came to dominate some of our meetings: Is there any other industry in which workers bear such risks and so often get defrauded as well? In fact, with leasing, the New York City taxi industry anticipated practices that would be perfected in other parts of the global economy only decades later. Today we hear a lot about outsourcing, subcontracting, downsizing, and business process re-engineering. Multinational corporations do these things in order to farm out risk to individuals or smaller firms. Outsourcing, downsizing, making workers pay for their own health insurance, and hiring temporary workers are a few ways big companies offload their risk onto workers. Over the past decade, such practices have come to define neoliberal economic practice at the level of the firm as well as at the level of the state, which has eliminated welfare nets and other basic services for the most vulnerable. But the taxi industry was way out ahead on this trend. The scores of illegal leasing operations that flourished under the TLC's nose in the early to mid-1970s became models for the industry's standard method of operating in the late 1970s and early 1980s.

Why did these practices begin in the taxi industry?

What distinguished the post–La Guardia taxi industry from most other industries of its time was its structural inability to implement the prevailing mode of labor control, known as Fordism. Inaugurated in the United States in the early 1900s, Fordism derived its name from the Ford Motor factories. A worker in a Fordist factory worked an eight-hour shift on the company's clock. During the hours for which the worker sold his or her labor, the assembly line would structure his or her work almost completely.[8] The specific activity a worker undertook on the line and the length of time it required were determined by management. The worker could not escape that regimen during his or her eight working hours.

A Fordist structure of labor control could not possibly work in the taxi industry. A driver did begin and end his shift under the watchful eyes of the fleet owner; however, once that driver was out of the garage and on the streets, he could not be supervised, nor could his work be structured. A driver could choose the number and the timing of his or her own breaks. How fast he drove, and how carefully, were the driver's own choices. After having worked his first eight hours, a driver could theoretically take his last four off if he felt he'd made enough money.

The ownership tried everything possible to produce some form of Fordist control over drivers' work. That was part of the purpose of the commission structure, which provided the driver with an incentive to keep earning more money for both himself and the owner. But every time the owners cheated drivers out of their wages, reduced the commission rates, or otherwise took money away from drivers, the response was an increase in what were called "arm jobs." An "arm job" was a fare for which, rather than starting the meter, the driver would negotiate a rate with the passenger and pocket the entire sum. Because of this, the industry ownership, which could not fully control its labor, tried instead to rob drivers of their earnings through corruption. In connivance with the bosses of Local 3036, the ownership put spies on the street. As Kevin explained, "Under commission, the owner's greed did not control the work of the driver." Rather, the medallion owner's earnings were determined by drivers. Something had to change.

Leasing was the answer. Leasing signifies, in many ways, the core of neoliberal economic practice and its logic of shifting risk downward to those who have the least power within the system. Such business practices that shift risk downward to those who have the least power have been variously referred to as neoliberal or globalized or post-Fordist. Of these various options I prefer the term neoliberal economic organization or neoliberal economic practices because of its specificity and more rigorous intellectual history.[9] When multinationals outsource their production to the Third World under the aegis of globalization, the effective change is that the risk of production is shifted downward to a Third World worker. When a credit card company outsources its marketing, customer support, and billing to the Third World call center, there is nothing left in the First World except the profits. When a Third World farmer produces cash crops for a First World multinational under the logic of leased farming, the risk of crop failure and price gluts are all pushed down to the impoverished farmer in rural Peru or India. In the end, then, the taxi driver in New York City and growing segments of Third World labor are connected by more than ethnicity—they are connected by the position they occupy in the long chain of neoliberal economic organization. And it is in industries such as the taxi industry, where Fordism's "imperfections" were apparent, that this form of economic reorganization was experimented with.

4

THE REINVENTION
OF THE YELLOW CAB

THE MIST HUNG low over LaGuardia airport. From our vantage point in the US Airways holding lot we could usually look across the open airfield. Today, we could see little. The lot was jammed. Not a single flight had landed in well over an hour. It was several weeks after the May 1998 strikes, and we'd come to the airport to talk to drivers about the upcoming mobilization to undercut the TLC's seventeen new rules through city council legislation. We had just come out of the council's transportation committee hearings on the subject that week. Bhairavi stood at the bottom of the lot, explaining the legislative process to the drivers. Six months later, the city council would pass our bill, Intro 376A, which undercut the most draconian of the TLC's new rules by defining a new set of conditions under which they could be implemented. It was the Alliance's first encounter with the legislative process. Through it, we learned that the idea behind legislation is not to simplify but to complicate matters, so that an aggressive bureaucracy can be held in check.[1]

While Bhairavi worked the bottom end of the lot, I hovered near the food truck. I told the drivers about the transportation committee's hearing the previous day, at which the TLC chairwoman, Diane McGrath McKechnie, had testified. "We have a problem here in Guiliani and McKechnie," I said. "Yesterday she ended up calling drivers rapists and murderers." My words met with a minute of shocked silence. I continued, "See, in the hearing, some of the transportation committee members began asking her questions about double ticketing and why the TLC felt the need for it. She had no real answer, and so she ended up asking the council members and the audience if they wanted to have their mothers and daughters driven around by murderers and rapists."

This time the floodgates broke open. One driver said that I was exaggerating. Another opined that she must have been drunk. "You can check the record, brother," I said in response to the first driver. "It's in the hearing transcript." Mansoor, a driver the Alliance had known for a while, reacted sharply. "How can she get away with it? . . . First the police commissioner calls us taxi terrorists and now she calls us rapists." As the murmur rose around me, I wondered about that first minute of silence. Perhaps people under constant attack learn to be judicious in their reactions, since they cannot respond to every insult and every attack.

Claude, a burly, outspoken Haitian, suddenly exploded. He had been standing just a little apart from the crowd around the food truck, looking disinterested.

"What the fuck do they want us to do?" Claude demanded now. "I mean, how do they want me to behave? Docile, polite, meek, quiet. . . . Should I bow, should I say yes sir, thank you sir, all right sir, each time I speak? I don't understand this, man. How do they want me to be?"

Claude's question stayed with me for a long time after that afternoon.

The mist rolled off the LaGuardia strip, and the planes began landing again. The Alliance won the legislative campaign, saving many drivers' licenses, and yet I remained troubled by the question of how the driver fits into the industry's story. Leasing was brought in. The medallion was extracted out of monopoly and fragmented. The risks of earning were all shifted onto the backs of drivers. With all these changes, somebody must have had an idea of what the shape of the industry would be. It was important to understand what fueled the changes in order to answer the question of how the Third World immigrant driver fit into that picture.

One place to begin was by asking who gained from the changes in the industry starting in the 1970s, and how. Of all the industry's stakeholders, the two segments that amassed and retained the most power over the next decade or more were the TLC and the brokers. The fleets gained financially, but their power in the industry had been significantly weakened by the fragmentation of the medallion and the emergence of the brokers. Local 3036/74 had already announced its death by playing such serious footsie with the owners and the TLC. That left the TLC and the brokers.

Neither the story of what the TLC attempted to do, nor that of how the brokers reshaped the taxi industry through the 1980s and into the 1990s, can be told without also telling the story of the larger changes reshaping New York City itself.

New York emerged in the 1990s as the key site in finance capital's global expansion. A wide range of scholars, including Saskia Sassen, David Harvey, and Doug Henwood, have documented New York's emergence as a "global city." But less is known about the history leading to that point. How did New York transform through the 1980s?

In his monumental *The Assassination of New York,* Robert Fitch tackles these questions as nowhere else. He documents in painstaking detail the manner in which manufacturing was driven out of the city and replaced by FIRE: Finance, Insurance, and Real Estate. How do the TLC and the brokers fit into Fitch's analysis? Without the context such an analysis provides, the story of the consolidation of the TLC and the brokers through the 1980s simply comes across as a tale of corruption and self-interest. There were TLC commissioners who went to prison. There were brokers who invented new scams and experimented quasi-legally with insurance and financing for taxi medallions. Does such corruption and scamming make sense in its own right, or is there a deeper and more comprehensive meaning to be uncovered if we tell these tales through the lens Fitch's analysis provides?

THE TLC: A NEW AGENCY FOR A NEW CITY

Two of the first three TLC chairmen were convicted of fraud. The first, Michael Lazar, took a circuitous route from the TLC to the city's Department of Transportation and then the real estate business before landing in prison. Jay Turoff, the third chairman, went straight from the offices of the TLC to house arrest. Only Moses Kove, the second chairman, escaped such ignominy.

There is good reason to revisit these early scandals. No commissioner, especially not one appointed chair, has ever been anything but a political appointment. As Kevin never fails to point out, Lazar was a Democratic Party insider from Queens. When the Lindsay administration created the TLC, Lazar's appointment to its chairmanship was most likely the mayor's payoff to the Queens Democratic Party machinery. Turoff, a small-time Brooklyn rug merchant, was brought in as commissioner on the last day of Mayor Abraham Beame's term—one day before Ed Koch took office. The Lindsay-Beame-Koch years were the central period of New York's transformation into a FIRE city. Focusing on lower Manhattan and the expansion of the financial district, Fitch writes:

> The 1961 zoning laws vastly shrunk the areas in which manufacturing was allowed . . . the successful zoning battle led by the Committee for Modern Zoning represented a postindustrial shift *avant la letter* . . . [it] narrowed the ring on manufacturing all over the city,

but Manhattan suffered the most. Manufacturing was
made illegal on Manhattan's East River side. The
Hudson River side was initially affected much less . . .
[in accordance with] the DLMA plan which initially
foresaw the location of the World Trade Center on the
East River—where coincidentally the project would
add value to the Chase Manhattan Bank.[2]

The Lindsay administration began the city's reorganization
with the vision of turning New York into a national center. Over
the course of the 1970s and 1980s, this vision was expanded into
one that saw New York as a global city. Reporting on a 1979
statement by the Twentieth-Century Fund Task Force, Fitch records the following:

We have a vision for New York City. . . . It is a vision
of a city increasingly oriented toward white collar employment . . . a vision of New York City as a true
world capital, the principal marketplace and cultural
center for the world. . . .[3]

Fitch connects this vision to the specific interests of the FIRE
lobby and the buildup of office space in both midtown and
downtown Manhattan. He writes:

It was an intoxicating prospect. Tourists dancing to
disco rhythms, Asian immigrants thronging into
Queens, turning the No. 7 to Flushing into the "Ori-
ent Express," new capital streaming in from Saudi
sheiks, leaders of Japanese keistrus, Mexican millionaires, French business magnates fleeing the Mitterand
socialists—the investors were all thronging to New

York to buy just what New York's families and institutions had lots to sell—office space.[4]

Against that backdrop, a series of scandals rocked the TLC. First came that of the Research Cab Company in the mid-1980s, a scheme hatched by the TLC's then-chair, Jay Turoff, with one of the largest fleets of the time, Midland. After the scandal broke, Midland was transformed into Midtown, still owned by the same Sherman family that controls the fleet today. Kevin had the following to say about it:

> As a scheme it seemed fair enough. The TLC wanted to conduct research into the feasibility of diesel-powered cabs. Of course, by the early '80s it did not need much research to show that diesel had little future, but that's another story. Surely Midland should not have had to pay for TLC research and so the assumption that a handful of "free" R medallions would ease the problem of Midland tying up its own medallions in a research study. The problem was that it was not a handful of medallions. When the figures came out after the investigation, the number of R medallions issued to Midland were recorded as 127 for a seven-year period. Clearly the Shermans made millions off this deal and we can surely guess where some significant part of those millions went. When the case went to court, a deal was worked out: ol'-man Sherman took the rap and did time, while Ron, the current fleet owners (MTBOT) president, was let off the hook and inherited the millions and the business.

Yilma, another Alliance member, confirmed Kevin's story: "Papa Sherman didn't stay in the locker too long. He was allowed to come back home. But he wore some kind of a brace that told the cops if he left town. He seemed like he was under some kind of house arrest."

Later came the Compumeter scandal. Yet again, Turoff was involved. Kevin was, as usual, an excellent source: "Of course I remember them . . . who wouldn't! Before they introduced electronic meters it was the regular wind-up kind of meters or the semi-automatics — Haldas, I think. Those were some meters. You could bash them with a baseball bat and nothing would happen to them. And instead they introduced electronic meters or rather electronic nightmares. They were so bad nobody would even steal them. There was one company you could buy them from: Compumeter, if I remember right. And when the mist cleared, years later, we learned that Compumeter was owned by Turoff's mother-in-law!"

These tales of corruption are interesting on two levels. First, they demonstrate the intertwining of local politics with the larger politics of urban transformation. Fitch writes about the transformative Koch years:

> . . . in the invisible bureaus and agencies, such as the Parking Violations Bureau, Department of General Services, and the Taxi and Limousine Commission, where rich opportunities flourished to steal in the dark, the mayor chose the nominees of the klepto-cratic county leaders.[5]

In other words, the Democratic county machinery was a kleptoc-racy, and in moments of major urban transformation, the minions of local politics made full use of opportunities to pursue their own interests.

The Turoff scandals—the diesel testing and the electronic meters—also offer two examples of the city's intense focus on the passenger's experience in a taxicab. At the time, there were many efforts afoot to recraft the yellow taxi, to make it different than it had been in the past, to experiment with new possibilities. In the 1980s, the search was on for a cheaper and fancier cab. These new priorities reflected the industry's reorganization. Under the commission system, owners were preoccupied with controlling labor, but after the emergence of leasing and the transfer of the industry's risks to the driver, worker control was no longer a concern. The city and the industry could instead focus on the passenger.

The central question became, "Who is this new passenger?" As the city was transformed, so was the taxi ridership, which consisted more and more of white-collar executives and of tourists who came to visit the global city. This new passenger was almost certainly white and middle class. Often he or she was a commuter. New York's entire transportation infrastructure had to be re-imagined in the city's new image. Thus the 1980s witnessed heavy reinvestment in the city's subways as well as in the final consolidation of its commuter rail system. Both New Jersey Transit and Metro North emerged in their current form in 1983, when they were pulled out of Conrail.

That the TLC deliberately positioned the yellow cab as a vehicle for the white middle-class consumer is evident from the fact that in the early 1980s, some yellow cabs began operating as radio cabs only. That meant that instead of taking street hails, these cabs would serve corporate accounts. The TLC specifically banned this practice, limiting medallion yellow cabs to street hails, but at the same time, the TLC acknowledged the necessity for more radio-based transportation in the central business districts of Manhattan.

It developed a new elite force of Black Cars (also called limos). These were radio operations that worked primarily on corporate accounts. Recalling this period, Harjit, an old Sikh driver who began driving in the mid-1980s, observed that, "When the limo business started, driving yellow cabs became less attractive. . . . We were already running taxis in that area—weren't we? And if there was a shortage of cabs, why could they have not issued new medallions? That's more than enough to show that there was some other plan. . . . What do you think, brother? If more medallions had been introduced, that would have meant more of us small people (*chote log*) who would have bought it . . . but no. . . . Instead, a new business was created for the businessmen of the industry to run, and the drivers were left with more competition on the streets."

It was clear that the taxi industry was being structured to offer different types of service to different kinds of people in the city. The limos would serve the new FIRE sector's lavish corporate expense accounts, while the yellow cabs would serve Manhattan's throngs of white middle-class passengers and tourists. The livery industry would meet the needs of the working poor in the outer boroughs. This restructuring, initiated under Turoff, was seen to completion under the next two TLC commissioners, Gorman Gilbert and Jack Lusk.

The final chapter in this story of implicit redlining and structuration of services came thanks to Fidel del Valle, an appointee of Mayor David Dinkins and the first and only TLC chair of color. Del Valle made it his task to legitimize and rationalize the livery industry that operated in the outer boroughs.[6] In doing so, he completed the TLC's decade-long project to restructure the taxi industry by defining different service modes for the different populations that were to inhabit the new New York. The only thing that could upset this finely calibrated apple cart, it seemed, would be if those on whose backs the system was built—the immigrant drivers—rebelled.

HEADS I WIN, TAILS YOU LOSE: THE INSTITUTION OF TAXI BROKERAGES

If the TLC was the institution that facilitated the transformation of the taxi industry as New York emerged as the new FIRE city, the transformed industry itself reflected the logic of the FIRE city. Brokers were, as we briefly discussed in the preceding chapter, not a new phenomenon in the taxi industry. The earliest brokers, including Oscar Katz and Haber, functioned well before leasing began in the late 1970s. They were small operators who settled medallion deals, bought and sold insurance for taxis, and lived off the periphery of the industry. They had no control over the medallion itself. Their emergence at center stage was an immediate consequence of Haber's innovation and the almost simultaneous creation of leasing. Kevin summarized the conditions created through these two changes: "Keep your focus on those two events . . . the first the conversion of the fleet medallion to individual medallions, and the second, leasing. All your explanations lie in there. Look at it this way: brokers were small-time operators—they sometimes sold insurance, they ran around between fleets, and if one fleet had a medallion to sell, they spoke to all the other fleets they were in contact with and sold the medallion and took a commission. They were the minor bells-and-whistles people while the fleets owned the real shit. But Haber and leasing changed that forever. The TLC was trying to create an industry that would free up the fleets to exploit the drivers every which way they wanted and they had no clue that what they had created alongside was the new and powerful broker.

The basis of the brokers' new power was simple. At the start of the 1970s, the brokers had little or no real control over the medallion. The Haber innovation busted the fleets' monopoly over the bulk of the medallions. The La Guardia plan had ensured that 60 percent of the medallions were to be fleet medallions while 40 percent would be owned and operated by individual owner-drivers. With the Haber transformation, these 60 percent (approximately eight thousand medallions) were now suddenly available to individual operator pairs.

The industry fragmented quickly as fleets lost their medallions to two-person operations that brokers helped start up and managed. By the mid-nineties, the brokers controlled most of medallions. The fleets that had once controlled in excess of 60 percent of the industry now barely controlled half—approximately 25 to 30 percent, or around four thousand medallions. The number of individual owner-drivers had also gone down, especially with many retirements leaving approximately two thousand owner-drivers in the industry. Brokers then controlled close to 50 percent of the medallions—around six thousand "mini-fleet" and private owner-driver medallions. Maged Gabriel, a private medallion owner-driver, is precise in assessing the impact:

> Look at it this way . . . now for any of the medallions owned and operated by individuals . . . the broker becomes more critical. Let's say one of them turns sixty and wants to retire to Florida. He is done . . . wants to leave. He could sell the medallion and leave or he could go to the broker and hand over the management of the medallion to him. He is off to Florida—no worries! The broker promises to pay him $1,200 per month. The $1,200 plus his social security is a fairly secure income for the retired driver and the broker now leases

the medallion out to two drivers for approximately $3,000 a month. Granted, he pays the insurance on the medallion—say, a maximum of $250 a week or $1,000 a month—but he is still making $800 a month on a medallion for doing nothing. The owner gets $1,200 for not driving the cab, the broker gets $800 for not driving it either, and the driver gets shit for driving the damn thing. What is more, that medallion which used to be under the roof of a fleet is now under the roof of the brokerage. The broker now controls the medallion and the fleet does not.

The broker owns nothing but controls a large segment of the medallions in the industry. He assumes no risk because he neither owns nor works the medallion, but he is connected to the owners, the drivers, the car dealerships, the insurance companies, the advertising companies, the meter shops, the TLC, and the repair shops. He makes money off of each of these connections because he takes a small cut of every transaction. That's all it takes for his risk-free millions to roll in.

Haber's innovative transformation of fleet medallions into individual medallions dramatically fragmented the industry. As owner-drivers moved around, changed professions, and needed new drivers to work their medallions, they turned to brokers to help them consolidate the transactions required for their medallions' maintenance. Had the commission system, with its employee-employer structure, persisted, the brokerage would not have become so important, but the combination of leasing and industry fragmentation (itself partly a result of the creative exploitation of loopholes the TLC had created) opened a space for brokerages, which were perfectly situated to manage the agreements among "independent contractors."

Rizwan offered me one of the best accounts of how risk-free the brokerage operations were. Following September 11, 2001, when New York's airports were closed for several weeks and the streets of lower Manhattan were blocked off for well over two months, the taxi business took a major beating. Tourism was at an all-time low. Businesses—from Broadway theaters to neighborhood bars and restaurants—faced an unparalleled downturn in business. The effect on drivers was profound. Taxi riding was down by 50 to 75 percent in the months after September 11. Rizwan's broker, being mildly considerate, reduced the amount of his weekly medallion lease by $25. One might think that this meant the broker took a $25 loss on every medallion he managed. But Rizwan explained otherwise: "He [the broker] told me what he did . . . he was laughing when he said this. He did give me a $25 break. But you know what he did while giving me a $25 break? . . . He went to the medallion owner and told him that business was bad and that his medallion would come off the road unless he agreed to a $100 cut in his take! Can you believe that? He gave me a $25 break, kept me driving, and made $75 extra in the process by cutting his payments to the medallion owner—probably some old man sitting in Florida—by $100."

So a downturn in business actually allowed the broker to make more money. Now that's a risk-free operation! The broker successfully outsourced the risk to the owner and the driver, both of whom rely on the broker for their basic income. By virtue of this entirely legal operation alone, the broker could easily be termed a shark. But brokerages frequently do much worse. Maged laid out the basis of the brokers' extralegal power as follows: "If you own a medallion, you need to be connected to a broker. One way or another . . . all the information that you need can be gotten only through a broker—insurance, refinancing . . . everything, you need a broker for—and with everything he takes money out of your pocket. . . ."

Once a medallion is in the hands of an individual, whether or not it was originally a fleet medallion, the broker's business has begun. Every individual medallion owner needs a broker to manage his medallion. The degree of dependence on brokers varies. An active owner-driver may depend on the broker for nearly everything (from insurance to buying a new car), but not for his daily income, whereas a retired owner-driver may depend on the broker for everything, including his weekly income.

When I met Maged in 1999, he had been driving his own medallion for three years. He was up to his neck in debt and very frustrated by the dirty tricks his broker had pulled on him. He had developed a detailed understanding of how brokers screw over every party in the industry for their own profit. Over many cups of sweet chai, Maged told me of horrendous scams:

> You remember Simon? Look at what he used to do. He advertised that he pays $1,700 for a medallion per month . . . this was three or four years ago . . . most owners were getting $1,200 or $1,300 from other brokers at that time. . . . Nobody could believe it, but it was true . . . and he would sweet-talk them up shit creek. . . . He got them to sign . . . $1,600- or $1,700- per-month three-year contracts. Simon would be responsible for managing these medallions for three years. The medallion owners walked away not knowing his game plan, and they paid dearly. . . . What he did was play with the statute of limitations on medallions. When he promised to manage somebody's medallion for $1,700 per month, the medallion owner assumed that this meant that Simon would handle all costs associated with the daily running of the medallion.

He of course promised them this. However, he didn't do anything like that. For instance, medallion owners have to pay fines to the TLC for many different kinds of violations—nonworking equipment, failure to appear for a TLC hearing, what have you. If the statute of limitations on a medallion for non-payment of owner summons was three years, then for the entire three years he would not pay a single owner summons. If the statute of limitations on medallion renewal–related costs was two years, then Simon did not pay for the last two years of the contract. He would let medallions run on the street without adequate insurance and if it landed with liabilities he would hold off the collection agencies till the end of the three-year contract. In other words, he ran up debts against the medallion. The owner did not know, because all bills, notices or other communications relating to the medallion came to Simon's address . . . that was what managing the medallion meant. What was the point of the owner getting the bills if Simon was going to pay them?

At the end of the three years he gave the medallion back . . . declared his brokerage house bankrupt and walked away. . . . The poor old man got $1,700 a month, alright, but suddenly when control of the medallion reverted back to him, he found out that he had numerous outstanding bills . . . debt in excess of 20 or 30 grand was owed . . . and Simon of course was nowhere to be found. . . .

In other words, not only were the brokers ripping off lease drivers, they were also fleecing the small medallion owners. "Take my own case," Maged told me that evening, as I sat cross-legged on the floor taping his stories while he sat in an armchair. "I kept getting screwed over and kept fighting my way out. First, I was sick of driving on lease. I had to find a way out, so I decided the quicker I owned a medallion, the better. But I had no money. All I had was a car. So I went to a broker: the most crooked of them all, Favio on the West Side. . . . I had to go to the worst of them because I had absolutely no money to put up for a medallion. Favio gave me a loan, fifteen grand at 24 percent, and I walked into the bank and claimed it was my money. Now remember, Favio is not legally allowed to do this. And in return, what did I have to do? I had to allow Favio to take out a lien on my medallion even as I bought it. So there you are: I had just tried to switch sides, and what do I have in return? A broker's lien on my medallion."

The down payment is the bare minimum amount of money that a prospective owner of any property needs to have to establish a basic infrastructure of credit. Favio had dragged in Maged, who had no such credit line, and loaned him the amount at an illegal interest rate. Maged continued his story: "Many drivers in my position . . . they pay the fifteen grand off but the broker doesn't take the lien off . . . the fifteen grand is unofficial. There is no real paperwork. So unless I got the lien off once I paid my $15,000, he could still execute it any time. . . . It took me quite an effort to get him to take the lien off."

A lien is a way of holding an asset to guarantee collection on a debt. It doesn't come into operation until the asset in question is dissolved. In our specific case, a lien of $15,000 on Maged's medallion meant that if Maged were to try to sell the medallion, Favio would have access to $15,000 of the cash generated by the sale. But Maged is a gritty customer and he did work his way out of the lien—only to land in other troubles with Favio. The next phase involved refinancing the medallion. As he explained, "The

rule in the industry is never to have any equity left on the medallion. Always pull out all the money that is available. In my case,
I was driving alone and trying to meet all my payments. The value
of the medallion had climbed in the months after I bought it, and
I had also paid off some of my debt. So the broker, at an appro-
priate moment, got me to refinance the whole deal. He got me to
the bank to refinance the freed-up equity on the medallion."

Equity on an asset is the difference between what you owe the
bank and the current market value of the asset. Thus, if you took
out a loan of $200,000 for a house, and on the day you moved in
the house was valued at $220,000 in the open market, you would
have an equity of $20,000. Maged explained his situation with
the medallion: "The medallion when I bought it was valued at
$160,000. It had moved to 180 grand and I had paid off approx-
imately 10 grand in little over an year. The bank gives you 80 percent of the available equity. In my case, I had 30 grand of equity
freed up on my medallion: the 20 grand that the medallion had
gone up by, and the 10 grand that I had paid already. The broker
worked with me and the bank and got 80 percent of the freed-up
equity, around 24 grand. . . . But that's not all . . . it's after this
deal with the bank that the broker steps in. He gives you more—
the remaining 20 percent at differential and exorbitant rates. Up
to 90 percent on 11 percent, 95 percent on 14 percent, etc." The
broker effectively reads the situation of the driver. If the driver
came to him to get the equity that had been freed up out of the
bank, he is aware that the driver needs the money for some reason.
If it seems like the driver is faced with some crisis, the broker then
offers him the rest of the equity over and above the 80 percent
that the bank paid at illegal rates of interest, all of it often secured
through a lien on the medallion.

Maged's story got more complicated by the minute; the broker
insinuated himself into every deal the driver had to make: "See,

a broker knows when you are in trouble because he is the person you are always in touch with because of your payments, or because of your insurance, or what have you. He constantly sweet-talks you. In my case for instance, Favio was waiting [for the time] when he could screw me over. . . . At one point I was just far too much in debt to drive alone anymore. And Favio knew that. I went to him and said I needed another driver. 'One hundred bucks and I will get you a driver right away,' he said. I agreed and gave him a hundred and he found me a driver. All the while he kept warning me, saying that if I put a second driver on the car and started paying insurance for him then I would have to pay for at least six months. . . . 'You sure, aren't you?' he kept asking me. 'Once you start the insurance you cannot cancel it for six months.' I agreed. A couple of weeks later my new driver quit . . . and I was back at Favio's. Now he knew how badly off I was . . . but the guy, he said another 50 bucks. . . . Well, I got another driver and he quit too. . . . I gave up and went to Favio to cancel my insurance and he said, 'I told you, six months . . . nothing I can do.'"

Maged was now paying insurance for a driver he didn't have. In desperation, he approached his friends who knew the industry a bit better than he did: "Now, but for the fact that I had some truly good friends who knew the industry, I would have continued paying the slimeball the money. I didn't know that you could cancel your insurance with a moment's notice."

But as if this were not enough, the broker had gone to even greater lengths to bilk Maged. The rate card is a document issued by the TLC that certifies that a medallion (and therefore the taxi) is insured in case a passenger sues for damages—say, as a consequence of an accident. It is expected to bear the names of the drivers who are authorized to drive the car, meaning those whose names have been given to the insurance company as the cab's official drivers. The amount of insurance you pay depends on the number of drivers. In the case of garages, the TLC issues an "Un-specified Rate Card," which is valid for any driver with a valid hack license. In the case of a brokerage, the names of the drivers have to be specified. However, the TLC fails to check each time a driver's name is changed on the rate card to make sure the broker has actually bought the insurance coverage. In Maged's case, the broker hadn't: "Favio had put the second driver's name on the rate card but had never gotten the additional insurance. In other words, for months he was doing a Simon on me. I had not only been paying for insurance that did not exist, but any accident the other driver got involved in at that time would have meant in all probability a lien on my medallion for the amount that the injured party sued for."

I recounted Maged's stories to Harjit, the older driver who has been driving since the mid-eighties. He confirmed them: "*Bhaisaab* . . . most of the brokers are like this. . . . The popular joke amongst the sardars about most of the big brokers is that they will sell their mothers. Look at all the older Sikh drivers. . . . Many of them deal with just one broker—the one or two brokers whom they trust."

The more drivers I spoke with, the clearer it became that brokers work in close cooperation with other actors in the industry, making money off of every little transaction through myriad legal and illegal practices. None of these transactions incurs any risk for the broker. Said Harjit, "See, it's all information. The driver has none, and the broker has it all, because everybody works with him as he screws the drivers. Everybody—the insurance companies, the TLC, the meter shops, the credit unions and the banks . . . they all work with the broker because each time he robs a driver they get a cut of some sort. . . . What they don't realize is that each time they cooperate with the broker, the broker is getting more and more out of control. . . . That's why insurance companies and the TLC are always uncovering new scams that brokers are pulling off. . . ."

The brokers operate primarily by building private relationships, which allow them to strike deals under the table. As Maged explained:

> Let us say a driver has an accident. The insurance company and the broker will work to ensure that the claim is not settled for as long as possible. On one pretext or another, they will push the case on because they know that it is possible that the medallion owner may want to sell the medallion at some point. Now, when I want to sell my medallion it is probably because I have to, because I have some kind of an emergency. The insurance company will at that point tell me that I cannot sell the medallion without the closure of the case and that the settlement could be potentially more than the maximum I am insured for. What do I do with this information? I go back to the broker, and he of course is acting as if he is willing to die for me but really he is in full cooperation with the insurance firm. In the end I strike a deal with the insurance company to release me from any liability in the future on payment of a part of my equity on the medallion . . . like if the equity left on my medallion is $50,000 I may agree to pay $10,000 to the insurance firm to get them off my back. And in this game the broker cooperates fully with the insurance firm . . . for what benefit to himself, we can only guess. . . .

Maged copes with the anguish brokers have caused him with grace and a sense of humor. Over those endless cups of tea, he told me about his life. He had emigrated to the United States from Egypt at age twenty-one, lean and mean and ready to take on this new world. But once he bought the medallion, the world crashed in on him. As the debt mounted, he fell into deep despair. "There were days when I would not be able to get out of bed," he told me. He described a condition most psychologists would recognize as clinical depression. He overate, lost interest in social life, fell out of contact with friends, and borrowed heavily on his credit cards to make up for the many days he just couldn't leave home to work. "In a little more than a year that I was down and out, I must have put on more than fifty pounds," he said showing me a photo from his slimmer days. Listening to Maged, I kept thinking of a book I had read a longtime ago—*The Hidden Injuries of Class.*[7] Yet he maintained a sense of humor that I am not sure I could have managed in his situation. "Hey, I wouldn't be this good in this game but for them!" Maged laughed. "It's a game and you have to know its details. See, the brokers control the whole business. If I want to sell my medallion, I cannot do it without a broker. And the broker sets up everything. He will decide where the auction is going to happen, when it is going to be, how to advertise or get the word out, how much the auction fee is going to be. . . . He knows how many liens there are on my medallion, how much the insurance company is going to suck out of me . . . everything. And all of them cooperate with him because otherwise their plans won't work either. . . . And the broker, he probably gets a cut out of everything."

The more I investigated, the more ridiculous it seemed. There were no fixed auction fees, no specified auction places, and no information outlets. This meant that the broker could set the auction place and fee and collect a cut from the auctioneer. For that matter, he could have the auction at his office and appoint one of his broker friends to be the auctioneer, letting him collect the fee.

He can to some extent control how many other brokers show up for the auction, and if he chooses, he can drive the value of the medallion down, collecting a cut of the difference from a pre-arranged buyer.

RISK FOR ONE AND ALL

The broker stands in the middle of every deal that involves a medallion. He farms out risk, legally and illegally, to every party possible, but primarily to drivers and private medallion owners; he takes no risks himself, and he makes more money than anybody. He does this by holding valuable information close to his chest and preying on workers and old people. He is able to operate in this way because the TLC doesn't regulate brokerages. "The driver," Harjit told me, "never knows the deal . . . he has to guess. The brokers, on the other hand, have closely worked out interests with everybody, including the TLC."

I cannot help but agree. In just the previous few years I had seen various TLC officials end up representing the interests of either the fleet owners or the brokers. Fidel del Valle was the official consultant of the Livery Owners Association after his term as TLC chair ended. Noach Dear, one of the TLC commissioners and an ex–city council member from Brooklyn, is openly acknowledged as MTBOT's close friend. And most recently, Joseph Giannetto, the first deputy commissioner in Giuliani's TLC, became one of the official representatives of the Safety Council, the brokers' lobbying association.

Arguably, the taxi industry as it was formed in the 1980s reflected the globalized world of finance capital. Bhairavi summed it up perfectly: "Who is a broker, after all? . . . It is somebody whose stakes are low because he is playing a game with somebody else's money. Everywhere in the world you will find groups of people who have made that their profession. They take one thing that somebody has and sell it to another person and make a cut in the process. . . . When they are in the taxi industry they are called brokers. And when they are part of banking and finance they are called finance capitalists and Wall Street brokers. . . ."

The governing logic of the neoliberal economy is that of farming out risk, something most easily done when you work only on margins offered by trade. Enron picks up energy cheaply on the open market and resells it to California at exorbitant rates; the financier George Soros moves money in and out of financial markets to secure gains in currency rates; and taxi brokers sell the use of medallions at a margin. All of these actors follow the same logic. Top management at companies like Enron and Worldcom worked a range of financial scams in which, like the taxi brokers, they spiked their earnings well beyond the rates available in the game of margins by leveraging information that they had and that the ordinary employees, like taxi drivers, lacked.

The taxi industry since Haber has been characterized by an ever-expanding series of scams. In legalizing leasing, the TLC made the brokers' exploitation of the system possible and any effort to rein in such abuse all but futile. The system the city set up is entirely stacked against the regulation of brokerages. The sham the city perpetrates as a "regulator" is that in facilitating a series of independent contractor relationships, it makes ambiguous its role as a regulator. Thus, like cops in a Hollywood film, the regulators always arrive late—after the scam has been in operation for years, if not decades—whether it be by Enron or Favio. In the end, the city government can't control the brokers for the same reason no federal administration can rein in the Enrons and the Worldcoms. And whereas Enron put the paper shredders at Arthur Andersen to work, Favio didn't even write any of his dealings with Maged down on paper.

But Maged's and Favio's stories must be told to the end. Maged finally quit the taxi industry in 2001. Favio Dias, the broker who "managed" Maged's medallion, has since been arrested. In early 2004, he took advances from at least ten drivers as down payments, promising to sell them medallions. Having collected large sums from the drivers (and possibly others in the industry), he vanished. The rumor for many weeks was that he had left for Europe. Six of the ten drivers who were scammed came to the Alliance, which helped them file cases against Favio. The latest industry rumor is that Favio has been arrested in Florida. This end to the Favio story not only highlights the fact that he continued to run his scams all along between 1999, when Maged first told me of him, until 2004, but also that the TLC did not act till it was too late.

But this nexus between the TLC and the brokers is not simply about corruption or greed. The two ascendant forces in the industry need each other. The TLC is keen on reinventing the yellow cab with the global city's white middle-class comfort as its main goal—without, of course, passing on the costs to this new elite. Each "service improvement" means additional costs, and if the fleets had held sway they would surely have resisted this imposition. The brokers, on the other hand, could not care less. If the TLC decided that the stockbroker in the backseat deserves to control the air conditioner, the broker would have no objections; he simply would pass on the costs of the required new plumbing to the driver—who, after all, "owns" the car. If the TLC decided that all taxis must have scratchproof partitions so that passengers can have an unhindered view of the driver, then neither the TLC, the broker, or the passenger would pay for that viewing pleasure. It is the driver who would. It is an alliance that so perfectly reflects the logic of our time—risk to the poorest.

5

PUNISH AND DISCIPLINE:
RACE IN THE NEW URBAN SPACE

AS THE GLOBAL city bloomed into full life in the 1990s, all of its requirements seemed to have been met. Downtown was more or less completely cleared of industry. Midtown was heavily built up. Old working-class neighborhoods like Hell's Kitchen were heavily gentrified. At the same time, the taxi industry had also been neatly segmented: yellow taxis served the white middle class and tourists at the wave of an arm for short runs between corporate offices or bars; the limousine business served those using corporate accounts; and finally, the livery industry flourished in upper Manhattan and the outer boroughs.

The TLC had emerged as one of the taxi industry's core institutions. It now affected every aspect of life in the industry, from licensing to lease rates. Brokerages, too, entered the 1990s strong and gaining in power. In just two decades, brokers had assumed control of a large number of both fleet and owner-driver medallions.

To any observer, it would seem as if Giuliani had inherited a fully reformed industry, and yet, as the season of strikes faded, the question still hung in the air: What was Giuliani attempting to do with his "safety reform package" of seventeen new rules? Was he trying to put a certain segment of drivers out of business? Was he after the brokers? What about the traditional fleets?

In November 1998, the Alliance hosted its first annual membership dinner. It was an occasion for drivers from a diversity of backgrounds to meet, and for the drivers' families to be part of a conversation with the core Alliance membership. The Alliance had begun to emerge as the drivers' core institution, and if it was to be a union that transcended the narrow economism that had hindered the union movements of the past, we needed to open up spaces that acknowledged and welcomed drivers' lives beyond their work.

By around 7:00 P.M., Twenty-seventh Street between Sixth and Seventh Avenues was a sea of yellow. More than a hundred drivers participated, many bringing their families. Hot korma, glistening kabas, and a steaming pot of rice and beans dominated the center of the room. One could hardly hear oneself talk over the hubbub of conversation among drivers and their families.

Bhairavi walked up to the top of the hall and announced, "All of us should be proud of what we pulled off and for proving to the world that New York City yellow-cab drivers are going to resist strong-arm tactics from Giuliani." A thunderous applause erupted. After a minute or two of speaking, she turned the floor over to the drivers. "What do you all think? How do you think it all went?" she asked.

A hushed silence descended over the room. Nobody knew how precisely to approach the aftermath. Little by little, driver members and the organizing committee members began to detail the various efforts the city and the ownership had made to break the strikes. Slowly the discussion wended its way to the central question of the evening: "What is Giuliani trying to do?" Kazem asked, "Who gains from this? . . . The value of the medallion has fallen considerably. I just heard that it stands at around $170,000. Am I right? . . . and if so who gains? . . . Clearly not the ownership. . . . And why is Giuliani interested in bringing the value of the medallion down? Does he care? . . ."

Again, a silence descended over the hall. But the discussion that followed reflected a sentiment that Louis put bluntly: "Giuliani is anti-immigrant. . . . He is racist and his pro-immigrant election rhetoric was just that—rhetoric." Jean Paul, a Haitian owner-driver, concurred: "You see, even before he became mayor, Giuliani had trouble with the Haitian community . . . and you know, many of the owner-drivers in the industry are Haitian. . . ."

Giuliani, the drivers suggested, was unhappy about the growing immigrant presence in the ownership ranks in the industry. But while Giuliani had not demonstrated any particular tendency to advocate for immigrants, the argument that he opposed immigrant ownership in the taxi industry didn't completely add up. For one thing, the number of individual owner-drivers in the industry had sharply declined. And for another, Giuliani had initiated a 1996 medallion sale in which a large number of the investors were Sikh and Haitian. The conversation began to meander. Ghulam chose this moment to drop his bombshell: "I know what Giuliani wants to do . . . haven't you heard? . . . He is preparing to sell the taxi industry to Disney. . . . I have been hearing about how he is planning on selling all the medallions to Disney for a few months now . . . that's it . . . that's it. . . . In the next four, five years he is going to sell it all to Disney . . . and Disney has the capacity to fund a presidential campaign, not the brokers or the garages. . . ."

He trailed off. Yet again, the crowd sat in stunned silence. Mamnun and Rizwan both corroborated Ghulam's theory. At the airports and garages, many drivers had been saying that Disney was looking to take over the yellow-cab industry. "Everybody is speaking about it," Rizwan added, "that Disney, is going to buy up all yellow taxis. . . . The rumor is so big that even [radio station] 1010 WINS did a story about it just a few days ago."

The story sounded like a conspiracy theory, cautioned Kazem. I was inclined to agree that the rumor had the ring of an urban legend. But there was something fundamentally appealing about the theory, which neatly concretized the idea of industry consolidation.

If Giuliani's intent was to somehow bring the fragmented taxi industry together, then why wouldn't he invite a large corporation like Disney to invest in it?

The room bubbled over with loud conversation. Most of the drivers present had heard the rumor but had been careful not to put too much stock in it. Now that they were openly discussing it, the logic was compelling. Somebody called out that he had heard it was Warner Brothers rather than Disney. Another driver said that a group of Haitian drivers at the airport had told him that Disney was actually interested in the monorail from JFK to the city, but for some reason that idea had been stalled, and so as a second option the yellow-cab industry was being considered. Surinder said he had heard that Disney was interested only in some part of the taxi industry, such as a new premium service out of the hotels to the airports. Each story was crazier than the last, but what struck me was the theory's fundamental appeal as an explanation that could link Giuliani's drive to discipline the taxi workers to his forcing down of medallion values. Kazem again interjected a note of caution: "I am not sure . . . it sounds too good to be true . . . it sounds too big and too much conspiracy. . . . We should be careful and not accept this rumor too easily. You see, conspiracy theories work because they make easy sense. . . . I think there is another explanation . . . the attack is most directly on drivers. Why? Just to reduce the value of the medallion? I doubt it. I think Giuliani and Diane want to bring drivers under control. He may feel that this industry is too much outside his control and he wants to bring the drivers to play by a set of rules . . . something by which he can control the industry. . . . He does not like a situation that he cannot control. . . ."

Kazem's explanation, which was as low-key and humble as the Disney theory was dramatic and sweeping, found its reluctant audience. Bhairavi jumped in, attempting to bring the discussion to some kind of closure. "I agree with Kazem," she said. "We need to be careful how much we put into the rumor. I agree that this whole thing has much to do with controlling drivers, and maybe even controlling the brokers and garages. Maybe it is not Disney, and maybe all Giuliani wants to do is to push out the individual medallion owners."

Her response encompassed the twin themes of control and consolidation. A consensus emerged that if Giuliani was primarily interested in control, consolidation was one way of getting it. But the appeal of the rumor did not fade. Said Kevin, "If Disney or a few corporate garages control the whole industry, then control becomes so much easier. Our capacity as drivers to bargain for something will go down considerably if there are only a few owners."

Nonetheless, we had made progress, and we had managed to extract the important themes from the discussion of the rumor. It had been a productive dinner.

THE URBAN SUBURB

It was close to midnight when most of the OC members left that meeting. Rizwan and I drove uptown. There was no rush, and we slowly worked our way up Sixth Avenue. The night's discussion had followed us into the car.

"Why would people start talking about Disney if there were nothing to this?" Rizwan insisted.

We swung onto Forty-second Street going west. I replied, "But, Rizwan, that's precisely how conspiracy theories work. . . . If you're asking how somebody thought of putting Disney into this frame, then you are bang on target."

A tourist bus had blocked off one lane, leaving us stuck, halfway turned onto West Forty-second Street. "Assholes," Rizwan grumbled, not so much because he had somewhere to be as because he knew that if he had done the same, he probably would have gotten a ticket.

We rolled slowly toward Seventh Avenue. It was a mess out there, with traffic on Broadway hardly moving, causing everything else to slow down. One light later, Rizwan's foot was about to hit the gas pedal when a group of giggling, screaming kids decided to cross the street. He slammed his foot on the brakes and muttered *"Kahan se aa jate saale."* With the typical New Yorker's attitude of superiority toward weekend revelers from New Jersey, he had said, "It's bloody midnight and look at this place."

The flashing lights on every storefront—Planet Hollywood, the Disney Superstore, Virgin Records—hurt my eyes as I watched the kids hurry across the street. They seemed like the bunch that gathers each day outside the MTV studio at Times Square, hoping to get on TV. I could see Rizwan's expression change as a few of those who had just crossed the street decided to turn around and cross back the other way, this time right in front of Rizwan's car. He lifted a hand from the steering wheel momentarily, slamming it back on the horn. A couple from among the revelers jumped and then turned, looking straight into the cab and laughing, half at themselves for being frightened and half at Rizwan as if to say, "Easy, man, we're having fun." Rizwan's window was down and his head was half out of the cab: "Screw off, will you . . . go back to Jersey," he yelled. I laughed. Rizwan pulled his head back in and cursed one last time, half smiling by now, as the light turned yellow. The kids made a face at Rizwan, and he gave them the finger before bursting through the light, barely beating the red and giving the kids another scare. We could hear them screaming behind us.

As we cleared the intersection, the neon from outside accelerated through the cab as it picked up speed. I grew quiet. A thought skipped through my mind, as if wired to the rapid flashes of the neon that slid through the car. "You know," I said eventually, "Disney doesn't matter. It's just a way of saying it all."

Rizwan turned with a quizzical look, his irritation fading. I continued, "That [with those kids] was precisely what Giuliani is trying to get you not to do: abuse the suburbanites." I laughed, banging the dashboard.

Rizwan's face lit up; he knew we were onto something. "Yeah . . . he wants me to shut the fuck up and behave, so that those kids don't have to listen to shit from an immigrant driver."

Our conversation sparked. By the time we were racing up the West Side Highway to the Henry Hudson Parkway, we were both animated. Finally, outside my apartment building in Washington Heights, we summed up the discovery we had made. Said Rizwan, "You are right. . . . Just six years ago, Forty-second Street was very different. After around 10 P.M., you zoomed through it . . . it was empty. . . . I mean, many people considered the area dangerous the later into the night it got."

I remembered my first trip to New York in 1993. Around Times Square, sex shops lined the streets like cells of forbidden pleasure: big ones and small ones, garishly lit, their cheap neon unable to compete with the grandeur of the giant Sony TV sign that dominated the space. Late at night, sex workers, pimps, and customers cruised the streets around the Port Authority bus terminal. Experimental pleasures, segmented and streamlined, were laid out for the enterprising tourist and the intrepid New Yorker alike in the row shops and on the street. Today, one sees little of that. Giuliani's Times Square is home to mall-sized stores run by every entertainment and specialty goods multinational. One supermall is entirely Disney's. There's a Planet Hollywood, a Virgin megastore, Universal Pictures, Gap. Applebees and other such quintessentially suburban bars and eateries dot the several blocks around the square. The Seventh Avenue line subway station has been remodeled and illuminated to reflect the Disney motif, with flashing lights and painted doors.

The transformation of Times Square from red-light district to megamall affects drivers' daily lives in innumerable ways. For the day driver, Times Square's traffic has gone from bad to worse. It was always a segment of the city best avoided, except during the morning rush hour, when the avenues on both the West and the East Sides carried the spillover from overcrowded highways. Now Times Square is impassably overcrowded all day. For the night driver, the old, seedy Times Square was mobbed only during the early hours of the night, because the tourists vacated the area at around 9 or 10 P.M. After that time, only the seasoned New Yorkers remained, along with the most intrepid tourists who sought pleasure in dark corners of the streets or in the private cubes of sex shops. Now the night, like the day, bustles with hordes of white middle-class visitors who scurry in and out of megastores and in and out of cabs, often distracted and disrespectful. The tourist family stays out until 11:00 P.M. or midnight; the white yuppie enjoys the megabars. Rizwan's response to the transformation of Times Square was not about whether he liked the change or not. It is far more an observation of the changed racial and class composition of those he found on the streets and what was expected of him as this change of clientele emerged.

To drivers, the Disneyfication of Times Square means traffic congestion at 11:00 P.M. and dozens of new No Right Turn and No Left Turn signs. Thanks to Times Square's transformation, drivers experience a new level of police harassment around the Port Authority terminal, and they have to negotiate streets disrupted by constant construction as Giuliani's billion-dollar corporate welfare project known as the Times Square Business District/42nd Street Re-development Plan unfolds. As they urge passengers not to use the Eighth Avenue entrance to the Port Authority terminal because often cabs that do so get ticketed on one pretext or another, drivers plan their quick exits from the overcrowded area with its self-absorbed passengers. "You know," Rizwan tells me, "now I know why my day partner hates Times Square so much. Any business anywhere else in the city is so much better than getting stuck in that mess. . . ."

But the mess that Rizwan is talking about is more than a traffic snarl. Cleaning up Times Square was presented to most New Yorkers as a moral imperative. It was about making the streets safe for children. The Giuliani administration's stated rationale was that it sought to ban sex shops from operating within a certain distance from residential spaces. When offered such a moral choice, many New Yorkers felt obligated to agree with the mayor. But drivers heard the celebration of Giuliani's great court victory against sex shop owners on 1010 WINS even as they watched the Disney stores fast replacing the sex shops. They could without any effort see the "battle against sleaze" as a battle for the multinational.

Of course, many others in New York saw this corporate takeover for what it was. Many debates unfolded in the liberal media on what Giuliani's real intent was. In some progressive and civil liberties circles, too, discussions on the tension between freedom of expression and popular morality took place. The difference, however, for a taxi driver was that the transformation of Times Square was a focused instance of the changing race politics of the new global city.

And so Rizwan continued, that night in Washington Heights, placing the rumor in context: "When you asked me if my question was 'Why Disney?' rather than trying to actually verify if Disney had paid off Giuliani, it all made sense. . . . We are right on target when we say that for drivers it was never 'Giuliani is right in banning sex shops.'. . . It's far more correct to say that the prostitutes are not good for the business of Planet Hollywood."

He stopped and began to laugh. "*Aare yaar,* this is too much," he said, the joke still running around in his head. "If one kind of for-hire people, the prostitutes, needed to be brought under control as part of cleaning up Times Square, then why not another type—the taxi drivers? You know what the commonplace word is for prostitutes in Pakistan, don't you . . . it's *taxi!*"[1]

Thus the Disney "conspiracy" emerges not as a rumor that needed verification for its factuality but as a metaphor for a larger transformation of New York City as drivers experienced it. The city was remade for the multinationals and the white middle class in the 1990s. Kmart, Best Buy, The Wiz, Whole Foods, Starbucks, and Blockbuster all entered the city, challenging the bodega at the corner, the small mom and pop video stores, and the relaxed coffee shops in which you could sit and smoke for hours on end.

Specifically with relation to Times Square, transformation signifies both a past "space" and a present/emerging "space." This necessarily also implies the destruction of the old space and the production of a new one. These notions of "destruction and production" are not merely physical concepts. A space must necessarily be understood as signifying a certain order—a specific environment that constitutes a social, physical, and visual whole, an identity that makes the space somebody's. The old Times Square thus "belonged" to a segment of New York that has its characteristics—of class, race, gender, and sexuality. Its "visual order" was "noir"; it was possibly more male than female, colored, with a diversity of sexual identities, and a class basis that was difficult to define. Whatever the specifics of this old identity, it certainly excluded one group—the suburban/neo-urban white middle class. To deliver this space to the white middle class entailed destruction/production of the space both through "domination" (the physical tearing down of older buildings and the construction of new ones or the deployment of excessive police force) and "appropriation" (such as the remodeling of the subway stop or the reshaped inclusion of the corner newsstand). Disney is the perfect metaphor not just because it has such physical presence in the new Times Square but also because it is the quintessential symbol of suburban America and its idea of pleasure. It is in this sense that to understand the transformation of Times Square is to understand the transformation of New York City as a whole.[2]

How do we characterize this change and how does control over taxi drivers fit into it? The prededing chapters offered part of the answer to this question by explaining the economic basis of the transformation: as New York became a global FIRE city, the TLC and leasing were supposed to create an efficient and solicitous taxi service that would meet that city's changing demands. The Disney metaphor, as set out above, helps us to go beyond the economics to understand the city's social transformation. Many theorists of globalization have attempted to analyze the new urban space by looking at structural similarities among large cities all over the world, including New York, London, and Tokyo. Such global cities serve an accelerated world economy, which is dominated by finance capital and manages the reinvestment of productive capital in every part of the globe. One of the most important of such theorists, Saskia Sassen, does identify the creation of an environment that appeals to a mobile professional class as one of the social characteristics of a global city but leaves it largely underdeveloped.[3]

Such analyses less frequently investigate the effects of globalization on the internal politics of these cities. Every global city, after all, has an existing politics, which emerges both from its national context and from the specificity of its local history. In the case of New York, globalization has produced a whole new race and class dynamic. Three distinct but parallel stories explain how that happened: the arrival of a Third World immigrant labor force, the redefinition of the role of the African American worker in the city's economy, and the reentry into the city of a white middle class, availing itself of new opportunities.

DISCIPLINARY STRATEGIES OF THE GLOBAL CITY: GIULIANI'S QUALITY OF LIFE CAMPAIGN

American racial politics has had distinct material consequences throughout the period of globablization. For much of the twentieth century, most of New York City's workers were white Euro-Americans. Indeed, until well into the 1960s, the majority of taxi drivers were white. During the postwar economic boom, which is so often extolled as a time of rapid class mobility, the logic of American racism dictated that these gains be distributed unevenly. A majority of the white working and middle classes benefited far more than African Americans did from the industrial prosperity and the share of such gains that unions garnered for the working class. This was most apparent during the period of rapid suburbanization, beginning the late 1950s, when upwardly mobile whites left the city in droves.

The black working class of the 1970s and the 1980s got left behind without a safety net in decaying urban centers. In fact, as manufacturing left the shores of the United States, African Americans were victimized twice: first, because they didn't get their fair share of the postwar prosperity, and then again because they were excluded from the postindustrial urban economy. An entire generation of African Americans lived through a period during which their immediate economic environment could not sustain them. The suburb was out of reach and the city was in decay. When New York went global in the 1980s, however, the economic elites sought to lubricate the city's new service economy by "rebuilding" its racialized urban space. New York City was not only to be "renewed," but that process was to take place on the backs of urban communities whose welfare and survival had interested nobody for the better part of two decades.

When Third World migrants entered the United States during the Kennedy era, they were generally professionals who were quickly integrated into white suburbia, where they remained just as isolated from the hollowed-out urban economy as did most of the white middle class.[4] It was not until the mid-1980s that working-class migrants began to enter the United States from the Third World, heading, as the poor had always done, straight for the cities. These migrants were predominantly dislocated males, unencumbered by the trappings of the full lives they'd left behind and unfamiliar with the underbelly of the American mythology of success.[5] They formed an ideal workforce for cleaning up the city's debris, and they soon comprised the bottom end of the new service economy, including janitors, gas station and parking lot attendants, newsstand and deli workers, restaurant workers, and taxi drivers.

The arrival of this new immigrant workforce partly solved the problem of labor in the emergent global city, but a regime of labor control was still needed. The vulnerability of the new immigrant workforce did provide some means of control, since workers who were only liminally legal were bound to play carefully by very rigid rules. Most African Americans, meanwhile, were subject to an entirely different regime of control: one of criminalization and brutalization. This period, beginning in the mid-1980s, saw an acceleration in the imprisonment of blacks. Today, the rate of incarceration of African Americans is four times the rate of incarceration of native South Africans at the peak of the apartheid regime. Approximately 800,000 African Americans are in prison today, which is equal to the number of African Americans in chattel bondage in 1820. If the current trends continue, in fifteen years there will be more African Americans in prison than those in chattel bondage at slavery's peak in 1860.[6]

Even as immigrant and African American workers suffered these indignities, the white middle class benefited from the emergence of a range of white-collar jobs in the new FIRE economy. From gated communities in Hoboken, these white-collar "executives" arrived in the city's financial district by express bus. From the blooming Newport-Pavonia section of Jersey City, infrastructurally sealed off from the rest of Jersey City, they could go straight into the World Trade Center on the PATH trains without even setting foot on a city sidewalk. From as far south as Princeton, New Jersey, as far east as New Haven, Connecticut, and as far north as Albany, commuters came and went every day on Amtrak specials, New Jersey Transit, Metro North, and the Long Island Railroad. The old white middle-class neighborhoods on the Upper West Side and Upper East Side were back in business and outfitted with new conveniences, including gourmet groceries delivered twenty-four hours a day by Mexican workers, and building-by-building dry cleaning concerns run by Chinese workers. Real estate prices soared as the white middle class repopulated the city in a wave of gentrification that swept from Park Slope in Brooklyn to the East Village and parts of Harlem and Washington Heights.

This was a white population that for decades had distanced itself culturally and ethically from the complexities and contradictions of urban America, choosing instead the isolated and segregated security of the suburbs. Large segments of those born during and after "white flight" grew up taking such security for granted. Now they staffed the white-collar information sector of New York's newly globalized economy. In class terms, this population was not perfectly homogenous; rather, it included "executives" spanning the gamut from the new keyboard wizard securities trader for Morgan Stanley, to the first-generation college-educated white professional working her way up the Starbucks franchise corporate ladder, to the immigrant programmer on contract for Citibank.

One thing these white-collar "executives" did share was a significant distance from the city's working-class communities. Whether they lived in the city or in the suburbs, they entered and occupied the urban space on a limited and specific experiential basis. The new city strove to accommodate them with an urban space that would provide suburban comfort, pleasures, and security. How this could be done was the fundamental social question to which Mayor Rudolph Giuliani's Quality of Life Program provided the answer. The white middle class, accustomed to suburban life, wanted Mickey Mouse pleasure, and those charged with its seamless production were immigrant, African American, and Latino workers. The only problem that remained was that this workforce had to meet the disciplinary standards of Mickey Mouse pleasure.

As we've seen, Disney itself was not very important. I realized that the drivers' perspective on this was best understood by reading the rumor as a metaphor for New York City's transformation. Giuliani's Quality of Life Program reproduced the suburbs within the city for the new urban white middle class, and it did so by harshly disciplining poor people of color. Its method was twofold: Giuliani sought to exert control over public space through a range of zoning policies, legislation, and litigation on the one hand and through recasting the police force on the other. In 1997, just before the showdown with taxi drivers, the program included a series of attacks on economically marginal "entrepreneurs," from curbside squeegee boys who washed car windshields to immigrant newsstand owners. In the period immediately following the taxi crackdown, Giuliani went after food vendors and street-side artists. During this time, the number of police and other uniformed personnel grew dramatically. Between 1993 and 1999 the number of police, sanitation, corrections, and fire-fighting personnel grew by 3,375, to a total figure of 69,937, while civilian employees in city agencies fell by 2,649, to 17,265.[7] Before Giuliani, the TLC's taxi inspectors, who were city employees with the status of peace officers, administered the city's taxi drivers. The NYPD could stop a taxi only for traffic offenses. But Guiliani more or less phased the TLC inspectors out of street work and created in their place a special unit of armed policemen whose job was solely to police the taxis—the NYPD Taxi Unit. Numerous other city agencies' security functions were similarly redefined as NYPD work. This transfer made city cops, who were empowered to make criminal arrests, into the enforcers of TLC policies, such as the cleanliness of taxicabs. As Kurshid said one day, angry and humiliated after a police officer had held him up for an hour checking his cab, "This is all so screwed up. What can I do? I am sitting there thinking, if I say or do anything I could land in jail and once I land in jail, you never know. So all I said to him, for everything he said, was 'Yes, sir.' I don't even remember what all the cop told me. He spoke to me a lot. . . . I just was not listening . . . I just kept saying 'Yes, sir.' I think maybe I didn't answer some of his questions because I was so afraid, and that got him even angrier and that's why I got so many tickets."

For example, in the months after September 11, Kurshid reduced his driving to three days a week, making just enough money to pay the very basic needs. "I have to get out of this industry," he told me, "and right now my wife has a job in a beauty parlor and I can afford to stay off the street."

Driving a yellow taxi in New York City makes you publicly visible and exposed every minute of your workday. "I don't know, man," Yilma Wolde-Mariam, a member of the Alliance OC, told me, "but I try to limit my interactions with my passengers. It's not that they are all the same, but there are enough of them who abuse you that you feel the terror all the time."

In the new global city where the comfort of the white middle class translated into a Quality of Life Program that segmented and attacked working people of color openly, the result is a psychological state produced by a sense of constant threat—something akin to the impact of a regime of biopower, in the words of the French philosopher Michel Foucault.[8] Subjecting oneself to such a sense of fear is not what anybody would do out of choice. Hence we must acknowledge it as produced by a regime of control that seeks to do precisely that. The claim is not that every immigrant worker or every taxi driver feels precisely the same way. But in the first eight months of 2004, three drivers were hospitalized, two of them brought into the hospital in a state of coma, after being attacked by their passengers. If such is the state of affairs, how should a driver feel when a passenger gets into the taxi and reads his name on the hack license out loud repeatedly? How is a driver to feel when a passenger feels compelled to ask him when he will leave the United States? How must he think when a passenger asks him, "Do you know Osama?" and laughs loudly after this disgusting "joke"? Is it an error to say that the moment of physical attack is not too far off when these questions are being posed? Will not avoiding a physical or abusive confrontation necessarily mean that a driver will just have to swallow hard and not respond? What then of the psychological state that is produced as a result? The racial politics of a global city has today seamlessly melded with the post–September 11 sanction of open expressions of racism.

The psychological sense of terror that an immigrant or African American worker feels is not without its mirror image—the sense of power felt, consciously or unconsciously, by those to whom this global city belongs. As Bhairavi has repeatedly insisted, ever since the Giuliani administration labeled cabdrivers "terrorists" and "rapists," the sense of power that passengers feel over drivers and the resultant abuse that follows must be attributed to the "environment that has been created," in which it is perfectly legitimate to hate an immigrant. Under the Quality of Life Program, the police were no longer tacitly racist but could be overtly so. Not just the needs but the pleasures and conveniences of the white middle class took precedence over all other aspects of city life. Giuliani insisted on keeping the sidewalks free of vendors for the walking pleasure of the new urban middle class; he banned protests from being held in the parks;[9] and he prohibited the taxi demonstration across the Queensboro Bridge to Fifty-ninth Street because he said it would inconvenience businesspeople. Parks, long a public space for citizens' protests, became increasingly inaccessible for anything but the leisure activities of middle-class New Yorkers. Because the Quality of Life police were responsive to the desires of the white middle class, the two groups forged a bond. Rizwan put it best: *"Aare yaar* . . . I am not worried about the blacks. They have a fight with you right then and there if there is a problem. . . . I am most scared of that white guy. . . . They enter the taxi thinking they own it . . . drunk . . . they will puke in my cab or smoke in it and if I fight with them, they will not say anything but complain to the TLC."

Throughout the 1990s, the TLC acted in every way possible to control drivers and to promote the middle-class passenger's pleasure and safety. That was the sentiment that came through the TLC chairwoman's May 1999 comment, at a city council hearing, that drivers could be rapists and murders into whose hands council members' wives and children should not be entrusted. The TLC's view of the urban working-class immigrant was as fearful as the colonial master's view of the native man. Many months later, a driver, Brahima, was attacked and killed by a white civilian to whom he refused to yield a parking space. Kurshid remarked, "*Kya bole yaar* . . . What is surprising about this? Nothing. . . . Your mayor and your TLC has made it clear to the public that nothing they do against a taxi driver will be held against them . . . the taxi driver you see is an animal and needs to be worked in chains only." Many drivers expressed similar sentiments of anger and humiliation. Rizwan asked, "Tell me, how does a loser standing on the sidewalk have any understanding of what a problem is between a passenger and a driver? Recently, I was dropping a passenger off and was arguing with him about why I had not followed his instruction and stopped the cab at the intersection when an idiot who was standing on the sidewalk came up to the cab to tell the passenger that he should not argue with me, but should instead complain to the TLC and get my license revoked."

We hear such stories daily in the Alliance office. Babul, a driver with more than eight years of experience, explained it best when he came into the office seeking help. He had been spat at and punched by a young, drunk white man in a stretch limo when his cab came up parallel to the limo at an intersection. He wanted to press charges, but this was what happened: "The limo driver . . . he came to help me. He stopped the limo and refused to go any further till I said I was okay. . . . I said I wanted to call the police and when the police came it was crazy. They came asked me what had happened and when I told them, they quickly took the guy away to the side and had a conversation with him in private . . . and then came back and told the limo driver that he could go on. . . . What was he to do? He didn't want to leave but he had no choice. . . . Then the police began to argue with me . . . and in the end just left. . . . They refused to register charges, saying they didn't know who the guy was."

Drivers who needed to see TLC officials at the agency's Queens licensing facility had to line up outside as much as a night in advance, even in the dead of winter, with no protection from the rain or snow. The later they arrived, the higher the chances were they'd be turned back without service and asked to return the following day. As the backlog accumulated, drivers began queuing up earlier and earlier. This continued until the Alliance mounted a campaign which converted a three-block-long line outside the TLC offices into a protest as drivers angrily chanted slogans: "Down with TLC, We Want Justice." Faced with the prospect of a spontaneous rebellion, the TLC brought the situation under control in less than three days.

Each of these stories says something about the ominous new social contract that was created in New York City in the 1990s. Rizwan's comment that TLC was essentially a complaint registration body for the white middle class, Kurshid's fear of the police, the overnight lines in the deathly cold, the killing of Brahima, the abuse of Babul, and the TLC chairwoman's claim that drivers could be rapists or murderers all marked the evolution of a compact that catered to the safety and pleasures of the white middle class while devaluing the safety and dignity of immigrant workers. These were not isolated incidents but repeated patterns. Taken together they revealed a systematic strategy of labor control in which Third World immigrants were meant to labor in a state of fear and to expect that they would be treated very differently from the white middle class.

The notion that the white middle class occupied a space apart from the complexities of class and race found powerful expression in the distasteful advertisements one saw on the subway for several years after Giuliani banned panhandling there. The ad positioned a thought bubble directly over a subway seat, as if to represent the thinking of the person sitting there. The "thought" was a response to a panhandler: "Oh no, I hope he doesn't come up to me," it began, neatly encapsulating the middle-class fear and distaste for the urban poor. It matters little as to whether every person caught under the bubble thought that way. What matters is that it was what the Giuliani administration wanted and encouraged the middle-class commuter to think. More importantly, it legitimated that fear, both through the advertisement itself and through the policy it was intended to announce.

Race and gender are social relations that are generally defined through either skin color or sex. But class has a long history of resisting such easy reduction. The complexity of class relations—even the well-off know that what separates them from the poor is entirely socially and economically determined—was what suburbanization had destroyed. The middle class so completely isolated itself that the poor and the worker became abstractions to which middle-class Americans bore no real relationship. To reenter the urban space was to come suddenly face to face with the human reality of class again. It was the task of a neoliberal mayor like Giuliani to protect these new middle-class New Yorkers and to ensure their daily safe passage through the city undisturbed by the complexity of class relations that would otherwise stare them in the face. As a historically specific social relation most easily available for manipulation, race became, in this case, the fundamental mode of managing class relations. The Quality of Life Program therefore provides a perfect window through which to view the deliberate ideological and physical transformation of New York.

PEOPLE OF COLOR:
THE POLITICS OF THE POSSIBLE

So far this analysis has focused primarily on the relations between the working poor and the new urban middle class, along with the urban transformation that brought those relations into being. But there is another relationship that is equally important—the one between the new immigrants and the city's long-standing African American working classes. The nature of this relationship will determine in some part the political possibilities of the future.

During the time I spent examining Giuliani's Quality of Life Program, I got to know Hakim Hasan, an African American book vendor who used to conduct his business at the corner of Greenwich Avenue and Sixth Avenue. Hakim had a remarkable ability to keep track of our conversations, which sometimes extended over many days, despite constant interruptions by customers and street noises. One such conversation was about relations between immigrants and African Americans, and it has stayed with me ever since.

I was sitting comfortably on a milk carton next to Hakim's bookstand, and he had just asked me some questions about the economics of the newsstand business and the small tobacco and candy shop business. "I am asking all this because, you know, nobody in my community knows shit about how this all works," he told me. "All we know is that Indians and Pakistanis are in all these businesses. . . . We need to talk to each other and inform each other . . . know what it is like for each other . . . maybe help each other."

I asked Hakim why he felt this conversation was so important. His response was striking: "You know . . . I can be curious. . . . I can try and understand, hell, because I am standing out here selling books and I see the newsstand right around the corner . . . I see the cabs fly past me . . . I can say, hey, maybe I can make more money there . . . but that is not the main reason for me. . . . I am quite happy selling these books as long as Giuliani leaves me alone . . . but the point is that if we don't talk to each other. . . . If I am not talking to you and you with other brothers and sisters, then we will find that the white man will decide how and who will speak to whom. . . . We won't have any control over how we understand each other."

Not three years after this conversation, in one specific public policy initiative, the Giuliani administration collapsed two aspects of the "globalized" moment into one: African American–immigrant relations as the potential domain of resistance, on the one hand, and the disciplining of the city's "colored" workforce as it served the new urban middle class, on the other. With "Operation Refusal," the Giuliani administration managed to transform a moment full of promise for a new negotiation of relations between the African American community and the immigrant community into one centered around a pathetic display of immigrant demonization.

In November 1999, Danny Glover, the famous Hollywood actor, was refused a ride by many drivers of empty taxis as he waited on Broadway attempting to hail a cab. Glover, angry that he was not being picked up because of his skin color, first complained to the TLC, but then decided that a much better approach would be to open a dialogue with the New York Taxi Workers Alliance. Two entirely disconnected responses unfolded.

The first was "Operation Refusal," the city's response. The second was a set of initiatives devised by the Alliance; Glover's lawyer, Randolph McLaughlin; and other African American activists. The difference between these two responses is a fascinating study in the basic assumptions from which they emerge. Operation Refusal not only assumed the worst about all immigrant drivers but cynically wove itself into the Quality of Life logic. It became a money-making and fear-inducing scam. The Alliance's response, which acknowledged real difficulties in immigrant–African American relations arising from complex patterns of both racism and xenophobia, attempted to turn the incident into a moment of consciousness raising.

The Giuliani administration slapped together "Operation Refusal" in a little more than a week. It was essentially an entrapment procedure. As publicized, the entrapment procedure was as follows: A two-person team of undercover TLC inspectors, one black or Latino and the other white, would hail a cab. The two inspectors would place themselves on an avenue at a distance of a half block from each other, the African American or Latino inspector farther up the street and the white inspector a little way down. As cabs came by, both inspectors would hail one. If a driver were to bypass the African American inspector and stop for only the white inspector, then he would be booked for discrimination, and suspension or revocation proceedings on his hack license would begin.

On paper this program sounded fair. Its obvious liberal sentiment prevented the media from investigating it with any seriousness. In practice, though, the program was a sham from the beginning. The scope of the scam is so extensive that it defies explanation unless we can look at it from within the framework of the Quality of Life Program and against the backdrop of a racist white establishment.

On the first day of its implementation, only seven out of more than seven hundred drivers tested were penalized for discrimination—that is, fewer than 1 percent of drivers proved to be "racist." The media and the public lost interest in the story after that, assuming that all was well because a system was in place that would deter some drivers from racist behavior. But very shortly after the press published this statistic, the Alliance received its first Operation Refusal case. Ali Baig, a driver with five years of experience, came to our office just as his license was about to be revoked. He was one of the seven picked up, allegedly for racism, on the first day of the program. He swore that he would fight the charge. "I did nothing wrong," he insisted. Baig had been at his shift change at Houston Street, just about to begin his night shift, when he realized that his meter was out of paper. To be unable to provide a receipt to a customer is an offense, according to TLC rules.

Baig decided he would go to the Lahore Deli a block away to buy some meter paper (which the deli stocks because its clientele consists mostly of drivers). Just as he was setting off to the deli, two white women approached him and asked to be taken to Fifth Avenue and Eighteenth Street. Baig explained to them that he was on his way to buy meter paper and was therefore unable to take them to their destination. As the women turned away, two undercover inspectors from across the street raced down and impounded Baig's cab and suspended his license. One of the inspectors ran after the women to ask them for their names and addresses so that he might use them during the trial. The two women brushed the inspector off, jumped into another cab, and went on their way. Baig spent the next ten months of his life trying to get his license back. On day one, Operation Refusal was already visibly nothing more than a program of harassment and a money-making venture for the city.

Beginning with Baig, the Alliance received more than twenty-five Operation Refusal cases over the next year, each one further illuminating how a crass, simple-minded antiracism program could go awry. Of course, there were a few cases in which the Alliance organizers felt that the drivers' responses were racist, but a large majority had little to do with racism. For instance, less than a month after Baig's case, we received Aslam Khan's. After he dropped off a white passenger, Aslam was hailed by a black undercover inspector operating alone. When Aslam refused, explaining that he was headed for his garage because his door was not working, the TLC inspector did not check for a malfunctioning door. Instead he impounded the cab and suspended Aslam's license. Aslam tried to explain that he had realized that his rear right-side door was broken only when the previous customer had been unable to open it from the outside. But the explanation fell on deaf ears. Even though his garage testified and produced evidence that the door was indeed malfunctioning, Aslam could not get his license back.

As a range of cases came in through the door, it became patently clear that the "noble" objective of preventing discrimination was merely a cover. As the Operation Refusal cases went to trial, the TLC violated every due-process rule in the book. For all regular summonses it issues to drivers, including those responding to customer complaints, a TLC administrative law judge (ALJ) presides over a hearing and makes a guilty or not-guilty decision, which is then subject to appeal. The ALJs who preside over these cases are employees of the TLC, often on short-term contracts of a year or less, and they report to the chairperson.

This already forms a biased basis for a court system, and drivers have long insisted that the TLC court system was a sham. However, in cases like those under Operation Refusal, in which the TLC is itself the plaintiff, the TLC cannot conceivably provide a fair trial, and so the agency is forced to send the cases to an independent authority. Because the same requirement would hold in similar situations for any city agency that has the power to prosecute, the city possesses such an independent authority: the Office of Administrative Trials and Hearings (OATH). In the cases it handles for the TLC, an OATH judge, who works for the city but not for the TLC, is to hold a hearing and recommend a course of action. The TLC can then accept or reject that recommendation after the full commission, made up of eight commissioners and the chair, read it, allow for comments, and vote.

As Operation Refusal unfolded, the TLC found it difficult to justify the on-the-spot suspension of a driver's license. Such measures amounted to sentencing a driver without a trial. Hence the

TLC decided that in the interest of serving the public, it would suspend the license on the spot but grant a hearing within five business days. What it failed to reveal was that the hearing it promised was not really a hearing. In what was called a "summary suspension hearing," the driver appeared before a TLC administrative law judge (ALJ) and had his entire record evaluated—not just the facts of the current case. Based on what the judge thought of the driver's entire record, and of the often trivial offenses therein (perhaps a conviction for failure to maintain a trip sheet five years ago, or an alleged "unsafe" drop-off twelve inches off the curb three years ago), he or she would then decide whether or not to continue the suspension until the real trial.

In short, the TLC used any means it could to make the case that the suspension it had instituted under Operation Refusal was justified and should continue until the real hearing. The problems with this are obvious. Virtually any driver who has spent, say, three years driving yellow cabs in the city has a TLC ticket somewhere on his record, followed by a guilty verdict in the kangaroo court of the TLC. What such past incidents, for which drivers had already been penalized, had to do with the alleged racism of which these drivers now stood accused was entirely unclear, but in the roughly twenty-five cases I followed, no driver who went through the summary suspension hearing came out with a reinstated license. In other words, it was a sham hearing that allowed the TLC to continue the suspension indefinitely, even while keeping the liberal elements of the press off its back. Furthermore, in every case that the NYTWA was involved in, the OATH judges refused to recommend license revocation on grounds that such a recommendation would violate other city laws. In some cases the judge went as far as to rap the TLC on its knuckles for violations of due process. And when the TLC considered the judges' recommendations at its mandated hearings, in all the cases we handled the chairwoman tried desperately to bully the commissioners into overruling the OATH recommendation and proceeding with revocation, but the commissioners could not agree to do so.

The first such hearing I attended was that of Mohammed Khan, who was later to become one of the core Alliance OC members. The OATH judge had only recommended a fine, but when the hearing began, TLC chairwoman McKechnie went berserk. She refused to stick to the facts of this case and of the OATH recommendation, attempting instead to put Khan's entire six-year history as a driver on trial. She produced drama: "For heavens sakes," she shouted at the other commissioners who had disagreed, "he has had a customer complaint before. . . . Isn't that enough for you?" Commissioner Torres, the most strident of the dissenting commissioners, looked confused and went back to his papers. He clearly had difficulty suppressing his annoyance. "I am a lawyer," he reminded her, before explaining patiently that while Khan did have an old customer complaint in his record, the facts of this case were simple: Khan had been found not guilty. Torres was at pains to explain that to suspend the driver's license on the basis of the old record, especially where the driver had been found not guilty in the case at hand, was the worst practice of double jeopardy. In the end, Khan got his license back because four out of the seven commissioners present at that hearing agreed with Torres. But by then he had spent more than six months without a job.

Unable to revoke licenses in many cases (although by the time the OATH verdicts came through, most drivers had already suffered anywhere between six and ten months of suspension), the chairwoman, a direct Giuliani appointee, decided to take the law into her own hands yet again. She brought about two changes in TLC policy. First, the commission was no longer required to give the driver a summary suspension hearing unless the "driver demanded it." Second, the cases would no longer go first to OATH but would be handled by a TLC ALJ, whose recommendations would be considered only by the chairperson herself, not the full commission. In other words, the driver would now be suspended without even a sham hearing, and when it came to the driver's future, the chairwoman could now do as she pleased without having to meet any onerous standards of evidence or due process. She proceeded to revoke licenses on the feeblest of charges.

As the Alliance fought the grossly unjust Operation Refusal, one thing was clear from the chairwoman's attitude and method: if ever we needed a confirmation that the primary objective of the TLC under Giuliani was to strike fear in drivers and thus to discipline them, the series of public hearings we attended was more than enough evidence. The anger, contempt, and desire to punish that McKechnie carried into the room each time spoke volumes of a clear-minded policy of aggressive punishment on flimsy charges to create an environment of fear that would in turn produce the "obedient driver."

The Alliance had to file two lawsuits in federal courts to force McKechnie and the TLC into a less aggressive posture. The first case was for damages, due to the improper processes associated with Operation Refusal. The second was directly against the chairwoman for misuse of her office, in a case in which she had gotten a North African driver's license revoked through a complaint in which she was the plaintiff before an ALJ, who was her employee. In that second case, Hasan Suleiman had an angry exchange with a woman trying to cross the street while he was attempting a legal right turn on a green signal. The brief altercation ended with Hasan's exchanging a few angry words with the woman and speeding away. Several weeks later he received a customer complaint summons. At the hearing, the woman took the stand against him. The ALJ threw the book at Hasan, revoking his license. Afterward, Hasan saw the woman leaving the building with an entourage of deputy commissioners, secretaries, and even security guards standing to attention. He put two and two together: he had run afoul of the TLC chairwoman. He came to the Alliance several months later. The case went to court, and Hasan received a good settlement and his license back, though not until a cover story on his case in *Newsday*[10] (and a few other embarrassments) forced the chair to leave office seven months before her term ended.

The Operation Refusal case took longer to resolve in a federal circuit court. In the end, the judge ruled that such operations fell within the jurisdiction of the TLC, but that the TLC had indeed violated due process and had not paid enough attention to evaluating the merits of the cases. Overall, fourteen drivers who went to court as petitioners with the Alliance received a total of more than $100,000 in compensation.

It was remarkable that Operation Refusal, an initiative that paid so little heed to simple matters of justice and process, abused immigrant drivers in the name of combating racism. By contrast, when Danny Glover reached out to the Alliance, the driver community responded very thoughtfully in a series of public meetings in Manhattan. All the parties involved—Randolph McLaughlin, Glover's lawyer; Glover himself; Virginia Fields, the Borough of Manhattan president; Bhairavi; and a whole host of African American riders and immigrant drivers—offered explanations and suggestions. At a public meeting in Harlem, Javaid laid out the situation from a driver's point of view:

> Let me be honest and tell you what I do when I drive. I discriminate. But I discriminate not because I have anything against any one community but because I have to pay the lease. If I get a ride to the Bronx during rush hour when I make most of my money in Manhattan,

I am screwed. It takes me, say, forty-five minutes to go to the Bronx and another forty-five to come back . . . this is if the traffic is heavy but moving, as it should be in rush hour. But if I get stuck on the FDR, as it happens all the time, then you can add another half or full hour to the time lost. I would have made fifteen dollars in two hours whereas I could have made up to forty or fifty in the city. If I make fifteen in two hours during rush hour, you can bet I am going home with empty pockets. So guess what I do . . . I try and see who might go outside Manhattan and avoid him or her. . . . I do this to Indians and Pakistanis. . . . I don't want to go to Flushing or Brighton Beach during rush hour. . . . As a matter of fact, going to Wakefield in the Bronx is far better than going to Flushing or Jamaica.

Of course, late in the night I am looking out for fare beaters. There are hundreds of them in the city, black and white and brown . . . people who get into your cab, take you for a ten-dollar ride and then get out of the cab without paying on a one-way street and run in the opposite direction. What can I do? Nothing . . . write my ten dollars off and come back. And of course, I am sometimes simply afraid. . . . I look at somebody and am scared. You can tell me that I am racist at that moment because the only way I come to a decision that somebody is dangerous is based on some stereotypes . . . and I will agree . . . but I have been mugged at gunpoint while in my cab and I am not going to take any chances.

Many of the reporters who attended the Harlem meeting or interviewed drivers on this issue chose to highlight the last aspect of

Javaid's testimony—fear—rather than the first, which was a racial coding of a class dynamic. It reminded me of Hakim, the book vendor, and his prediction that immigrants and African Americans would lose control over the conversation between them. In projecting what is essentially a white middle-class fear onto an immigrant, a far more complex class dynamic was deliberately obfuscated. In contrast, by openly admitting that he sometimes operated on the basis of stereotypes, Javaid was demonstrating a willingness to take responsibility for his attitudes and to engage in discussion. The Alliance found, when this crisis erupted, that such honesty and openness among drivers was common. Immigrants carry racist stereotypes about African Americans (just as African Americans carry xenophobic attitudes toward immigrants) with them from home, often from the flourishing American media presence in the Third World—from Clint Eastwood films, in which the black male is alternately a wastrel or a violent, crazy person. Media images of African Americans in much of the Third World until very recently were almost consistently negative. Such stereotypes, combined with home-grown attitudes about color and caste, produce a complicated field of racial dynamics within immigrant communities.

Nonetheless, most immigrants living in cities have a very keen awareness of racism. They may fall into it, in spite of such awareness, because it is easier to be racist; the system is set up that way. This is critical to understand, because it is the fundamental difference between middle-class immigrant racism and working-class immigrant racism. The driver uses racial coding, even against his own community, because he feels he has no choice given the lease that sits around his neck like a noose. He has no illusion that it is okay to be racist; he just responds to the traps of daily life in the ways he can. This explains why, when the Glover crisis hit, drivers' first reaction was very consciously defensive. In contrast, I have had numerous conversations with middle-class South Asians isolated in the suburbs who speak prejudicially about African Americans without any self-consciousness. With a little prompting, they will say the same kinds of things about the South Asian working class. Inasmuch as middle-class immigrant communities see themselves bound to white America by reason of class, there is no material basis for building solidarity between them and impoverished communities of color. On the other hand, for immigrant working-class communities, the very conditions of their daily material existence form the basis for such solidarity.

When the Alliance evaluated its work on the Glover crisis, it concluded that the drivers' responses had been very positive and hopeful. McLaughlin and Glover suggested training programs recognizing the problem as one borne not only of race but of a lethal and complex intersection of race and class. The Alliance issued a full proposal in response to the crisis. We suggested that all new drivers be trained by a team of older, more experienced drivers and civil rights activists. We also proposed reevaluating redlining in the industry (something for which the TLC was responsible), and we offered some suggestions to ensure that drivers would not be penalized for accepting out-of-borough fares at peak time. Speaking at a forum at Pace University, Bairhavi explained the redlined nature of the industry thus:

> If we are really serious about understanding and solving the problem, then we need to look at a series of historical mistakes and begin a process of redefinition. For instance, the taxi industry is what it is today because of the TLC. Prior to 1970s when the TLC did not exist, there were only yellow cabs in NYC. The TLC created a three-tier system of taxi service in the city. At the top end are the elite limo services for the high-end

executive, a service operating only on corporate accounts. Then you have the city's yellow-cab population that is available for street hails and are under an entirely horrendous leasing structure where a driver has to make more than $20 per hour to make for himself anything close to a reasonable income and thus finds it necessary to stay in the central business districts to make ends meet. Finally, you have the car service sector of the industry, cars that are, on paper, meant to be on call but that are available for street hails in the outer boroughs and upper Manhattan. It's a taxi service that primarily serves the poor. Who created this system? The TLC. And if we are to recognize this as the basis of the problem, then we need to attack this to find a solution. The NYTWA is therefore proposing a reevaluation of the city's transportation infrastructure and the taxi infrastructure with upper Manhattan and other outer-borough residents' priorities made central. We argue that we need such an effort with African American and immigrant workers leadership.

The TLC chose to ignore all these suggestions and instead stuck to its own "sentence and execute on the spot" practice, Operation Refusal, which served mostly to manage the public relations side of the issue. As the months went by and racism within the taxi industry faded as a public issue (though it remained important to African Americans and to drivers), TLC inspectors ran amok in a blitz of entrapments. Waheed was one such victim: "I was in a hotel line in midtown . . . number three in the line, when an African American person approached me and told me that he wanted to go to the Bronx. I told him that I was in the line and that he should go up to the first taxi in the line. He went away and stood away from the taxi line, till I reached the first place and the doorman asked me to pull up and take a customer who had just come out of the hotel. At this point the inspector intervened and told the doorman that I was not to be given the passenger and that he was suspending my license."

The inspector/customer was enforcing an obscure law in the taxi rulebook that says that a passenger can choose any taxi she wants at a hotel line and does not have to get into the first available taxi. Waheed was livid: "In every other place, the airport or Port Authority or Penn Station, the dispatcher goes by order . . . customer after customer into the first taxi in the line. How am I to know that at a hotel this rule does not apply? He [the inspector] did not approach me again when I was first in the line. I was at the first position for more than a minute waiting for a passenger to come out of the hotel. Should I have noticed that he was standing there and asked him again? If he was really testing me, why didn't he come up again to me?"

It is clear from Waheed's experience and those of many other Alliance members that inspectors used the rules created under Operation Refusal to victimize drivers. However, it would be wrong to conclude that the problem was merely one of bad inspectors. The larger context was one wherein it was not just acceptable but actually TLC policy to strike fear into drivers, through a whole range of disciplinary techniques. The policy's purpose was once again to assert a new level of control over the driver workforce. Whether it be the "Disney rumor" or Operation Refusal, both point to the same logic: a project to discipline drivers into providing suburban-style bliss to the city's new white middle class. In the end, the primary goal of many of the Giuliani administration's policies affecting the taxi industry was to create a more subservient driver who, as Kurshid put it, would even under duress say only, "Yes, sir."

6

THE BORDERS OF GLOBALIZATION:
NEGOTIATING THE METROPOLIS

MALIK MAJID DROVE a cab in New York City for several years. He died in Pakistan on November 24, 2000, just a day before he was to return to New York. I last saw him on June 12 of the same year, the day I left for India. We met up at the New York University Immigrant Rights Clinic to do some translation work on his brokerage case. Then he drove me to Forty-second Street so I could collect my plane ticket. After all the work was done, we pulled up in front of a deli and I ran in to fetch two cups of coffee. As we sat in his cab drinking our coffees, Majid reflected on how lucky we were. "At least we can go home," he said.

The conversation was a long one. We knew we would not see each other for many months, because he would leave for Pakistan before I returned from India. We spoke about his family, part of which was in New York and part in Pakistan. He was a U.S. citizen, but even those family members already in the United States (his wife, two daughters and a son) were not. Three sons and three daughters remained in Pakistan, and he spoke of bringing them over. "But it is difficult now," he lamented. "Four of them are already adults, and it is going to take years to get them here." There was also another daughter—not his own, but the daughter of a deceased friend. Majid was her guardian in Pakistan. "I will never be able to get her over," he told me. "My greatest concern is to get her married."

When Majid died of a heart attack, questions about the fate of his family troubled me. Would his family members in New York be able to secure citizenship, now that he, their sponsor, was dead? What about those still in Pakistan? Would they ever be able to join their mother in the United States? Or would she just go back to Pakistan? What would happen to Majid's adopted daughter? Who would get her married? Who took care of her now?

Majid had always resolutely insisted that his youngest son, who was nineteen when his father died, should not work. "Let him study. Once he begins to work, he will never again study," Majid told me once, when he brought his son to the Alliance office to meet with Bhairavi and me. "He has all sorts of crazy ideas . . . in Pakistan all he wanted to do was to cultivate the little land we have . . . he went and did a degree in agriculture. . . . In Pakistan . . . as if that was going to get him anywhere . . . and now here, he keeps asking me if we can get a plot of land for him to farm. . . . I presume that's the only thing he knows."

Would Majid's son go away to Pakistan to farm, or would he become a taxi driver? Or would he fulfill his father's hopes and continue his studies? I have no way of knowing.

In many ways, Majid's story was structured around borders. He began his adult life as a locomotive engine driver, working the steam train on a route that crossed the Indo-Pakistani border at Wagah. The track that ran across the no man's land between border posts climbed a steep gradient from Pakistan into India. As he tells it, "You have to know that slope well . . . else you cannot ever get past it . . . you have to get a pick up and then run full steam up hill and only then will you be able to get across. Once an engineer came from Lahore. He pushed me aside and said that he was going to take the train across that day. I tried to tell him that he had to deal with the gradient. But he didn't listen and the train came to a grinding stop in the middle . . . something you are not allowed to do. Once the train leaves Wagah, it is not supposed to stop. . . . You know how the train is escorted don't you . . . there are Pakistani Rangers and Indian Border Security Forcemen racing their horses alongside, up and down, up and down to prevent illegal crossings."

He reflected that we as Indians and Pakistanis get a chance to get past that border here in the United States: "Here the union is our new world without borders. . . . We have built it so that an Indian and a Pakistani can be brothers . . . where an African and I can be united . . . and there, just like here, it has to be people there who will make that decision to get rid of the division."

THINKING THROUGH BORDERS

I have often reflected on that statement of Majid's. It seems remarkably true; only those whose lives are integrated culturally, socially, and economically can overcome the regressive logic of nationalism.

My conversations with Majid, I've realized, always returned to the subjects of division, separation, and borders. He was a man of the border and understood its artificiality completely. In his days as a locomotive driver, his life was deeply transgressive, because he built relations on the "wrong" side of the border. In New York, he tried to do the same: to connect with all of us in the Alliance entirely outside the frame of nations and nationalism.

When I think about Majid's life, stretched between the Wagah border and the shores of the Atlantic, I cannot but help but feel that his story captures a basic truth about immigrant working-class life. We live a fundamentally divided existence, wherein the life we have known for generations has been torn asunder. And yet, at the very moment that the familiar social order has been nearly annihilated, the possibility of a new one emerges. That's the union of which Majid dreamed. In the months after Majid's death, when I spoke to other Alliance members about their experiences as immigrants in the land of the gold rush, the stories Majid told me repeatedly resurfaced in my mind.

The stories of migration are not easily told. Full of pain and regret, they circulate in whispers among confidants who know each other well. The more such stories I hear, the more strikingly they seem to contradict the conventional wisdom that globalization has made the world smaller. The world is allegedly easier to traverse than it used to be, and staying in touch across great distances is supposed to have become simple. But how does a family that is divided between at least two continents, with little or no prospect of reuniting with any regularity, reflect a smaller world? How does the presence of a large male workforce in New York, with workers' families stuck all over the Third World, unable to join their husbands, sons, or fathers, make for a world where staying in touch is easier? We discussed these issues heatedly at Alliance meetings. Surinder was candid: "The last time I went home, Delhi had changed. There was McDonald's and Pepsi, KFC and Baskin-Robbins. It is easy for them to get the permits to open up everything they want in Delhi, but its almost impossible for me to get a green card for my father and mother. And even if I did, will they want to live here? I thank God all the time that my brother is still there in India to look after my parents because given how it is, I cannot even think of taking my family to India every year. It costs too much. . . . For all of us to go, just the tickets will cost six, seven thousand. I cannot afford it. If I can go once every three years, I am lucky."

In the age of globalization, the world is indeed becoming smaller and easier to traverse—for capital and for those who manage and represent its interests. But for those who labor, the nation and its borders have thicker walls. To them, national boundaries sometimes seem as formidable and impenetrable as the barbed wire surrounding a prison.

THE PREHISTORY OF A NEW YORK
TAXI DRIVER

Like Majid, Awan and Asif are both older immigrants. "I never thought I would end up in America," Awan told us one day. "The first time I left Pakistan was in 1974. I went to Afghanistan and from there to Iran, Iraq, and Turkey . . . all of this is by train, you know . . . and from there to Hungary and Czechoslovakia before finally working for nearly a year in Germany. Then I came back home and got married. But I didn't stay long . . . in two years I was off again . . . again through Europe. This time I worked in Belgium and Germany for nearly two years before going back home. I stayed for a while before starting out again. This time I finally ended up in England and after working six months there I got a chance to come here. It was simpler then . . . you could go from country to country very easily. Now look at the situation. I am a citizen and just to get my son citizenship papers is so difficult. I have sent the application and the fees three times already . . . and now they tell me he is over-aged and cannot get the papers through me. Now he has to apply independently."

Awan's story testifies to the fact that the borders of nation-states were far more porous when we might have least expected them to be. Common sense would lead us to associate ease in traversing the planet with globalization and a world of closed borders with the Cold War. But Awan's experience demonstrated the exact opposite trajectory.

Like Awan, Asif left Pakistan early, in 1973. He went to Libya and later to Saudi Arabia. As the oil economies of the Middle East began to slow, he found his way to Texas through an oil company. *"Hum tho Bhutto ke aulad hai janaab,"* he says with a smirk. "I am a product of Bhutto. I was one of the first to leave my town, just months after they opened a passport office."

Pakistan emerged from British colonialism with the partition of the Indian subcontinent in 1947. Among other things the subcontinent inherited from colonial rule was the Punjab Land Act, which created large land holding, all over Western (Pakistani) Punjab and Sindh, and small but very productive land holdings in East (Indian) Punjab.[1] Within a very short period after independence, Pakistan became a client state of the United States. As its economy was integrated into a system of U.S. client-state economies, one early change was known as the green revolution, and it involved introducing large scale mechanization and capitalization into the agricultural sector.[2] As a result of mechanization and capitalization, tens of thousands of landless workers had no choice but to migrate to the cities. The cities, however, had not begun to develop the anticipated industrial base, largely because the United States flooded the Pakistani market with its own cheap manufactured goods. Tensions ripened. Zulfikar Ali Bhutto, Pakistan's second democratically elected prime minister, came to power on a wave of popularity when he offered the dream of socialism to unemployed, newly urbanized youth. Awan remembers clearly what he saw in Pakistan in the late 1960s and early 1970s: "And what were we to do? No land, no education. My father joined the army. And with all the savings that he could put together as an ordinary soldier, he finally bought a patch of land in our village near Sargoda. But that didn't mean anything. My brother and I left after we finished high school . . . to Karachi . . . the land is still there . . . but it cannot even support my parents. After I came to the United States, we built a house on that land for my parents . . . and now we have built two more."

Bhutto never delivered socialism, nor did he develop much by way of an industrial sector; instead he struck upon the ingenious idea of exporting the unemployed. Instead of socialism, the

Pakistanis got passport offices in every small town. As the oil economies of the Gulf grew, so did the export of labor.[3]

The green revolution came much later to Indian Punjab, and India's experience was different as a result. Pannu Saab, as he is popularly known, is a veteran editor of *Naya Zamana,* the newspaper that was once run by the Communist Party of India. "Indian Punjab," he told me, "is a very different case from Pakistani Punjab." The essential difference is that in Pakistani Punjab the Zamindari system was in place, meaning that a very small number of families held land on a large scale. Land-holdings of more than two hundred acres are common in Pakistan. In Indian Punjab, the case is very different. The most fertile stretch of Indian Punjab is called the *doaaba* (literally "two rivers," or the land between two rivers; *do* is two and *aab* is river in Persian). In the *doaaba,* the largest land-holding was not more than twenty-five acres, and a large number of farmers held as little as five to ten acres. In other words, the Pakistani farmers—the Zamindars—had significant access to large amounts of capital, while the Indian Sikh farmers of the *doaaba* were prosperous but did not enjoy the same level of access to capital because their land base was smaller. Pannu Saab analyzed the Indian case for me: "The *doaaba* region was the region that experienced the green revolution, and you will find that most of the Sikh migration to Britain, Canada, and the United States from the 1970s onwards comes from the *doaaba*. The smaller the land holding, the quicker you thought up the idea of sending at least one of your sons abroad. If you were a small farmer, there was no way, at least initially, you could afford the tractors and the threshers. And if you managed to find a way to get your son across then there you are, you have immediately found the answer. You will find records of U.S.-manufactured tractors and other equipment being imported based on payments already made in the United States through the late 1970s and even up to the early 1980s."

Such dramatic changes in Third World economies are common themes in taxi drivers' stories. "I am a farmer, man," Theodore told me one afternoon at the airport. "All this union stuff . . . I don't know, man. I just work here so that I can go back to Haiti and farm my land." Again, Theodore's story is one of American grain and American meat entering the Haitian market. "Have you heard of the *couchon creole*?" he asked me, detailing the fate of the Haitian pig, which he explained was fundamental to the Haitian economy. Pigs required little investment and were particularly hardy and sustainable assets to "the small farmers and the poor people of Haiti." He continued: "Gone . . . you won't find one in Haiti now . . . all killed, shot dead, and hunted out for immediate annihilation . . . to be replaced with the hybrid American pig supplied to us by USAID. . . . Which of course needs a special feed and special injections which only the rich farmers and the companies can afford."

The Haitian government, in cooperation with USAID, had sent out armed men to capture and kill the local pigs. Then it introduced the American pig. The logic was simple: Haiti would now supply a new market for the U.S. agribusiness firms that sold not only the new pig but also its specialized feed, inoculations, and other animal husbandry resources.[4] Theodore says, "I don't want to be here. But for me to have a decent life in Haiti I have to spend five or six months here." His life, I came to understand, is entirely patterned around Haiti's agricultural seasons, and it has been painfully and concretely reshaped by the neocolonialist forces that would probably seem distant and abstract to many of his passengers.

To note these large-scale agrarian changes in India, Pakistan, or Haiti is not to argue that all Third World migration into the

United States is connected to changes American-inspired "developmental" regimes induced. (The International Monetary Fund and the World Bank inaugurated such soft imperialism in the 1950s. It turned into a more brutal structural adjustment program only in the 1980s.) Clearly, these trajectories merged with earlier and later migratory patterns. For instance, the British colonial army recruited large numbers of Sikhs after 1857; many such soldiers found themselves in Hong Kong, Singapore, and Britain after the Second World War.[5] The Sikh communities established in the United Kingdom, Canada, and the United States during this time would help lay the foundation for a new wave of migration in the 1970s.

Rizwan, who came to the United States on a "lottery" visa,[6] characterizes this confluence as follows: "Once migration starts from a region for one reason or the other, then it picks up speed. You will find one out of every three Pakistani drivers is from one area in Punjab: Gujarat. It's a rural area. Many of the drivers support their families back at home . . . maybe there are one or two brothers who are still there farming. But once it starts then other reasons come in. For instance, during Zia's time, many political refugees came out of Pakistan . . . students who were involved in the democracy movement."

Whether the precipitating event was the green revolution or the brutal military dictatorship of General Zia, Pakistan's ruler from 1977 to 1988, Third World labor migrated into the First World generally due to shifts in the global economy. As globalization bloomed into its full form in the 1990s and the new century, its dynamics exerted ever more formidable control over the flow of labor.

Over the years I've known Kurshid, every day, without fail, he has done one thing before leaving for work each morning at 5:00 A.M.: He makes a one-minute phone call to his ailing mother.

Kurshid is in the United States for good, living a life of isolation here to ensure that he can pay his family's medical bills back home. He is caught in a bind only partly of his own making. He tells me often that if he had his way he would go home. But he can't. That Kurshid must instead make his daily phone call demonstrates how tightly borders are controlled in the contemporary economy—not for capital, of course, but for workers.

One chilly November afternoon in 1997 I stood outside the Al Fala mosque in Queens, waiting for the Pakistani embassy to give us an NOC (No Objection Certificate) to transport the body of Agha Saleem, a comrade who had died unnoticed and undocumented. Saleem was one of the early taxi driver organizers, and the friend through whom I began working in the industry. His lonely death exemplifies the strange limbo of migrant male working class life, where family is often ten thousand miles away. As Saleem's body was lifted into the cargo hold of a Pakistan International Airlines flight, the thought that preoccupied those of us who stood by, teary-eyed and at a loss, was about the tragedy of a loving person being reunited with his family after ten years—but in a body bag.

In the last three decades, "globalization" has, ironically, depended on shoring up the borders between nation states, especially those between the Third World and the First. What is even more important to note is that since September 11, 2001, those borders have hardened more than ever before. As thousands of working-class and poor immigrant men are plucked from their homes, detained, and deported without any semblance of due process, the immigrant's internal sense of incarceration intensifies. "I sometimes feel I should stop driving," Kurshid told me one evening, months after September 11. He had just encountered a passenger who kept calling him Al Qaeda: "I know I am perfectly legal . . . my wife is after all an American citizen. But these days, you don't know, they will find something about you that you don't even remember and lock you up for months. It's just not worth it . . . you know . . . I have always said that driving is a strange life. You are constantly surrounded by people but you are all alone . . . and every passenger who sits in your cab is an unknown entity."

Such acts of individual racism, which had sharply declined in the post–civil rights era, come back to the fore at moments such as September 11 because racism has merely been managed in this country, not wiped out. In post–September 11 New York, institutional racism, too, became starkly manifest. The Immigration and Naturalization Service, the Federal Bureau of Investigation, and police departments all profiled Arab and South Asian men.

Just days after September 11, the Alliance received calls from drivers saying that Guiliani had declared that yellow-taxi drivers were not eligible for emergency assistance. The Federal Emergency Management Assistance (FEMA) program turned drivers away at the door; they were not even permitted to fill out a form. In March 2002, the Alliance held an open public hearing on emergency assistance at Hunter College. More than three thousand drivers attended, packing the auditorium and spilling into the foyer. More than three hundred drivers signed up to testify at the hearing, but in the end only forty got to speak. One of them was Javaid Chaudhury. He recalled: "I dropped off a passenger, an elderly Jewish gentleman, at the World Trade Center on the morning of September 11. Just as I was about to pull off the curb after dropping my passenger, I heard the roar and then saw the first plane go into the tower. I was frozen but then recovered and ran for my life."

Javaid's cab was never recovered. It was probably buried under the rubble of the collapsing towers. He tried several times to obtain emergency assistance, but he was always turned away. "What else can I say?" he asked. "If I am not an affected person, who else is?"

In his public testimony Javaid only spoke of losing his car. But outside, while we smoked a cigarette, he told me another story: "When I ran from my cab, I was so scared . . . but then once I was a few blocks away I stopped, like many others, and began to watch. It is at this point that a new fear took control of me. I had no idea what to do . . . I started running back toward my cab . . . I wanted to get to my taxi and get my hack license and rate card out of the cab . . . I don't know what happened . . . but I kept thinking . . . I am Muslim and if they find my identification under the WTC, they may think that I had something to do with the attack."

Javaid never made it back to his cab because even as he began his fearful sprint back, the second plane crashed into the second tower. But in that moment when Javaid felt the need to get his license out of the taxi, the power of institutionalized American racism stands framed. Clearly Javaid's was an "exaggerated" fear in as much as his taxi's presence in the rubble did not cause him any trouble. And yet we know that thousands of Arab and South Asian Muslim men were detained and held (and continue to be held) in jails for several years after 9/11 for no fathomable reason with no due process at all.

Sami, a driver of more than ten years, came into the Alliance office months after the FEMA public hearing. He needed help filling out the forms for the rental and mortgage assistance program FEMA had launched in response to our mobilization. By the time the program came to an end, the Alliance had processed at least four thousand such forms. Sami had been evicted because of nonpayment of rent. His concerns, however, were larger: "This cannot go on like this. Today they picked up more than sixty people from Midwood. If it continues like this, there won't be anybody left in the neighborhood. . . . What are they thinking . . . that they can make somebody legal any time they want and then declare them illegal six months later . . . it just makes no sense . . . there is no legal framework left in the United States."

It sounds hyperbolic to say that there is no legal framework left in the United States, but it is fundamentally true. What is truly contradictory about this condition of unabashed and undisguised profiling, harassment, and detention of large numbers of Arab and South Asians is the response to it. At one end are the working-class and urban immigrant communities, along with the political left, who understand the phenomena for what it is: the destruction of the liberal state and the emergence of a neoconservative repressive state. At the other end are the neocons themselves for whom the terms Muslim and terrorist, for instance, merge. To profile and detain a human being for his religious or ethnic identity is perfectly legitimate within this framework. A state that does this is not just acceptable but preferred. It is the people in the middle that are the most interesting. A large part of this segment that identifies itself as liberal finds itself incapable of a systemic critique. For them, the liberal state still works. And when the specific failures of the liberal state stare them in the face, the ad hoc critique that is produced is always that of exception. Within this logic, the detention without trial or sham trials of thousands of immigrants is an exception for which the solution lies within the state itself. For them, Abu Ghraib prison in Iraq is an exception. For them, the war on Iraq matters mostly at the level of the fact that Bush lied about weapons of mass destruction (WMDs). Bush becomes the exception, inasmuch as he lied, because American presidents and the liberal state do not lie. That the war is imperialist, with or without WMDs, is not part of their critique. Javaid's and Sami's fears would seem truly irrational to this segment for they have neither the experience of such treatment nor do they have a theoretical framework that lets them see the

exception itself as the emergent rule. It is precisely the same segment that failed to notice, and when they did notice, dismissed as
an exception, the systematic brutalization of the African American
communities over the last three decades.

In this context, the FEMA victory is significant because it tested
the Alliance like nothing before had. Under conditions of spreading state terror, we produced one of the largest mobilizations in
our history. But we were also painfully aware that the racism of the
INS and FBI continued unchecked. Surely the thousands civilians
killed and brutalized in the Iraq War, and the prisoners of war un-
protected by the Geneva convention in Guantanamo Bay, had it in-
comparably worse than New York's taxi drivers, and we should
never make the mistake of equating the two. But internal incarceration and external war both have their appeal/acceptance in American racism. Sami was livid: "We are all terrorists . . . pick anybody
up whenever you want to . . . all because you have a Muslim name,
and then say you are the best democracy in the world. What is the
use of that rule that Clinton passed that said that we are allowed to
regularize ourselves . . . what their president said is just thrown
away . . . I will tell you this much, there is no worse democracy
than one that just pretends to be one."

Since September 11, most working-class immigrants, those
who have labored in America for years and were deemed legal by
previous administrations, still have no certainty about their status.
What exists in the United States today is not an extraordinary circumstance, but a perfectly ordinary one legitimated by a claim of
extraordinariness.

THE SOCIAL SPACE OF FIGHTING BACK

What is the nature of social life for someone whose daily existence
is defined by isolation and increasingly hostile borders? How does

that person remain culturally whole and retain meaning in his life?

Globalization, as it affects the lives of immigrant workers, most obviously produces a deterritorialized culture, including such phenomena as ethnic restaurants, films, parades, and associations. Immigrants produce this culture with some ease in the United States because of recent advances in media and transport technologies. Anthropologist Arjun Appadurai describes the experience of an immigrant taxi driver who ferries customers through the streets of Chicago while listening to a Saudi religious cleric on tape. The cleric's voice is muted, hardly audible in the back seat. But for the driver, that tape allows him to create a sense of meaning as well as to retain some part of his culture of origin in his everyday life. In recounting this anecdote, Appadurai participates in white America's fetishization of the religious Muslim immigrant. But there is also some truth in the idea that immigrants who experience extreme alienation and dislocation sometimes attempt to reproduce a semblance of the familiar using packaged culture. Still, this experience is often more complicated than Appadurai's stereotypical image—the Muslim driver listening to the voice of Saudi mullah—might lead readers to believe.

"The fatso has gone to sleep," a driver shouted across the crowded room. He was referring to the Pakistani batsman Inzamam Ul Huq, on whom all the Pakistanis in the room were pinning their hopes as the match between India and Pakistan in the 1999 World Cup reached its final stages. The Himalaya Restaurant, just outside the Port Authority bus terminal, was packed. Two rooms with two televisions overflowed with cricket fans. Indian and Pakistani drivers were glued to the screens, and good natured gibes filled the room. Somebody called a Pakistani bowler a reptile, and the room exploded as every Indian player was immediately associated with every possible animal out of a biology textbook. The Indian drivers joined in, correcting the Pakistanis:

"What are you calling him a toad for, brother, I object . . . he is more like an ass . . . I haven't seen him do one small thing right in his entire cricketing life . . . I wonder why they keep him on the team."

Now kababs were making their way from the kitchen to the counter, threading through a forest of immobile human bodies. And slowly, as the tension of the cricket match built, the crowd divided, until the Indians occupied the outer room and the Pakistanis filled the inner room. As the last ball was bowled and India registered its victory, the crowd melted away. There was no great display of national pride from the Indian drivers, nor any loud lament from the Pakistani drivers, whose team had just lost a match to its traditional rival on the subcontinent. Those who stuck around analyzed the game in detail—sharing theories about how the Pakistanis had been paid off to throw the match, or opining that India could never win a match without Sachin Tendulkar, or observing that the Pakistani middle order was of entirely suspect quality.

Matches like this one illustrate the numerous ways in which immigrants reproduce cultural meaning, however deterritorialized and dislocated. Cultural nationalism falls apart in such spaces. Everybody understands the limits of nationalism in a workers' space—one where immigrants, mostly men who work twelve-hour shifts, take their breaks. Within these men's countries of origin, the same match would have been far more easily packaged and experienced as a nationalist event. But when the same "product" enters an immigrant space, its meaning is different, because immigrant workers do not live in a homogenous ethnic space. Instead they must constantly negotiate differences and antagonisms. Although borders and boundaries still exist in an immigrant space, they are neither rigid nor incontestable.

In the Alliance, that negotiated sense of difference is always in order. It is Majid's borderless world, constantly in formation. For working-class immigrants today, in a city like New York, life is bounded by the rapid growth of seemingly impenetrable and incarcerating regimes of borders, which isolate immigrants from their homes and families back in the Third World. But at the same time, daily life is characterized by an engaged and deepening understanding of the production of difference. Such consciousness has great potential to shape political life. In the OC meetings of the Taxi Workers Alliance, and sometimes in the relaxed conversations that follow these meetings, touching on the fragments of family back in Dar-e-Salaam, Dacca, or Dakar—conversations full of humor and anger about national identity and nationalism—there are two conversations that stick in my mind.

The first involves a Sikh driver, Paramjit, whose father was a Naxalite (an armed Maoist revolutionary), whom the Indian state captured and tortured until he lost his mind. But he had taught his son many things before his arrest, when Paramjit was still a teenager. Parked outside my apartment building in Washington Heights, Paramjit told me story after story: of the immense revolutionary potential of the green revolution; of its failure and the emergence of the separatist Khalistani movement; and of how Pakistan hangs as a shadow over Indian Punjab. "My generation has some distance," he said. "But my father's generation saw partition as a betrayal, especially by some elements of the left who went with Pakistan . . . you know, I don't think my father ever understood Pakistan. . . . And look at me here . . . I have two lives. I go to the Gurdwara with my family because that is the only way my children can know what it is to be Sikh, but I also reject everything some people in the Gurdwara say about Islam, because I know so many Pakistanis in flesh and blood who are of my own land and share a world with me . . . Punjab is etched into them in the same way as it is written on me."

Paramjit's embrace of Maoist revolutionary thought, Sikh

identity, and his Pakistani brethren encapsulates the contradictions and the potentialities of immigrant working-class life. His is an instructive example I carry with me.

The other story is Rizwan's. After gradually developing a long-lasting relationship with a set of Bangladeshi drivers, Rizwan told me one night: "If I had remained in Pakistan, I don't think I would ever be able to understand what the Pakistani army did to Bangladeshis. The sheer lies that are taught to us are so complete that I would never have been able to go past them in Pakistan. It is here in the United States that I have found the means to face that truth . . . it's a truth that fundamentally changes my relation to Pakistan."

THE ANTITHESIS
OF MONOCULTURALISM

This characterization of immigrant drivers' lives offers an immediate contrast to the lives of the white middle-class passengers and, for that matter, to the lives of immigrant professionals. For every driver who has not seen his family in years, there is a passenger sitting in his cab who works for a multinational corporation and travels to the driver's home country, returning when he pleases to the security of his home in a U.S. suburb. The pathways of American professionals are startlingly distinct from those of working-class immigrants. And immigrant bourgeois life is a mirror image of white bourgeois life.

In response to Cold War fears of being technologically outstripped by the Soviet bloc, the United States relaxed immigration restrictions for professionals in the 1960s, touching off a wave of professional migration that is well documented (most recently in Vijay Prashad's *Karma of Brown Folk*). Since the 1960s, immigration quotas for technical workers have expanded, delays have been few or nonexistent, and an orderly visa process has allowed immigrant professionals selectively preferential treatment as well as a relatively painless transition from student status to resident alien status. Following September 11, while America's working-class migrant population reeled under an intensive wave of racial profiling and detention, immigrant professionals faced the occasional racist civilian or cop, but no dramatic foreclosure of opportunities.

Just as the working-class immigrant and professional immigrant negotiate the national borders in dramatically different ways, so to do they participate in different cultures. The immigrant professional's suburban life is almost an exact replica of that of the white soccer mom, who drives her children from piano lessons to soccer practice and Kaplan classes. It is true that instead of piano lessons or ballet classes, she may ferry the kids to Bharatanatyam lessons or Muslim cultural centers, but the core idea remains the reproduction of exclusive cultural privilege, or cultural purity. The immigrant working class, meanwhile, occupies the more complex, globalized urban sphere, which offers the possibility of radical cultural unity. A reemergent politics of class, engendered from within a politics of color, is possible within this frame, and it is postnationalist and postethnic. But how is such a politics to be negotiated?

It was late—well past midnight—when Rizwan called. The note of panic in his voice warned me immediately that he wasn't just calling to chat. *"Miya . . . buray din aa gaye yaar,"* he said, trying to lower his voice so as not to betray the fear of the "bad days" that he had just announced: "I just threw a guy out of my car and I am sure he is going to complain . . . he has my medallion number . . . and I am sure he made sure he got my name off the hack license . . . and the motherfucker said I will hear from him again." He paused. "I tried not to react . . . but it was too much."

Rizwan had picked up this passenger near Grand Central

Station, heading for the East Eighties. He had completely forgotten that he'd tuned in, like he normally did at the start of his
shift, to the liberal-left WBAI 99.5, New York's Pacifica station,
until the passenger began shouting: "What the fuck is that on
the radio? Is that the radio? Really? Or are you listening to some
fucked-up tape?" Rizwan informed the passenger that it was indeed the radio. In fact, WBAI was airing a program on New
York City schools. As the host detailed the racist aspects of the
education system, the passenger grew angrier by the minute:
"This cannot be on the radio . . . it's disgusting." When he got
no response from Rizwan, he exploded. "Ask them all to get out
of here . . . who the fuck wants them here . . . leave, man,
leave . . . if you don't like it here." Now Rizwan had a choice:

> But somehow I felt that I should not shut the radio off
> at this moment. To do that would be really bad . . . so
> I let it play on . . . and he just lost it . . . he started
> banging on the seat and calling it all fucked up and
> that we should all get out of here. Here is where I
> should maybe have kept quiet, but I couldn't. I asked
> him if he knew who the person on the radio was and
> of course he didn't and so I told him that the host was
> an African American activist . . . but that didn't shut
> him up . . . He kept saying that he couldn't care who it
> was . . . I knew the guy was Irish by now . . . I had
> guessed it and so I asked him if he was Irish. Now that
> surprised him . . . and he stopped for a moment and
> then said yes . . . I could again have stopped here be-
> cause my question had kind of tripped him a bit. But I
> didn't. I kept driving and in my calmest voice told him
> that we should work on it together. I told him that the
> African Americans got here probably a hundred years

or more before his folks showed up here . . . and that
he should transport his Irish ass back to Ireland, and
then we should move the Italian ass back to Italy and
the German and the British . . . and then we could finally see if the African American should go back and
leave this place to the Native Americans. At this point,
he fell silent and I pulled over and asked him to get out
of my cab.

I asked Rizwan why he had taken the risk. He had many options. Simply shutting the radio off would in all likelihood have
appeased the passenger. He could have remained silent. He could
have asked the passenger not to yell at him. He could have said
something sharp to silence the passenger. In each of these scenar-
ios, he would have minimized the risk of a complaint that could
land him a $350 fine and/or a suspended license. After some back
and forth, Rizwan became silent for a moment, before he said: "I
don't know . . . once you see the connections, once you see how
the racism actually works, then you have no choice . . . it's the ba-
sics of solidarity."

And of course, he knew at the back of his mind that the Alliance would support him to the end on this one—a fact that, at
least unconsciously, must have emboldened him. A few more conversations with other OC members and he was no longer afraid.
That night, a number of drivers told similar stories of solidarity.
But for each driver who, like Rizwan, took a stridently antiracist
position, there are others who choose the safer option of silence.
For the first time in American history we are faced with a new possibility: a politics of class that is not directly forced into the contradiction of race. Of course, this is not yet a fully developed
consciousness in daily urban working-class politics. It is just
emerging, and it contains the seeds of a possible political future.

The most common understanding of globalization is the one I
have cited repeatedly as a foil. It holds that we are approaching a
world without borders—one that technology has made smaller,
and one whose only conflicts are cultural ones, soluble through
greater cultural sensitivity. Such is the view of globalization promoted by business schools and often echoed in liberal media
from the *New York Times* to CNN. After the collapse of the
Soviet Union, claim advocates for this vision of globalization, triumphant capitalism enveloped the world, bringing Western-style
prosperity to its every corner. When farmers in India destroy the
offices of Cargill or oil workers in Nigeria riot against Shell, globalization's apologists explain that such conflicts erupt for cultural
reasons: the farmers and oil workers are "backward" people who,
locked in their "traditions," reject modernity in spite of its
inevitability and liberatory nature. Samuel Huntington, in
his popular book *The Clash of Civilizations,* described Islam as
backward-looking compared to the secular, liberated West.[7] These
were theories shorn of all power relations. They ignored the possibility that the Indian farmers and Nigerian oil workers were responding to the fundamentally unequal class relations that had
been constructed through colonialism, postcolonial developmental imperialism, and more recently, the bludgeoning power of institutions serving global capital, such as the IMF, World Bank,
and World Trade Organization (WTO).

That the rich and powerful prefer the sanitized theory of globalization should not surprise us; after all, it helps them do what
they wish to do. The answer to the question of why large segments
of relatively disempowered white Americans believe in this theory
will constitute the bulk of the next chapter. But before we get
there, we need a more workable understanding of globalization—
one that explains the reality described so far in this book.

Broadly speaking, there are two other, competing theories of globalization. One is the brainchild of a group of theorists who have only recently found a label under which they band together with some difficulty: the postcolonialists. These are largely Third World scholars wishing to challenge most things "Western" or "modern-colonial," particularly Eurocentric assumptions and epistemologies. In examining the postcolonial view of globalization we shall use as an imperfect representative the anthropologist mentioned earlier in this chapter, Arjun Appadurai.

The idea of deterritorialized culture, exemplified by Appadurai's driver listening to the mullah, as a defining aspect of globalization is a pervasive and a resonant one. Such anecdotes perfectly compliment the neoliberal vision of a world where one economic form has triumphed over all others, auguring the end of history, and all conflict is essentially cultural conflict. Appadurai proposes that "migration and media" together call for an approach that is "explicitly transnational—even postnational," and wherein what must be underscored is the fundamental loss of "salience, both methodological and ethical, of the nation-state."[8] He deduces from the bourgeois experience a homogeneity in the condition of migration itself. However, workers' lives involve intense negotiations of borders that practically incarcerate them. These lives are constantly unsettled. In other words, the salience of nation-states in the social and cultural experience of the immigrant worker is the first thing that we need to acknowledge about globalization. Postcolonialist theories of globalization fail where they construct a false opposition between globalization and the territorial state, viewing such an opposition as if from the point of view of a middle-class migrant subject. The immigrant bourgeois, who shares with the white bourgeois the agency to negotiate the nation-state successfully, while reproducing deterritorialized culture in the isolation of a suburb, begins to speak for all immigrants.

In contrast, theorists such as Henri Lefevbre point to more complex readings of globalization, wherein globalization and the territorial states are not opposed to each other. Rather, for Lefevbre the global economy operates through a system of states, and it is precisely the normalization of such a system that makes globalization work. By this reading, globalization requires not a vanishing nation-state but its opposite, an increasingly well-defined territorial state, in order to organize space and provide "the regularization of flows and control of its networks." In Awan's and Asif's life stories, we located a moment during the Cold War when the nation-state was still being normalized, and in its emergent form, it was far more hostile to the mobility of capital and far friendlier to that of the intrepid immigrant worker than the system of nation-states today. In recent times, the nation-state has been brought into better congruence with capital.[9]

In the months I've spent trying to understand what globalization means to the immigrant working class, I've entered into a dialogue about another institution that seems to be fundamentally affected by the contemporary condition of globalized labor: the family. The first set of organizations that were created in response to the conditions of immigrant life were domestic violence groups. Just from that fact, it is clear that something had been dramatically altered in the relationship between the public world of capital and work and the private world of family and home.[10] Again, it took me years to understand that the effects were different for working-class migrants and professional migrants. But both groups witnessed the entry of pathologies created by the structures of public life into the private space of family and home.

In the case of the immigrant bourgeoisie, alienated and racist capitalist life, combined with older, feudal constructions of women's roles, produced a wave of violence inside suburban homes. Working-class immigrant families, too, were recast, but differently. The first time I got fully involved in negotiating family relations, it was at the request of my comrade Rizwan. The INS had detained Rizwan's brother, Imran, on the suspicion that his travel documentation was invalid. In February 2001, after Imran had spent nearly eight months in detention, Rizwan and I finally managed to get him on a plane to Pakistan. He even sent money to pay off Pakistani immigration officials so that Imran would not be harassed at the other end. For the first time in eight months, we sat down that night for a meal free of worry about Imran's detention. Rizwan had aged during those eight months. His frame had fallen, his hair had grayed, and he seemed incapable of having a conversation that didn't involve immigration. Said Rizwan: "I am worried about what we are creating . . . of what we are doing to ourselves. . . . All these days I just went about life here as if all this was normal, but seeing what Imran had to go through has really made me think . . . I think about my family all the time . . . their reaction . . . I cannot understand it . . . here was their son in jail in the U.S. and all they kept asking was if there was a chance of him getting in . . . just like Imran . . . even when he was inside, the important thing for which he was willing to hang on endlessly till it became hopeless was the chance of getting in here."

That night we talked about family. For me it was the continuation of a discussion I used to have with Majid—one that had come to a premature close with his death. Rizwan expressed many worries about his faraway family: "Will my son recognize me . . . ? Last time I went, he was too small . . . just a few months old . . . but now he is two . . . and all he knows of me is as a voice over the phone . . . each time I go away, will he forget me . . . ? And ten years from now, or even twenty, what kind of a relationship will he have with me . . . ?"

The nature of this destabilization of family is difficult to comprehend. Rizwan's reflections reminded me of stories other working-class immigrant friends had told me. I think of Saeed, who left Pakistan when his wife was pregnant with their third child and could not go back to see the child because he was afraid that his case for readjustment and change of status would be compromised while he was away, leaving him unable to reenter the United States. In my conversations with him, I was always aware that he spoke of his two elder daughters much more. After all, he knew them as real persons, as children he had helped to raise. After four years, he had still never seen his youngest daughter. It was only then that he finally managed to get papers allowing him to migrate to Canada with his entire family.

Years of separation would come to an end: the moment seemed one to celebrate. Saeed talked constantly about how he would go to Pakistan, sell everything he had there, and move his family to Canada. But something was missing. When he painted the picture of his family's new life in Canada, Saeed didn't seem to include himself. If anything, his passing references to his own imagined future suggested that Saeed saw himself continuing to drive a taxi in New York. At first I dismissed that impression, assuming I'd misunderstood. But many months after his big move, I ran into Saeed at the LaGuardia holding lot. He had indeed moved his family to Canada. His children were going to a Canadian school and doing well. So what was he doing back in New York? He had left Canada, used his Canadian papers to reenter the United States, and gone back to driving a New York City taxi. It dawned on me that Saeed may have a more ambiguous relation with his family than I had imagined. He never said it in so many words. But I could not help but feel that Saeed had known all along that he was going to do precisely this. He had, over fifteen years, grown accustomed to living a bachelor's life, punctuated by structured and limited encounters with the family. It was only after

September 11, 2001, that Saeed returned to Canada to live with his family.

In the months following Saeed's return to New York, Rizwan and I discussed family life more and more. Reflecting on another driver's choices, Rizwan remarked: "Look at Cheema . . . his wife is a school principal in Pakistan. He calls her most nights from here . . . but he has not been back for years . . . and his papers are all fine. . . . His life is driving, as late into the night as he can last out and then sitting on a sidewalk drinking beer with his buddies . . . by the gas station—it's a whole group . . . that sits there each night smoking and drinking and then, drunk at six in the morning, they call home."

The more we spoke about it, I realized that a significant part of the community I was part of was structured almost permanently into a culture of masculine bachelorhood. The only consistent aspects of this life were the act of laboring—driving taxis for ten to twelve hours a day—and brief periods of leisure—drinking a few beers at the end of your shift with a group of friends on the sidewalk or at one of the bachelor apartments. A small sample of restaurants where most meals are consumed, a Bollywood film on some weekends—and the act of sending money home to support one's family. These anchors hide a whole range of instabilities— many of the drivers are middle-aged men who have no investments of any sort in the United States, including Social Security. The structure of work—new driving partners at regular intervals, a different shift change location every so often—also necessitates a pattern of constant flux within the home space, as housing partners move in and out and apartments are changed. Often, the space of the home is valued only minimally, reflected, for instance, in a peculiar relation to commodity culture (a bare apartment that has next to nothing in it except a large television, sometimes bought for nearly a whole month's earnings. Many haven't seen a doctor in years, and even if they have, it would surely be a different doctor in a different emergency room each time. Rizwan had the most incisive comments on the condition: "I have to get Shamim and Hasan over here quickly, otherwise my entire life may be destroyed. . . . Think about it. . . . I got married. . . . I lived with Shamim for four months after marriage and then came away . . . then several months later Hasan was born. I was there for three months . . . and now again . . . when you go back every two or three years for three months, what do you make of that time. . . . Do I resume a relationship as if there was no break? What do I talk to my wife about? . . . After all, we live completely different lives . . . and my son . . . how long will it be before he makes some kind of a reconciliation about his absent father? . . . When I go home, I am not being treated like I belong there."

The family then becomes an extraordinary occurrence—something, one could argue, that is consumed as part of one's leisure time, rather than lived as everyday life. For men who grew up within relatively stable structures, who assume that the family is a normal structure of living, the condition of being immigrant workers slowly turns them into folks who reconcile and understand the family as an extraordinary unit—one located within the realm of pleasure every other summer.

I asked Aziz, who had been alone in New York for more than twenty years, why he did it, whether he missed his family, and how he saw his future. At first his answers were predictable: he hoped to reunite with his family soon; he was concerned about his children's education; and he was considering returning to Pakistan for good. But a few conversations later, the picture grew more complex. "I can't go back . . . what will I do there? There is nothing that I can do to earn a living there," said Aziz. "And when I go there this way . . . once every other year, it's so much better. . . . It's my holiday. . . . I can spend all the money I want. . . . I can have all the fun I want."

Aziz's conundrum is a common one. Pakistan's economy has suffered such a dramatic downshift that it has become impossible for many families to sustain middle-class lifestyles. Some have solved the problem by proletarianizing one member of the family in the West. That person ekes out a working-poor existence in the United States, sending remittances home to sustain the family's standard of living. Aziz relates to home and family as a holiday space. What's more, he continued: ". . . when it gets to a point where I am running out of money or when I have to deal with all sorts of problems there, I leave. . . . I come back here. . . . You see, I don't have the capacity to deal with daily problems, children's education . . . somebody's medical problems, sisters' marriages. . . . Don't get me wrong. . . . I support them all. . . . I sent the entire money for my sisters marriage . . . *bade shaan se hui*. The marriage was royal . . . and I financed it all."

After twenty years, Aziz has come to feel that the quotidian affairs of family life would be overwhelming to him. He has made his peace with this arrangement: "I don't want to bring my wife here. . . . What can I do with her and the children here? . . . Who is going to take care of them here? . . . In Pakistan they are okay . . . and if I bring them here then I have to worry about everything."

Even when the opportunity to reunite as a family unit presents itself, then, some immigrant workers may turn away from it. Men whose family life has become a distant, rarely visited place of leisure commonly come to abdicate the "normal" responsibilities associated with family life, with the exception of the most traditionally masculine one under capitalism: providing for the family. Other responsibilities—rearing children, supporting a family emotionally, participating in one's partner's interior life—languish.

Rizwan asks: "But even if the family comes here, then what? I look around and I am worried as to what it would be like for Shamim. At least we go out to work daily. . . . What about the women? . . . I see their lives here in our community—alone . . . a few women of the families that are together . . . but they live surrounded by single men. . . . I know its changing but I still see a problem . . . even if there are fifty families in this neighborhood I still see them as stuck here . . . nowhere to go but these few blocks."

The only way one can understand what is happening is by seeing that some segment of the Third World poor that has "globalized" itself has come to see the family as a bit of a lie—or at least as unrealistic. If the immigrant bourgeoisie holds in place a physically real family in the suburbs, which is by many accounts so pathologically mutated that it is incapable of being a space that reproduces anything that we understand as family, the working immigrant's family has turned this on its head and holds it up as simply unrealistic under global capitalism. As I spoke to more drivers about their families, I heard from one young driver who lives in New York with his father who said that his mother had lived in New York for a long time. "But she left. . . ." He said, "She went back to Pakistan with us—my brother, sisters and me. . . ." The driver himself came back a few years ago as a young adult and began to drive and go to school here. "She prefers being there," he continued, "at least she doesn't have to be poor." He stopped and then continued, ". . . and deal with an alcoholic husband. . . ." I was speechless. Just that morning I had had a conversation with another driver, Khalid, who had told me, "I can't manage this anymore. . . . I am sending her home." Khalid is in his late thirties. He had spent fifteen years alone in the United States and it was just a month since he had brought his entire family over, his wife and three children. He had spent five years following up on paperwork for family reunification. He was exasperated:

"What should I do? . . . Should I drive or should I stay at home? . . . My little daughter is ill and who else but me can take her to the doctor? . . . My older kids are at school but everything they need, I have to be there to get it. . . . Every time the phone rings, I am afraid . . . because I feel I may have to rush home and then how will I work?"

Khalid's situation, I realize, is a peculiar combination of factors. In some part it is the sheer difficulty of making ends meet with only one person working a low-paying job. But at the other end, it is also how he has come to live for the last several years with the most pared down of responsibility structures. He, like Aziz, no longer wishes to be part of the daily life of the family. I had tried to reassure Khalid that morning. "Look at Awan," I had said. "He too has three children . . . he is doing okay, isn't he? He just bought a house. . . . And more and more drivers are bringing their families over, aren't they?" Khalid was not easy to reassure. "Look at Awan," he retorted. "He is past fifty . . . and it is now that he is okay . . . that's because both his sons are earning and only his daughter is still in school. . . . What did he do? His family just came six years ago . . . and within a year his eldest son was working. . . . But my children . . . it's at least ten years before any of them can earn. . . ."

Somewhere, hidden in the several comments on family that I had heard, there was a critique of the family. For it is true that locked between the twelve-hour workday, and the time of rest and food that one needs to be able to work the next day, there is very little space left for the relationships that one nurtures. To think about one's child's health or education is necessarily reduced to a chore with no trace of spontaneity or meaning beyond getting it done. The immigrant worker communities are placed in a peculiar bind. As long as the structure of "one globalized body" away in the First World is kept in place, a large part of the rest of the family's class experience changes for the better. But the working immigrant "alone" in the First World leads a life that is significantly empty of the more enduring signifiers of a meaningful life—love, intimacy, emotional attachments, and the sensual. If, on the other hand, the family reunites in the West, then too there seems little space for a meaningful experience of the family. I cannot but, however hesitantly, agree with the young driver who had spoken to me about his mother's decision to move back to Pakistan with them, where "at least we had it good." It is in this context that one of the Alliance's earliest decisions—that we would be a union that is going to welcome "all" of the driver's life in—makes complete sense.

Was the family being "deconstructed" actively by the forces of globalization, visible differently within the immigrant bourgeois domain and differently in the immigrant working-class life? But it is just as true that whatever the nature of the deconstruction, some minimal structure of the family was still in place. Within the logic of the present global political economy, the act of laboring has been isolated. The family is relegated or reduced to another space in another nation-state. The imaginary is kept in place as leisure—men travel on vacation to live brief lives as family members and then return to live lives of long workdays and beers with the buddies on the sidewalk. And maybe this imaginary is not just one that the immigrant worker keeps in place but is itself critical to the continued existence of global capitalism. For without the fiction of the family as all-important—which is never to be realized but always to be idealized—why would anybody travel 10,000 miles to work twelve hours a day? The family is, as Engels wrote more than a century ago, the basic unit for the reproduction of capital. It serves as the space where gendered labor helps in the daily reproduction of labor. But even more importantly, as is so explicitly visible in the case of the immigrant worker, it is the fundamental unit of the "private" beyond the self, a core and critical requirement if the idea of private wealth is to be kept alive. The charade of the meaningful family must go on because it encompasses the idea of the "private" that makes all laboring under the worst of conditions worthwhile.

The contemporary labor movement understands its role as creating the social space for a fight back against neoliberal globalization. But if this vision is to be realized, then it must be a movement that produces a social space that is intensely meaningful for the worker. Global capitalism fragments labor not just because it seeks out cheaper labor but because it fundamentally fragments the lives of people. The labor movement, if it is to be a sustainable grassroots movement, must necessarily provide alternatives to the fragmentation of lives.[11]

However, at the other end of this challenge that class-based mass movements face in making fragmented lives whole is the critique that it faces on a daily basis: that the labor movement as a whole is too narrow and too economistic. Often this claim that the labor movement is too narrow is based on a critique that posits the sexism, homophobia, and racism of the working classes as evidence. Such a position is just as dangerous as the labor movement's inability to rise above narrow economism. Before reaching the state of being economistic, intersectionally progressive, and above all not prejudiced lies the necessary step of concretizing the gendered concerns of the working class in struggles that belong to their daily lives. In this sense, we must understand that a "living wage" campaign is not narrowly economistic. Instead, it seeks to fundamentally alter the ability of a worker to lead a life where there is time and space for building meaningful relationships. So, too, a campaign to naturalize immigrant workers must be seen as one that attempts to eliminate the flux and instability in living conditions that are fundamentally about race. It is, therefore, campaigns and work that imagine more broadly the life of a worker and seek to make it more whole that are the fundamental building blocks for a broader political movement.

7

IMPERIAL AMNESIA

ON AUGUST 9, 2000, Eric Asimov featured Chelsea's Eat Again Deli in his weekly column, "Under \$25," in the Dining Out section of the *New York Times*.[1] All New Yorkers, urged Asimov, needed to experience the food at two taxi driver delis: Eat Again Deli on Ninth Avenue and Lahore Deli on Crosby Street. He wrote mouth-watering descriptions of Eat Again Deli's makki di roti (a cornbread) and sarson da saag (mustard greens)—authentic fare enjoyed by the city's South Asian taxi drivers.

For years, Eat Again Deli primarily served Punjabi Indian and Pakistani drivers, who came in for very low-priced, healthy food or to use the restroom, all on breaks just a few minutes long. In the hot summer months, Eat Again Deli also kept large barrels full of chaanch, a very diluted and chilled form of spiced butter-milk, which drivers could drink for free before getting back on the road to finish twelve-hour shifts amid the heat and exhaust fumes.

The column was printed on a Wednesday. On Saturday of that week, I received a call from a professional middle-class desi (South Asian)[2] friend. He'd read the article and wanted me to join him for a meal at Eat Again Deli. It seemed as if every wealthy resident of Chelsea and beyond had the same idea. By the time we got there, the makki di roti and sarsoon da saag were long gone, and a long line of mostly white middle-class Americans still waited. The place was a veritable zoo, with people hanging onto every avail-able inch of the limited counter space. Andy and Mohinder Singh, the ex-drivers who owned the deli, and their limited staff were stretched to the limit; they seemed at a loss as to how to deal with this invading army of diners. Drivers came in, saw the scene, and left. After all, they couldn't wait in a half-hour line. Andy and Mohinder could not find a way to ensure that their regular clientele was served. That day they were lost in a sea of "yes sirs" and "no madams," as the mostly white middle-class New Yorkers ate rural Punjabi food.

A week or two later I returned to Eat Again Deli on some business. "So where are the white people?" I asked Mohinder. He laughed. The craze lasted exactly three or four days, he told me. "They must be at the place the guy wrote about this week," he said.

As it happened, for about a year before Asimov's column ran, Eat Again Deli had been the site of conflict between local Chelsea residents, taxi drivers, and the deli's management. The residents of the building that housed the deli, together with their supporters on the community board, wanted to shut the deli down. Failing that, they hoped to get rid of the taxi relief stand on Ninth Avenue between Nineteenth and Twentieth Streets. Their stated argument was that taxi drivers make a lot noise, litter the place, and piss on the streets. But in heated discussions, a deeper rationale often shone through: Chelsea was gentrifying, and the taxi drivers simply did not fit in. As the liberal city council member Christine Quinn once put it, this was a matter of the "quality-of-life concerns of the residents." These residents, led by a certain woman named Doris, who was always the most aggressive in the meetings we attended, regularly came into the deli to pick fights with its owners and clientele, in the hope of proving that the deli was a blight on Chelsea's landscape of fast-appreciating property values. Said Andy Singh, "*Aare yaar,* if there is actually a fight, who will believe me if I tell them that [Doris] came in and started it? That's why I tell everybody, whatever she says or does, don't start a fight with her." The Alliance had been approached by a small group of drivers who frequented the deli in a last-ditch attempt to save the taxi relief stand.

During the many months of meetings, which included every interested party from the deli owners and local residents to Quinn and the Borough of Manhattan Department of Transportation commissioner Joseph Albano, I collected some information on my own. I walked up and down the neighboring stretch of Ninth Avenue and the side streets in order to assess the extent of littering, as well as to count the clubs and bars from which drunk white men might roll after midnight and take a piss on the streets. I wanted to see for myself whether Eat Again Deli actually created a problem. The Alliance argued that the residents' complaint was racist. But those accused dismissed the notion with a wave of the hand. "I am not racist," one of the residents argued. "I've lived in Goa for a whole year." The residents mounted cameras on all sides of the deli, in the hope of catching the odd cabbie taking a leak. Finally, one fine morning the taxi relief stand disappeared. Christine Quinn's office insisted that the councilwoman had ample evidence of something she would not reveal, nor would anyone discuss the evidence with us—behavior that led us to believe that the "evidence" was doctored. Asimov's column featuring Eat Again Deli was run in the *Times* just months after the taxi stand had been removed.

My question is simple: what makes makki di roti so delectable and working immigrants the only ones who could conceivably piss on the streets? Is there something inherent to these times that makes it possible to keep the two issues separate? Why is it that Asimov would never call that column "Taxi Deli Subject to Racist Attacks Serves Excellent Food!" Or for that matter, "Food from the Front of the Cab: What Drivers Eat While on a Grueling 12-hour Shift"?[3] There is clearly an interesting disconnect here: food, made

by and for immigrant workers, served in a predominantly
working-class immigrant space lacking all the standard trappings
of middle-class sophistication is for a brief moment not just acceptable but celebrated, suddenly disconnected from the larger
frame of racism that marks the daily attitudes of the very same
resident community toward the immigrant worker. The question
simply is: how is this disconnect managed?

THE INVERTED RACISM OF LATE CAPITALISM

I invoke the idea of the "front of the cab," in contrast to, say, the
"back of the bus" not because I see any easy equivalence between
the oppression and exploitation of African Americans under slavery
and that of contemporary Third World immigrant workers but because I wish to highlight the simple fact that something that we may
often treat as trivial, such as food, has a sociohistorical meaning
whose erasure and "writing out" is itself indicative of a political formation. What is disturbing about the Asimov column, then, is not
so much that he wrote about somebody else's food but that he
obliterated the context in which the people who eat that food exist.
The argument here is not an "insider-only" one, that Asimov should
not write about any food but his own. Neither is the argument that
every article about somebody's food must be embedded in deep so-
ciological analysis. A quick sampling of the very same *New York
Times* section—Dining Out—will show us that history and sociology do get embedded into the writing when it is a "pleasant" or
"positive" story that's there to be told—food of princely traditions
or food of novel ethnic mixes. What we do have, then, is an inau-
gural question of how this "writing in" or "writing out" happens:
what is it about our times, about our ideologies, about our privileges that allows for this unconscious writing in or out?

American racism has reached a new level of sophistication based on the assumption that racism is over. To use June Jordan's formulation, this new idiom acknowledges difference without referring to power. It has a popular name: *multiculturalism*. For more than three decades now, multiculturalism and a "respect for diversity" has been trumpeted as the American solution to its racism.

Forty or fifty years ago, multiculturalism was a tool for minorities who demanded the right to mark themselves in particular ways in order to ensure that, in the battle against racism, white mainstream cultural forms did not determine what was and was not legitimate. But in today's milieu of late capitalism, the minorities' right to mark themselves has been usurped.

The civil rights struggle was primarily against the discriminatory legal structures that kept blacks and other colored Americans in their "separate but equal" spaces, a struggle that fought for a legal-liberal adjustment to American society. Having produced that formal equality in the "eyes of the law," society's racism was deemed to have been resolved through a respect for diversity—a granting of space for cultural expression. This is the new, "liberal" racism. Liberal racism functions by taking any two human beings or groups of human beings who have radically disparate levels of social power and claiming that they are "equal." A casual walk through housing court in any urban area experiencing gentrification will show you that large numbers of African Americans and immigrants come in there with no representation at all or with very poor-quality representation by overloaded court-appointed lawyers and face large real estate companies with a battery of well-paid lawyers. I have been to enough small claims court sessions with drivers to know that what is often practiced in reality is that unrepresented and incompletely informed poor people are forced into binding arbitration with corporations and collection agencies by courts that will not recognize the differential in social power. There are more blacks on television and in prison in percentage terms than in the general population. The former reflects the success of multiculturalism's alleged solution to racism—more representation means less racism—while the latter reflects the abject failure of liberal law. Thus liberal law and its claim of equality is a lie and we must call it that.

I deliberately used the term "sophisticated" to describe the current trajectory of American racism. Liberal law and its claim to equality is flawed by its inability to acknowledge the impact of real social power differentials, and is often enough called out as a sham. The market, however—the other institution through which racism is kept alive and well—is far more difficult to unpack, for it is indeed a very sophisticated institution and the racism it reproduces inherits all of its sophistication. Multiculturalism, the liberal resolution of racism in the post–civil rights era, is deployed most forcefully through the market—most specifically through one of the fundamental aspects of the capitalist market: the commodity.

The fundamental basis of racist multiculturalism lies in our culture of hyper-consumption. If the tourism industry of the seventies and the eighties sold the African safari—carefully delimited exotic jungles with the humans and animals of wildlife reserves as the exotic—then multiculturalism is your instant, street-corner safari available in the West Village. Each evening the white bourgeoisie excavates the new dress, the new music, the new plant, the new breed of dog, and that mouth-watering Thai curry, a short-shift safari that changes daily. Racism thus exists not in spite of multiculturalism as a failed solution, but because multiculturalism has indeed become the basic structure of racism itself. It is in this sense that Slavoj Žižek refers to multiculturalism as the "inverted racism" of late capitalism.[4]

Culture, as many scholars have pointed out, is a process,

produced by and producing social relations according to the logic of the larger trajectories in which it is formed, such as the media, politics, and the market. It is tempting to say that the market freezes cultural forms by commodifying them. This is true in some respects, but the late-capitalist market is far too dynamic an entity and the consumer far too sophisticated for this reading to suffice.

Let me briefly explicate what I mean by the sophistication of the consumer and the new dynamism of the market. As many— most recently, Naomi Klein—have argued, one of the major developments of the last three decades is the gradual but successful subordination of all forms of identity to that of a consuming subject.[5] The consuming subject is the primary identity of most Americans today. Even an individual's "outsider" or minority identity is produced through commodities. Nike's scouts in poor urban neighborhoods are, after all, not wasting their time. The development of this "perfect" consumer reflects the success of capitalism in restructuring all social relations in terms of commodities, as well as the fact that ordinary people are responding to an accelerating alienation through a rapid mobility as consuming subjects—demanding more, demanding greater sophistication and dynamic creation of pleasure.

NICE RACISM

I have, for a long time, been suspicious and uncomfortable with the "celebration of difference" and the demand to "be positive" in America. My visceral reaction always has been that I will not be positive on demand and thereby simplify something that is complicated and contradictory. Extracting that positive quality about anyone or anything is simply to dehistoricize that individual, group, or thing. The demand is to disconnect makki di roti from the twelve-hour shift of a driver, not to ask *why* the roti traveled

10,000 miles across two large oceans to be placed on a supermarket shelf, neatly packaged and ready to consume.

The demand to be "positive" fetishizes the domain of culture itself. Such an impulse hides the processes by which culture travels, forms, and changes, removing histories of imperialism and revolution from the cultural product as it makes its journey toward commodification. The apparatus of difference, positivity, and diversity as deployed by the white middle class allows a new form of ownership over a dehistoricized cultural segment, the boundaries of which are now located at the immediate experience of consumption—the purely sensory experience of somebody else's life and the taste of roti, rather than the driver's daily struggle to pay the broker. The demand for this cultural experience is always framed within an ambience of pleasantness—an innocent demand that is in itself seen as progressive inasmuch as it is an effort to recognize and embrace difference. In short, it is "nice racism."

A PEOPLE FREE OF HISTORY

Nice racism, then, is the process of cultural production where somebody else's life is segmented and isolated, and a neatly defined packet of pleasure is extracted from it and the "remainder"—the excess that is the pain and the history is erased. What allows the market to do this and the white bourgeosie to consume it all without sensing the contradiction? The answer is just as simple: what allows for this nice racism is white culture itself. If culture is a process, then mainstream white culture is significantly a product of its history of slave trade, dehumanization, exploitation, and imperialism. It is against this simple kernel of truth that we must evaluate America's persistent claim that it has neither history nor culture. It is a claim many of us have heard and maybe even made—that America is a nation without a deep history and only a shallow sense of the past because we are all so new here.

But we know this to be untrue. America's history is, simply put, the history of the decimation of the Native Americans, slavery, and the new colonialism/imperialism that began with the Phillipines and Central and Latin America as far back as the late 1800s. And yet the claim that there is no history rests on another claim to nationhood—as a modern nation. The discursive self-image of America is often that it is a "progressive" modern nation—with the only values at its core being the secular values of rationality, reason, efficiency, orderliness, effectiveness.

These are, incidentally, also the values of the market—the core values of a consumer. What is critical to note is that the rational-efficient value structure is itself a creative isolation of a larger cultural system—modernity. Thus what constitutes the American self-image is a certain extracted and isolated set of values of modernity that leaves behind the rest of the history of Euro-American modernity—racism, colonialism, and imperialism. I would argue that this process of abstraction has been part of the American nation since the inauguration of Jeffersonian democracy. It has gone through various stages of sophistication that are linked to actual material change, such as the Wilsonian rearticulation of a scientific America that coincided with the arrival of the industrial revolution in America, the articulation of a post–Franklin D. Roosevelt "equal America" of the civil rights movement that located the United States in the postwar/Cold War international framework, and, most recently, the reinvention of America as the global peacekeeper.[6] All these have the same foundation: an understanding of America as ahistorical with only the bare minimum values of modernity, rationality and efficiency, at its core. Multiculturalism is the newest twist on this fiction, America's ingenious way of abstracting and eradicating imperialism from the conception of

Western culture and history. To the abstracted set of rationality and efficiency we have added a new set of values that works in precisely the same manner—those of difference, diversity, and positivity. It is this value structure—rationality-efficiency/positivity-difference— that allows for large parts of America to "slip" into a belief that the American war and occupation of Iraq is legitimate, even as evidence mounts against it. The United States, after all, has no history of imperialism and is always about the most secular and modern of values, and that is what it will reproduce in Iraq. The mode of "othering" the Iraqi, the Afghani, the North Korean, or the Iranian, is always that of a complex culture full of irrationality, cast against the simplicity of American culture—the rational. Even our violence is intensely rational. It is for this reason that the "burning" questions are about whether Bush lied and not the fact that Iraq was aflame in resistance and that the war, whether or not Bush lied, was wrong.

And it is not just the white bourgeoisie that partakes of this culture of imperialism. Much has already been written about how the professional immigrant middle class uses its mythical model minority status to resolve the primary contradiction they face in the United States—that of race. If, as Fanon wrote, "the Negro is comparison," then multiculturalism offers a convenient answer to several difficult questions. As the perpetually empty urn of American culture is held up to be filled, the immigrant bourgeoisie is best located to offer its culture, a body of heritage and traditions perfectly reduced to symbols and presented as ahistorical material for consumption. Multiculturalism allows the immigrant bourgeoisie to present its culture as its positive offering in the marketplace, and thus locates itself perfectly in a white middle-class consumption structure. If race has always been a particularly difficult obstacle to surmount in the United States, multiculturalism offers the resolution of race through class in a very specific way. Thus the South Asian bourgeoisie could stand shoulder to shoulder with the white middle class in seeking out the makki di roti and sarson da saag Asimov praised. There were no Dominicans from Washington Heights and no African Americans from Harlem running in to see what food taxi drivers eat, but largely white middle-class Americans and a smattering of South Asian, African American, and other immigrant professionals. On the flip side, South Asian drivers do not follow the Asimov column each week and end up at the recommended Thai or Argentine eatery, but instead continue to eat in the same deli week after week. The capacity to be located within a white cultural frame of choice—the power to choose the flavor of the day—is a feature of class privilege rather than of race or ethnicity.

More recently we see the emergence of a further twist to this hegemonic method of American cultural formation. If, within the domain of the economic, the Asian as a model minority was the mode of disciplining the other troublesome minority, the African American, then in post-9/11 America, as a certain segment of the immigrant community is branded as the internal enemy, the African American emerges as the litmus test of patriotism. In broadcast after broadcast of stories that dealt with the immigrant—whether it was illegal detentions and deportations, the taxi driver's right to a livable wage, or the right of one and all to hold a driver's license immaterial of immigration status—the African American was positioned in these stories as the "mainstream." This placement of different minorities as the "positive" value in differential frames is the precise symbol of the hegemony of multiculturalism.

The fundamental success of multiculturalism is its rearticulation of race along class lines, vis-à-vis the commodity form: it allows the immigrant and African American bourgeoisie to switch sides equally. Multiculturalism lets the colored middle class participate in the imperialist culture and "lose" their history in the noise of the fetishized celebration of dehistoricized difference. Multi-culturalism works.

MULTICULTURALISM AND THE POLITICS OF "COMMUNITY"

I cannot emphasize sufficiently the importance of the origins of multiculturalism as a determined effort of people of color, women, and the gay-lesbian-bisexual-transgender movements to ensure spaces of cultural legitimacy outside of white-male-straight cultural hegemony. However, as the ideology of both the state and the market, multiculturalism also breeds an ideology of racism of a new sort. I emphasize this because, far too often, white leftists and liberals who are still stuck in some Enlightenment-based notion of the left project see multicultural-ism of the 1960s as the fundamental reason for the failure of the left over the last forty years. If given half a chance, they would run back to the same old "universalisms" of the Enlightenment. This way of thinking is clearly part of the problem—allowing people to partake of the Thai curry and then support U.S. imperialism in the name of Afghani women.

Thus, I am arguing that we should not take multiculturalism as inherently progressive anymore and should also hold some distance between what multiculturalism was at an important moment of ferment in the 1960s and its evolution, over the next four decades, as an ideology critical of the status quo. Such a distance is critical to begin a project that attempts to map the nature of political work that we could all collectively engage in. We must admit to the possibility that progressive politics has surely been affected by multiculturalism, just as multiculturalism has affected the market, the state, and class society itself. Any political work must now begin by asking how this process has shaped our political formations.

I want to guard against the error of homogenization. Of course state- and market-friendly multiculturalism is not the only important ideological force shaping progressive politics in the post–civil rights era. Rather, the political moment that emerges in the post–civil rights era is constituted by multiple political trajectories. Multiculturalism has provided a broad political framework sanctioned by both state and market, and thus allowed for a new politics to stabilize. Much has already been written about each of the other trajectories that have shaped politics and so I will provide here only very brief summaries, sufficient for us to begin thinking about a future politics.

I. **The Decline of Mass Politics.** The failure of mass organizing in the United States since the 1960s has fundamentally to do with large segments of the labor movement's leadership climbing into bed with corporate capital for well over four decades while others remained locked in a tight embrace with the CIA.[7] Only recently have they begun emerging from these self-created binds. The failure of mass-based organizing has also got much to do with the violent state repression of various mass/cadre-based organizations, whether it be the Black Panthers or the more militant of the AFL unions. Further, the traditional parties that would articulate a mass-based politics—the Communist, Socialist, or Labor parties of the United States—also fell into various states of disrepair. Faced with a repressive state and a Cold War environment where they were continually under attack, they failed to develop an adequate criticism of Stalinist politics and, by the end of the Cold War, exhausted, many did not know how to respond to the demise of the Soviet Union.[8]

II. Feminism and the Discovery of the Personal.
The most historic and revolutionary of feminist epis-
temological breakthroughs—the deconstruction of the
private/public divide as a way of making visible the operations of gendered power—was rearticulated into the
notion of the personal as political. This centering of
personal experience fit neatly with the multicultural
framework at many levels. The specificity of "an experience"—"the Asian experience" against the "Black experience"—became understood as a substantial way of
establishing difference. Further, to make one's personal
experience the grounding framework for one's politics
is intensely appealing, especially to the suburban disaf-
fected. If the suburb is a space of extreme alienation
(even more so for an immigrant), then it makes sense
that defining politics as a response to that alienation
produces a range of politics that centers around the
self. We find various strands of this logic articulated in
many commentaries on what is often called "the Reagan Generation"—a politics of self-expression rooted
firmly in a fundamental inability to create a meaningful
collective self within the context of suburbia. This is
not to say that this is a political domain bereft of progressive possibilities. Not in the least. It is the fundamental success of this response to suburban alienation
that we owe much of youth do-it-yourself (DIY) culture from punk rock to open source software, where
conventional notions of form have been thoroughly
broken down. But we must note the centrality of the au-
tobiographical in these forms of expression and ask what
that means. Similarly, in the current progressive context,
political work has to be immediately and constantly

responsive to the self and how it "feels." Politics remains strongly moored to individual experience. Knowledge is understood to be produced experientially, and any knowledge deriving from a source outside of the realm of experience is suspect. This sets up a fundamental divide between what is seen as experiential and theoretical knowledge, resulting in an anti-intellectualism that is difficult to combat.

III. **The Rediscovery of Community.** Along with the decline of mass politics on the one hand and the development of a new politics of the self came the revival of some older American traditions of political organizing. Given the long history of ethnically specific waves of migration and neighborhood development, the organization of communities had played a role in every aspect of American politics from electoral politics to union organizing. With the redrawing of the demographic map of America and new growth of the suburban population, a new politics of community organizing also emerged. Saul Alinsky and the many variants of his model of community organizing came to the fore. Alinskian politics represented a particular revitalization of the idea of grassroots politics which in many ways fit neatly with multiculturalism. It was deeply populist and tended to frame "community issues" with no external referents at all. In other words, for many organizers following this model, what mattered was what mattered to "the community." This articulation of the particularity of "a community's" issues was ideal for the age of multiculturalism. While some inspired by this model, especially in the domains of rural and ethnically mixed labor groups in and around

Chicago, did produce exciting local struggles, most of
Aliniskian politics was focused on the winnability of
single campaigns—getting a stop sign or bus shelter on
your block, for example—and thus often disengaged
from anything in the outside world, or outside the
"community's" immediate self-interest.

The net effect of these political trajectories was an inward
turn in politics—a politics constantly occupied with a particularity of needs, that is, as Bhairavi said at an internal Alliance
meeting, "never placed or understood in relation to other
struggles."

UNDOING THE DIALECTIC

The current politics of community representation evolved out of
a transformation of the basic symbolic material of social justice
activists. In the civil rights struggle, the goal was the elimination
of a regime of "separate but equal" laws and for the creation of
universal legal rights. Out of this context of a universal called
equality emerged an effort to give to each "community" the right
to mark itself as different. At the moment of the civil rights struggle the universal right to equality and the particular right to
mark difference were articulated in a dialectic. However, in
the framework of multiculturalism, this dialectic broke down and
the marking of difference was institutionalized in the separation of
communities at each and every level possible, thus creating a new
regime of "separate but equal." Thus the right to mark difference
was divorced from this dialectic, and "each" community then produced its own resources and institutions, its own priorities and
campaigns. The rearticulation was one that moved away from the
expressive universal of "all," instead crafting the idea that each

"community" had its own separate interests, hence the emergence and proliferation of the community-based organizations (CBOs) which form the self-fragmenting infrastructure of the American progressive movement.

This inward-looking, self-dividing politics operates on multiple levels. One of the domains in which the state/market model of multiculturalism becomes entirely visible in CBO politics is on the question of funding. Most CBOs have no mass base to ensure their minimal solvency. Nor do CBOs have large amounts of their annual budgets coming from "within the community"—say, through a small, door-to-door donations campaign. Most CBOs are almost entirely funded by liberal foundations. As funding goes, then the business of CBOs is a race to the bottom—where each "community" and its specific needs are framed as they compete for funds.

The fundamental reason why most CBOs are dependent on liberal foundations for support is because the "community" is not available to them. In other words, the "community" is not willing to support the CBO. This would suggest that there is some distance between the CBO and the said "community." The B in CBO may actually be the most salient letter—this formation is indeed only "based" in the community and does not belong to the community: the community has no ownership over the organization. If the community has no ownership over the organization, then it would be reasonable to assume that the organization itself owes little to the community. In other words, the notion of "community" is potentially the most misused and most easily bandied term going. Clearly the idea of a "community" is one of the most fundamentally underexamined concepts in American liberal politics today. The way the idea of community works is that it is always already formed and a fixed entity that has "needs," and the organization has an unascertained mandate to "fight" for those needs. If the community is not "inside" the organization, then what is the organization? The popular answer to that question would be an enigmatic figure called the "activist." Just one look at a funding agency application will tell this story in the starkest terms. Most progressive funders seek detailed information about two things: the preexisting community and the "activist" group. It does not take much to figure out that what is being sought is the uniqueness of the preexisting community—the specificity of the oppression, which justifies the granting of funds—bringing the race to the bottom as projects collide. What is also sought is the detailed information about the activist group—the board, the executive director, and other staff—an evaluation of whether this small group of "activists" have good liberal politics and are adequately representative of all the different axes of oppression.

This is a perfect politics of inertia. The activists feel morally superior because they have good politics, while the "community" can continue to exist in its loose and free-floating fashion, lending the organization a kind of authenticity. Such politics proliferates because it fits so perfectly into the multicultural model. The "activists" stand in for the community because they are ethnically insiders and thus have some strategic knowledge of the community. A group of five South Asian "activists" could, for instance, create a South Asian Tenants Rights Organization—where the organization is constituted by the five activists and the predefined ambiguous South Asian community exists as the organization's constituency. Clearly there is a necessity for such a group inasmuch as many new immigrant South Asians have all sorts of problems with their slumlords. If such a group is created, it would clearly do "good work" in responding to such needs, because these five South Asians would have the necessary insider information—an understanding of where the South Asian neighborhoods are;

which are the ones that are still developing; some language skills, such as which of the many South Asian languages are predominant and where; some cultural understanding of holidays, such as, say, Diwali or Eid,[9] and when such festivals show up on the calendar and which occasions may be good moments for outreach; and a capacity to negotiate with neighborhood "leaders," such as store owners or community boards. And clearly all this insider information will help them identify needs and respond to them. But since mass membership is not on the agenda, the "community" remains out there, its definition static and eternal, while the "activists" are located inside the organization. The organization's stated politics, then, is the politics of these five activists, fairly easy to achieve when it is just five friends who probably have fairly similar backgrounds and trajectories to begin with.

The flaw in this mode of organization lies around the question of the "community." Who is the "community?" What is the relation of the organization to the "community?" I would argue that the "community" exists inasmuch as a group of "activists" has knowledge of it, know important people within it, and understand its needs and possible resources, if any. However, the community has no political reality. It is not "organized"—it has no organizational or institutional roots and thus has no meaningful commitment to a long-term politics of social transformation. This produces in the end a politics of inertia where the community continues to exist as an alibi, activists walk around with perfect politics, and the mass of people who constitute the world we live in remain fairly isolated from politics outside of an occasional mobilization. Despite alienated lives as workers or women, Asians or blacks, they are not part of any structure that they can claim ownership over and embolden into action when the opportunity presents itself. "Communities" in the CBO world are not organized communities, but at worst tokens for the self-perpetuation of the activist class, and at best occasionally mobilized groups of people.

The "community" remains static in political terms because there are no spaces of progressive engagement to which it belongs. At the other end, the activist core of the CBO can lay claim to a complicated and perfectly intersectional universal space which they at best negotiate within a small cohort group and are rarely, if at all, forced to take out to the "community." It is then a politics where both the particular and the universal seemingly exist together and, inasmuch as the two exist, it can make a claim over a politics of transformation. However, the sham lies in the fact that while both the universal and the particular exist, they are fundamentally disconnected. The conditions under which the Alliance was established illustrate this case well. The Alliance began as a project of an Asian American antiviolence organization and was known as the Lease Drivers Coalition (LDC). LDC served primarily as an advocacy project for drivers who were victims of police brutality and other forms of harassment. In 1996 Bhairavi Desai was hired as a staff person. Under her leadership the OC came to a decision, after much debate, that the LDC needed to become a mass organization. This decision to become a membership-based organization, especially one open to all drivers and not just Asians, came under much criticism from the "activists" of the parent organization. Finally, just four months before the Alliance began its historic May 1998 strike, we left the Asian American organization to set up the Alliance. The level of mistrust of mass organizations came into full view when one of the "activists" asked me how I could ascertain that none of the members (drivers) were homophobes? Bhairavi herself faced intense pressure from the parent organization to be responsible to them and not to the mass base. Finally, when we left we had been forced out under ugly circumstances: Bhairavi was fired, our budget was frozen, and we were denied access to our membership database. This fear of mass organizing, along with the demand for a pure universal politics, is, as I have outlined above, the central failure to recognize the dialectic of organizing.

What then does it mean to create a politics that resists such disconnection? At the simplest level, it means creating organizational spaces and using them to consistently produce a politics of organizing rather than simple mobilization. The "community" needs to be inside the organization, taking ownership of it and setting its priorities. When this condition is met, then the possibility of the dialectic coming to life exists, and not otherwise.

While I do not claim that the NYTWA is in any shape or form representative of a perfect political model, I can surely say that there is much I have learnt and stated here that comes from being inside the NYTWA and its struggle to find a logic of organizing that creates the possibility of real and long-term social transformation. In the NYTWA, drivers themselves hold the majority of seats on the Organizing Committee. At this writing, for instance, the OC consists of eleven driver organizers and three non-driver organizers, including the staff. The space of the OC meeting, both formal and informal, is possibly the best place even to begin answering the question of how the basic dialectic of organizing is approached. An average OC meeting is largely spent discussing campaign strategies on some of the core problems that drivers face on a day-to-day basis and the simultaneous work of membership development. It is this fundamental focus on the core concerns of drivers that enables the organization's long-term engagement with the driver community and increasing levels of engagement with those drivers who enter the organization as members. Once drivers become members, their level of engagement changes dramatically: they come to the office to rest or to resolve problems they run into in the course of their work; they come to meetings, where they direct, maneuver, and make decisions; and newsletters, flyers, postcards, and pamphlets arrive at their doorsteps. The airport holding lot is for members, a space that is "organized" because when a member walks into the space, he/she is immediately part of a "community" of drivers who are organized as members and who will work together in engaging the mass base toward further organization.

The leadership emerges from this community of members—those who volunteer time for the work of the OC, which thus becomes a space of greater and greater engagement. While most of the time in an OC meeting may be spent on the core issues facing drivers, the meetings also wrestle with the universal. Since 2001 every meeting has had a significant discussion on imperialism and war, on oil politics and racism, on violence and solidarity. Apart from the OC meetings, in NYTWA retreats (day-long meetings) a large part of the day is always a discussion on ideas of large-scale social transformation. The point here is not that these discussions are smooth and well defined—far from it. But, I would argue, it is this space, where the discussion of the particular concerns of drivers is framed against the backdrop of more universal concerns, that helps keep the organization dynamically engaged in the work of organizing for broader social change. There are several levels at which this helps. Apart from the task of a continuous political education for all of us, it develops a sense of the real-political as also a capacity within the organization to respond to events and phenomena at multiple levels.

"Danny Glover?" Mamnun asked me, a half-smile playing across his lips as if he knew something that nobody else did as we stood listening to a heated discussion at LaGuardia's Delta holding lot. The discussion was on the fare increase proposal that NYTWA had blocked the previous December at the TLC. Inspired by the garage owners, the TLC had had a public hearing on a proposal for a 23 percent fare increase along with a 23 percent lease increase. The NYTWA had blocked the proposal with a convincing show of force and argument—that a 23–23 percent fare-lease increase was entirely meaningless to drivers. It had been a good four months since that meeting and, as the discussion on what had happened to the fare increase proposal continued, one driver came up with an alternate proposal. He suggested that instead of going for a general fare increase, NYTWA should seek specific increases: an increase in airport fares and an additional surcharge for out-of-Manhattan fares. He had hardly outlined these proposals before Abu, a longtime member of NYTWA who had thus far said little, jumped in. "Not possible, brother," he said. "You can forget about getting any extra money for out-of-Manhattan fares." The argument unfolded quickly, some saying that the TLC would never allow it, others positing that it was only fair that drivers get paid extra for out-of-Manhattan rides because "we lose so much time." A third group of drivers loudly asserted the position that to ask for more money to leave the island was discriminatory. "After all," said Abu, "who lives in Queens and the Bronx?" A loud murmur went up as some drivers agreed and others disagreed. "Find a way to take some extra money from your Upper East Side passenger . . . that you won't, but you want to charge some poor Chinese or black passenger more?" Abu fumed.

We left the crowd of drivers, still discussing the fare increase and its components, and it was then that Mamnun brought up Danny Glover. "I am telling you," Mamnun said, "there is no way Abu would have said that but for all our meetings." The Danny Glover incident (which I have detailed in a previous chapter), was an interesting moment where the organization most explicitly negotiated the tensions between the particular and the universal. Once the dynamic of racial coding as distinctly connected to the economics of the industry was made explicit, the NYTWA could potentially have taken a position that simply defended drivers' interests—that racial coding of passenger pickups would cease if out-of-Manhattan fares were differentially priced. But in flyer after flyer and meeting after meeting, the organization worked to bring out the implications of such a stand and, from there, progressively moved to a position that not only was racial coding wrong but, further, that differential pricing would be a racist solution.

In joint public meetings where both drivers and African American community members were present in large numbers, NYTWA articulated a range of proposals from training by civil rights activists on issues of racial discrimination to proposals to re-work Manhattan's public transportation infrastructure, including the taxi industry, to better serve poor people of color. In other words, over a period of three months of intense engagement with the membership base, many members moved from positions of defensiveness to positions of antidiscrimination and solidarity. In an organization that is predominantly immigrant in membership, the articulation of a political principle of solidarity with African Americans finally emerged from the Glover crisis. An organization that was narrowly focused only on the particular needs of a "community" would have either chosen to articulate those interests, wait out the crisis, or, worst of all, in typical CBO activist fashion, take a principled position on behalf of the organization without any engagement with the "community." In the case of the NYTWA, the OC had some very serious and passionate meetings during which the political position of the combined priorities of both the immigrant and the African American community were worked out. From the Glover incident to the Transit Workers contract negotiation (where a TWU strike would have bene-fited taxi drivers because of the increased demand on the streets but NYTWA decided to go on a sympathy strike) to the Afghan war (where it was again within the narrow interests of the drivers to distance themselves from any position on the war, but they came out against it), each of these have been moments of growth for the organization—not necessarily in terms of the number of members but surely in the members' development of a politics committed both to radical universalist social change and to the particular concerns of drivers. As an organization, I see the NYTWA as engaged constructively with the dialectic of organizing (producing a mass base) and promoting a broader politics of social change (engaging the mass base in issues well beyond the narrow range of "driver" concerns). The idea here is not to point to NYTWA as any kind of a model, for we too have failed, on occasion, in these efforts and have not worked out a framework for such an engagement of the dialectic of the universal and the particular on every occasion that we faced an opportunity. However, the example should serve us well in articulating two fundamental rules of political organizing that should lead us out of the morass of inward-looking CBO politics.

I. **The success of social justice struggles is dependent on a growing consciousness of a universal condition.** The invocation of a universal should not be mistaken for some backhanded support for Enlightenment universals. The specifics of this new universalism are not my task to unpack here, largely because I see it as something that is still in process. For now, its expressed politics is far easier to pin down. The best expression of it to date for me remains the call of the IWW: "an injury to one is an injury to all." However, having this wonderful political philosophy (after all, who could disagree with it?) is by itself not enough. This brings me to my second position.

II. **Social justice work is by its very definition success-
    ful only if it is mass-based political work.** In the
    long run, progressive political positions matter only if
    organizations come into place whose mass base is en-
    gaged with such positions and is moving forward and
    growing, however slowly. In other words, progressive
    politics limited to a few activists who run an organiz-
    ation in typical CBO mold, while valuable to some in-
    dividuals they may have helped, does not build much
    of a movement. I am not arguing that the work that
    CBOs do is unimportant. For many poor people, or-
    ganizations that help them gain their rights are very im-
    portant. However, CBOs need to define their relation
    to mass-based work. The reason for this is simple: po-
    litical empowerment is not an individual matter. The
    only way a community of people go beyond being vic-
    tims is by charting their own future and engaging in a
    process of fighting for it. Without mass organizations
    this is not possible.

One way of understanding this combination—the simultaneous development of a new universal and mass-based politics—and
the political possibilities it presents was best expressed by Bill
Fletcher, the ex-director of training for the AFL-CIO, at the 2004
Socialist Scholars Conference. In response to the title "A Better
World Is Possible: But How?" Fletcher argued that what we have
in the contemporary moment is a wide array of social justice
struggles without an understanding of how these will bridge to
the revolutionary.[10] His articulation of two levels—the domain of
social justice struggles and the space of revolutionary movement
building—as discontinous in the contemporary moment begs the
question of how we will bridge that gap. In thinking of a new

universal lies one of the ways of constructing this bridge to the revolutionary. This new universal, as I have already said, is in process, but its contours of formation, I would argue, lie around the idea of "justice." So many of the struggles around the world are premised on holding the state responsible for justice, each time defined in its own specific context. In a neoliberal world, as the state attempts to withdraw from historically produced roles and responsibilities, many social movements find themselves articulating a struggle against the state around the principle of justice. Justice itself is an interesting category, for it is in many ways, unlike laws and legislations, contracts and negotiations, a claim that exists prior to the state itself.[11] Each group articulates a notion of justice both in response to the state and private capital, but also by reaching for an utopian ideal that has valence for their collective self. In much of the Third World, social justice movements have gone as far as to reject hegemonic ideals such as bourgeois democracy, often articulating the idea of democracy as itself possible only under conditions of justice. Many of these movements demand of the state an idea of collective rights that is inherently impossible within the structure of bourgeois democracy. These ideas of collective rights emerge not from an understanding of citizenship in a bourgeois democracy but from differential and partial constructions of the social that are part of the tradition of such communities—traditions that may be rooted in ancient or medieval histories on the one hand or more modern ones of socialism and communism. Maybe our collective task here is to look carefully at the resurgent left social movements all across Africa, Asia, and Latin America and comprehend the ideas of justice that inhere within these movements and the historical memory they are rooted in. If bourgeois democracy articulates a notion of an equal citizen through the recognition of a formal legal equality that rests in abstract individualism, these new movements in the

Third World have turned this idea on its head. Democracy is not a process that yields a liberal society but rather a product when justice is ensured.

Many of the stories in this book are evocative of this politics. However, the stories in this book are necessarily incomplete, as are the politics. Rizwan and Mamnun continue to struggle with the question of whether to leave the industry altogether or continue to stay in it and fight. Kurshid still drives, but just enough to keep body and soul together. He says, "You have no choice but to cut down. If not, ten years from now, I will be the owner of a wasted body, and maybe making so little will force me to do something more sane than driving a yellow in New York City." Kevin has survived a heart attack but has no choice but to continue driving. He faces the fear of growing older and feeling the real impact of an impoverishing regime of independent contractorship with a smile and an attitude of defiance, as so many workers around the world do. Yilma and Ahmed continue in the industry and dream the universal in OC meetings. Almost all of them, including Tahir, Javaid, Kasif, Tasleem, and Surinder, struggle with the consequences of fragments of families in distant worlds. As the United States turned more and more inhospitable, Saeed was among the many Alliance members who moved to Canada. These stories have no heroic Hollywood-style ending. But what they do have is the possibility of a collective vision. It is in pursuit of this that I offer this book—as a hopeful new moment in a debate that will take us closer to the revolution. And Bhairavi? The politics of revolution certainly cannot do without her.

EPILOGUE: TRACKING TAXIS, WORKER AUTONOMY, AND NEW LABOR STRATEGIES

SINCE THIS BOOK was first published, the position of the Taxi Alliance both within the industry and within the broader labor movement has been significantly affected by three events: the formation of the International Taxi Workers Alliance (ITWA); the Taxi Alliance's developing relationship with the New York Central Labor Council (CLC); and the ongoing battle against the GPS–based Taxi Technology Enhancement (TTE) Program of the Taxi and Limousine Commission (TLC).

The formation of the international alliance of taxi workers is, at the most basic level, a result of the growth of the New York Alliance. The New York Alliance's multiple battles and its role in raising local and national awareness of issues facing the contemporary taxi industry prompted a range of new conversations and brought together several new and old taxi-driver organizing initiatives. As Thomas George-Williams of the United Taxi Workers of San Francisco said in March 2007 on the first day of the ITWA meeting in New York: "This is momentous simply because I had to come all the way to New York to meet two very successful organizers who have been organizing taxi drivers just miles away from where I live, but never had a chance of meeting. It just shows how fragmented we are and the role that you guys [NYTWA] have already played in changing that."[1]

Thomas was referring to Anwar Zadran, of the East Bay Taxi Drivers Association and Seyoum Asrat, the organizer of the San Jose Taxi Drivers Association.[2] As Ron Blount of the Taxi Workers

Alliance of Pennsylvania said in his capacity as co-chair (along with Bhairavi Desai) of the founding conference and its significance in bringing efforts together, "This is about us—we know we are here to support each other from now on!" In all, organizers from fifteen cities attended the meeting including Toronto, Boston, Chicago, San Francisco, Los Angeles, Philadelphia, Minneapolis, and New York.[3]

At the time the ITWA founding conference was being planned, the CLC made a historic decision to accept NYTWA as a full member. This was not just a matter of recognition of the consistent organizing work that NYTWA has done for over a decade. At a much broader level, it signified the development of a new consciousness in the mainstream labor movement (or, at least within some segments of the movement) toward an appreciation of the critical role played by the new wave of immigrant labor that has entered the United States over the last thirty years in crafting the future of the American labor movement. Ed Ott, the executive director of the New York CLC, reflecting on the entry of the NYTWA into the CLC, began by recognizing that there are "two working classes in this city." The first is made of those in the organized public-sector unions who "have a modicum of security," and the second is made of the new immigrant working class that labors twelve-to-fourteen-hour days. For Ott, it is clear that if the unions that represent the mainstream unionized workers think that their unions are sustainable with two working classes in the city then they need to understand that: "it's folly to think that . . . [respectable wages and benefits are] sustainable . . . carried around on the back of a working class that is living in poverty. In fact, the danger for the labor movement is that the mass of the working class would become the social base of their opposition."[4]

The formation of the ITWA and the Alliance's entry into the New York CLC are nestled within a period of the most intense struggle within the taxi industry—the city's and the owners' decision to impose a non-navigational GPS-based tracking system in all yellow taxis and the drivers' determined struggle against it. The GPS story is crucial because it gives us another glimpse into the strength of grassroots organizing and because it brings together several of the themes discussed in this book and thus sets the stage for understanding the new modes of structuring labor that we need to contend with.

CATCH ME IF YOU CAN: THE GPS STORY

The night had settled in but Bhairavi, Javaid, and I could not get out of the main taxi holding lot at La Guardia airport. It was the night of September 9, 2007, three days after the successful two-day strike called by the NYTWA. Under the floodlights, a large group of drivers had gathered by the photographs the Alliance had put up of the completely empty taxi holding lots at JFK and LGA. The pictures stood as a stark testimony to the success of the strike against the media spin that Mayor Bloomberg and the TLC had attempted to engineer. Mamadou, a lean wispy Senegalese driver whistled and said "Wow, we did it, man!" After a moment, laughter rose like a burst of sparks in the air. Javaid, a grin spreading across his face, broke in, "and this is the first time in forty years that we have created a strike entirely on our own strength with everybody else in the industry united against us. . . . This is entirely ours. We did it!"

A cheer went up, and the group broke into an animated discussion of what such unity could achieve in the long run. And it was true that every part of the industry had tried every trick in the book to break the morale and destroy the strike. The MTBOT, the garage owners' association, had begun telling drivers that the GPS was a "done deal" as early as May 2007 and that it "was a waste of time to strike." The TLC itself began sending out people to the airports with flyers advertising the so-called benefits of the GPS system. As part of the negotiations between the mayors' office and the NYTWA, Jeff Kay, the mayor's chief of operations, along with two underlings from the TLC, had come to the main lot at LaGuardia to "speak with drivers" and "understand their concerns." Closer to the strike date, as it became clear that the negotiations were not headed for a positive resolution, the TLC drummed up a PR campaign in which it made several false claims—including that tips were up by 18 percent on credit card transactions. The garages and brokers also, it seemed, hired a small group of drivers to try and infiltrate the Alliance and create trouble within the campaign.[5] The brokers stayed silent in large part but consistently refused to give drivers a break on their weekly leases throughout the strike.[6] In the same time period several brokers also increased the lease fee by an additional $1,200 per year, claiming that drivers now had to pay for the tax stamp, a cost that historically has been paid by the medallion owner; in reality they were essentially passing on the cost of the GPS system to the drivers. A week before the strike, several garages banned drivers from bringing pro-strike flyers onto the garage premises and put out offers for discounted lease rates for the two days of the strike. But with all efforts failing, the TLC and the MTBOT turned to their last hope—Fernando Mateo. Mateo had inserted himself into the industry in 2000 as self-appointed president of an organization called the New York State Federation of Taxi Drivers (NYSFTD). Between 2000 and 2005 his claim was that his organization represented car service drivers.

On August 30, we received the first reports that a new flyer was moving at all the airports—one that simply said in huge bold letters "NO STRIKE." It was signed by Mateo's federation but gave no number or address. By late that afternoon, reports were in from all the airport lots and from Penn Station, Port Authority, and Grand Central that federation "workers" were out in full force distributing flyers and trying to talk to drivers. Within a few hours, we figured out that none of them was actually a driver, but rather they were young teenagers hired off the streets of Washington Heights. As one of the kids told me late that afternoon at LGA, "Hell man, I don't know what's on this paper. I am getting paid for giving it out." It was an operation with money behind it. Every four kids, on the average, had a supervisor who was driving around the airport to ensure that the kids didn't throw the flyers into the closest trash can. On day two of the Mateo operation, the situation got ugly. Outside Penn Station, Grand Central, and Port Authority, Alliance organizers and federation kids battled it out. Qayyum and Tariq manned Port Authority. Billy, Tahir, and Osman took over Penn Station. Mor Thiam and Kavita were stationed at Grand Central. Bill Lindaeur coordinated logistics from the office and did countless shifts at Penn Station. Lakshman, Beresford, and Kasif canvassed JFK along with a group of airport regulars including Winston, Gogi, and Maninder, while Mamnun and Victor covered LGA. Tipu, Tasleem, and Khalid shuttled among all the mosques, and an additional team of thirty volunteers provided twenty-four-hour coverage of all spots. The Alliance strike machinery was in high gear. In the end, the day before the strike, the Port Authority, probably because of pressure from the city, blocked the Alliance from being at the airports and allowed the federation kids to stay, claiming—"they applied for and were granted permission to flyer." But by then it was too late. There was almost no driver who did not know what the flyer was about, and the federation's tactic had failed.

"So where is Mateo now?" asked Jean-Bapiste, one of the drivers who had been speaking openly against Mateo at the airport lots. Javaid laughed. "He is finished . . . this strike has certainly taken care of that."

At the other end of the lot a cheer went up. Bhairavi was there—surrounded by another large group of drivers. They had arrived at the same conclusion.

With no possibility of picket lines, driver participation in the strike was entirely voluntary. The sense of victory that drivers experienced in the days following the strike was immense. The drivers regarded everything the city said as spin, and very soon it began to fall apart. The *Daily News* ran a story two days after the strike that more or less said that the mayor's statistics on strike participation were fudged.[7] *Metro New York* ran a similar story on the drivers' having to pay for the system in spite of the city's claim to the contrary.[8] The *Village Voice* ran two stories in as many weeks that once again opened up the question of corruption in the GPS deal.[9]

From the lane farthest away, a driver shouted out, as he drove away—"Bhairaviji union ke saat hain sab log." His hand was rolled into a fist, and he slowed down for a moment as he passed by Bhairavi: "The union will be made this time." In so many ways the strikes of September and October 2007 were not only about the GPS system but also just as much about the final decision that a majority of the drivers had made—they had existed in the industry for too long without collective bargaining, and as independent contractors they would find some new way of creating a collective power structure for themselves.

A SHIFT IN POWER: THE ORIGINS OF THE GPS

A brief description of the GPS-based technology system that the TLC is seeking to impose on drivers is important if we are to understand the grassroots upsurge against it. The very origins of the TTE program speaks volumes about the relations among various

actors as envisaged by the TLC. The system was proposed at
the very end of the fare increase negotiations of 2004. Over
2003–2004 as the negotiations moved forward, one thing had become increasingly clear: the Alliance had placed itself in a strong
position. Part of the success of the Alliance's strategy was visible
from the way in which the categories of discourse that the Alliance had introduced dictated the terms of the negotiation. For
instance, early in the campaign, the Alliance promoted a bench-
mark for the proposed fare increase as securing a "livable wage"
for drivers. By the time the fare increase was approved in March
2004, several of the commissioners and the press were themselves
freely using the category of a livable wage as the core objective of
the fare increase.

All this signified a changed dynamic from what was commonplace in the taxi industry for the last several decades. It is easy to
see the GPS program coming in at the end of the fare negotiations
as a response to the victories of the Alliance. For the first time in
over three decades the ownership did not get anywhere close to
what it was used to getting out of a fare increase. The Alliance was
surprised when in one of the last negotiation meetings the city's
key negotiator, Iris Weinshall, suggested a new tech enhancement
package to "give back something" to the riders in lieu of the fare
increase. The TLC had a record of failed technology programs.
Their "talking meter" had failed miserably, and their Taxi TV program had not gotten past the pilot stage. Riders had hated both.
But Wienshall and her man-in-the-TLC, Andrew Salkin (soon to
become the first deputy commissioner of the TLC and the person
to head up the GPS project), were both determined, raising immediate concerns within the Alliance as to whether the new technology proposal was a "payback" to the ownership. However, the
precise shape that the TTE would take was unclear at that point. It
was only several months later that the TLC's plan of imposing a

GPS-based system began to surface. Three years, several delays, and many wranglings later, the system that emerged had four components, four vendors, and smelled of corruption.

THE FOUR VENDORS: THE SMELL OF CORRUPTION

Four vendors cleared the TLC's complicated and elaborate award process—Taxi Technology Inc., Digital Dispatch Systems, Verifone, and Creative Mobile Technology. The TLC claims a rigorous process for the approval of the vendors. And yet, it has been reported that the systems of all four vendors have experienced significant failure on the streets.[10] The full story of failure will emerge in time. For now, we know the first of the four—Taxi Technology—has already filed for bankruptcy, less than twelve weeks into the program.[11] Most Digital Dispatch systems installed are incomplete and are installations only for the record. Further, the grapevine indicates that Digital Dispatch Systems also has one of its subcontractors suing it for IPR violations. Verifone, the vendor with the most end-user contracts, has also been dragged into court for misrepresentation of its financial strength. Also, Verifone has failed to execute a corresponding GPS contract for Philadelphia taxis for more than two years, and the Philadelphia Parking Authority is holding back a large part of the payment due to Verifone because of nonperformance of its systems and has imposed a deadline for fixing all pending problems.[12] Creative Mobile Technology has had repeated failures on the street and is the only company among the four to have experienced several hours of shutdown at a time. How all four vendors could have such financial, operation, and contractual failures within such a short time of the launch of the program when the TLC claims it went through a rigorous three-year technical and financial evaluation of the vendors is a critical question to ask. Does not the abysmal mess just a few months into the program point to a fundamentally compromised process—where everything from an industry gun-on-hire such as Bruce Schaller was used in the RFP evaluation all the way to a complete failure in financial evaluation?

What adds much credence to the questions is the fact that of the four vendors, two—Creative Mobile Technology and Verifone—have taken approximately 75 percent of the contracts and are both old time industry insiders with significant contacts with the TLC. Verifone is owned by Amos Tamam, the industry's largest meter vendor, and Creative Mobile Technology's owner, Ron Sherman, is the president of the garage owners association. The TLC itself has a long history of corruption.[13] Several ex-TLC executives have moved from the TLC into employment with the industry ownership. In the case of the GPS systems for instance, Jed Applebaum, the former TLC commissioner for Safety and Emissions, and Joseph Gianetto, the former First Deputy Commissioner of the TLC, are both employees of Ron Sherman. The extent of corruption and the inability of the liberal establishment to respond to these collusions is deeply troubling. However, to examine this problem is outside the scope of this book.

THE FOUR COMPONENTS: GIZMOS NOBODY ASKED FOR

The first of the four components of a GPS system is a receiver, with an attendant dead-reckoning software that is integrated into the taxi meter, allowing it to record every aspect of a driver's movements whether he or she is on or off duty, whether the car is in motion or parked. The second is a high-resolution Passenger Information Monitor (PIM) built into the partition and seat just behind the driver, which puts the screen barely two feet from the

face of a rider sitting back in the taxi. The back end of this unit
sticks out into the front cabin of the taxi and is literally just a few
inches from the right hand of the driver, overheating the front
cabin, creating constant noise, and in some cases reducing the
amount of space available to the driver. Third is the Driver Monitor (DM), a monitor on the driver's side integrated with the GPS
receiver and used by the TLC to send directives and informational
text messages to the driver while he or she is in the midst of a
shift. These text message directives from the TLC could include a
demand on the driver to check if a rider has left behind a shopping
bag or that Lincoln Center has just spewed out a handful of potential passengers. Fourth, also in the back cabin of the taxi, there
is a wireless credit card reader that is not, and does not need to be,
integrated with the GPS receiver. While many riders do see the
credit card capability as a welcome addition, for drivers it involves
a double whammy. Not only is there no indemnification on failed
transactions, but the TLC/ownership has sneaked in a 5 percent
service fee on every credit card transaction to be split among the
credit card company, the GPS vendor, and the broker/garage —
amounting to an income cut for drivers.

To gain support for this GPS system the TLC has continued to
promote several features to the public. These include information
services via the PIM, a lost and found service, and credit card convenience for riders. In addition, it has touted the benefit of the information service for drivers on passenger availability and policy
data for the TLC.

The list of positive features is largely public relations hype that
does not take into account the disadvantages that are created in
their wake. The PIM in the back cabin of the taxi takes the notion
of a captive audience for advertising to an entirely new level. A
quick survey shows that a significant part of the airtime when the
PIM is on is filled with commercials aimed at the rider. Other ser-

vices being offered include news headlines, a map identifying the current location of the cab, and in some of the systems weather and other such trivia. Most passengers have already made it clear that they are not interested in being sitting targets for commercials. At the Penn Station taxi line, I interviewed more than one hundred riders. With few exceptions, most of them were clear that they wished for peace and quiet in the taxi and did not want to be targets for commercials.[14] The other services are either useless or simply uninteresting for most passengers. As Mamnun said, after three weeks of driving with the GPS technology in his taxi, "a large majority of my passengers just switch the system off minutes after they get in." Mamnun is clear about predicting the future of the system. "I get at least one passenger a day who yells at me for not turning the system off when he asks me to. All I can do is to tell him that I don't have the controls and that he should do it himself." Mamnun laughs at the thought of passengers using the map on the PIM to locate themselves: "Who would look at a map on a tiny TV screen in a moving car when they can just look out and read the street names?"

The lost and found service is the biggest hoax that the TLC has pulled off. Their PR efforts to promote the system have in a large part depended on the riders' desire to locate objects they may leave behind in a taxi. But the system in place does absolutely nothing. Says Osman, the famous diamond cabbie, so named by the media for his efforts to locate a rider who left behind several thousand dollars' worth of diamonds in his taxi. "You tell me. . . . If somebody leaves their wallet in the backseat, what happens? I drop the passenger. I have no idea that the wallet is there. The next passenger gets in within one, two blocks. And it's all over. The new passenger gets the wallet."

Any effective lost and found system depends on Reminder, Recovery, and Return. The TLC's GPS system does absolutely nothing on Reminder or Recovery and hence cannot produce any better rate of return than is currently available. Osman had a point to make:

> If the TLC was really serious about this then what they should have done is put a light in the back cabin of the taxi and a still camera (or a mirror) that comes on when the meter is shut off. That way I can see the back cabin within seconds of the rider stepping out and if there is something in the back cabin then I can simply yell out to the departing passenger, "my friend, your wallet is in the back seat."

This would have improved recovery and return a hundred fold, but the TLC does not believe in simple low tech solutions.

The case is not very different when it comes to giving information to the drivers about where passengers are available. For an effective passenger availability system, the TLC has to first institute a real time passenger locating system that then becomes the input for a messaging system that will inform drivers of where passengers are without any taxis in their vicinity. But there is no such real time system, and the order of complexity of any such system is humongous if not impossible. Without such an input system, any information that the TLC gets will either be irrelevant or already expired. Dhiren, an experienced driver with more than twenty years of experience behind the wheel, came up to the office recently laughing. He had just gotten a text from the TLC informing him that passengers were available at the Brooklyn Navy Yard while he was cruising uptown close to Columbia University. "It's ridiculous," he laughed, "what do they expect me to do. Rush to Brooklyn from uptown Manhattan? And this message came at least three times. Each time I have to open it, read it, and delete it. Now you tell me if this is dangerous or not?" In terms of real time taxi shortages that develop without pattern based on traffic and business on any given day, drivers often have far better solutions than the TLC can ever dream of. "Why do I need that bull****?" asks Naeem. "Drivers get to passengers because of their own networks. Every driver is on the cell phone with ten to fifteen friends who are driving in different parts of the city. So I get a regular update just by being on the phone about what is happening where. . . . This is instant information and no system that the TLC can give me can match this."

The absurdity of the TLC's claims around lost and found, passenger information services, and driver information on rider availability suggests they are merely part of a PR exercise and not the result of any serious study that would have ensured a better design. Beyond the problems with these functional features, this system also brings a taxi cab into greater risk of being out of service. "This monkey on the meter is a disaster in terms of service delivery," said Victor Salazar, an Alliance organizer, at the end of an early TLC public hearing on the GPS system. Without the GPS-meter integration, for a taxicab to be operational, it needs only a functional car and a functioning meter. The car itself is a fairly standard piece of equipment with a large infrastructure in place for its repair and maintenance. The meter, sans the GPS, was a simple piece of equipment that was fairly stable and seldom encountered failure. The GPS-based integration adds a complex layer of hardware and software and accompanying factors such as weather and signal strength to the capacity of a taxicab to deliver basic services—transport passengers from point A to B. Why an administration would create a new layer of potential for failure on a vital city service is a question that bears asking. In spite of the critique that I have already raised of the so-called functional features of the TTE, all of the services aimed at the customers (credit cards and video monitor) are fully deliverable without the GPS being integrated with the meter. In other words the TLC could have achieved the same degree of functionality as far as passengers are concerned without creating the risk of failure. The only feature for which the GPS integration into the meter is crucial is for the TLC (and the ownership) to collect detailed information about the driver. It should thus become palpably clear what the true purpose of the system is—monitoring and creating a new degree of leverage over the driver for the TLC and the ownership.

TILTING THE SCALES—STILL FURTHER

Thus the PIM and DM are both miserable failures, and all the claims of the TLC and the ownership are either functions that nobody asked for or ones that have no chance of working with the technology being implemented.[15] The two claims that have a grain of truth in them are the question of passenger convenience through credit cards and the collection of so-called policy data. What TLC means by policy data is essentially information collected off the meter-GPS integration, where the TLC and the ownership have the details of every trip a driver makes, including information about when a driver takes breaks and when the driver is cruising. The question is not so much whether the TLC could use this data, but much more. "What use will the TLC and the owners put it to?" Harjinder is clear again about the concerns: "The TLC has not ever been interested in drivers. So when it collects all this data on drivers it will be used to harm us. Surely, they will use it. If not today, tomorrow. But it will. . . . We have more than thirty years of experience on this."

Harjinder's fears are shared by a vast majority of the drivers. In the months before the strike, the Alliance had the most intense struggle trying to keep a balanced perspective in place with the drivers. "This GPS system is an insult and a complete big brother system," announced Gogi, a young Punjabi driver, to a group of drivers who were at the JFK lot. "Think about it," he said. "The GPS is connected to the meter and once they have the data of how much is coming into the cab, the IRS will be after you in a second. We will all be getting audited, and every single penny we make will have to be accounted for."

Early in the mobilization, Alliance organizers would insist that there was no evidence to suggest that this was going to happen. Most drivers' reactions were simple. "You tell me," Winston, a Jamaican driver asks his friend and NYTWA organizer Beresford Simmons, "Can the system deliver such information?"

"In technical terms, from what I understand, yes," says Beresford, guarded. "If the IRS or any other government agency subpoenas this information then they can get it because it is being captured."

"That's it then," is Winston's only response to an approving murmur from all the onlookers.

"If it is there, then given how much the TLC hates us, they will use it against us," says Asamouh, and a grave silence descends over the lot.

There were many such conversations. "You let this system go through, and you can be sure that sooner than later you will get speeding tickets by mail," says Ayub, who has been driving for well over fifteen years.

"Come along brother," responds Maninder Ohri, another long term driver, "let's not get carried away." He speaks in Punjabi but then switches to English, as he notes the African and Arab drivers standing around. "We can keep getting afraid. . . . They will do this; they will do that. . . . Let's not say these things till we know for sure."

Ayub doesn't back off from the point he is making. Several others join him in unison. "Who says I am afraid?" asks Ayub.

"It's got nothing to do with being afraid." The others approve loudly, and an Arab driver, Gamal, joins in. "And we cannot wait . . . to confirm or to not. . . . If we want to fight, it's right now."

Maninder is left silent for a moment. He waits for the loudest of protests to die down before he comes back in. "I didn't mean to say that it's good, this technology," he says. "I think we don't know everything, that's all. . . . We may be looking at the wrong things." Maninder is waiting for me to get a free moment. He gestures me over and says:

> You know what will be the greatest problem with this technology? It won't be the speeding; it won't be the IRS. It won't be any of that. The greatest problem with this technology will come because of the credit cards. Not only are they going to take 5 percent off every transaction, we have to depend on our garage and brokers to give us the credit card money, at the end of the shift or the week. You know what that means. . . . It means my broker, he has more control over me. It means I have to now beg him for my money. Earlier he never got to touch my money. Now even my money is with him, and I have to get on my f***ing knees to get it from him. . . . He will adjust the lease, then he will adjust parking tickets which I may or may not have actually gotten; he will adjust this and that, and in the end he will decide how much of my money I will get. You know what that f***ing means.

Maninder was angry—his voice rising. From a mildly analytical mood, he had turned furious in the course of a few minutes and I, like every other driver standing around him, nod silently. We are all wondering why Maninder is so upset, and slowly everything that he has just said begins to sink in.

"Yes, it's not just the 5 percent," says Gamal, and walks away shaking his head.[16]

I left the airport that night, a little after 9 p.m. All through my ride back into Manhattan, I kept turning these conversations around in my head. It is a complex class and race dynamic that frames the industry, and the TLC has not a shred of credibility with the drivers. Over the last year of mobilization the Alliance organizers were able to turn the issue of GPS-based data around and focus on more immediate issues, not long-term potential (mis)uses of the system. That the TLC only helps owners is apparent even on the simple day-to-day conflicts between drivers and owners. When a driver and an owner end up in conflict, the TLC has a long record of threatening to suspend a driver's hack license unless he settles with the broker or the garage. But, if the owner owes the driver money or confiscates his car illegally, the TLC always tells a driver that the contract between owner and driver is a private contract over which they have no oversight. Thus, for the Alliance organizers and over a period of a year of organizing, for most drivers, that imbalance of power between owners and drivers that the TLC helps create and reproduce on a daily basis is something that they see happening with the GPS-based data. Bhairavi elucidated this aspect to a group of drivers at a meeting: "The next time we go in for a fare increase negotiation, remember that with the GPS data, the TLC and the owners know every little bit about you and you know absolutely nothing about them."

And yet, even after the two strikes, the early conversations with Maninder and Gamal, with Harjinder and Mamadou don't leave me. Why, I ask myself often, do drivers end up with such an analysis? The conversation with Maninder, especially, never leaves me. For one, I realize that the drivers have shown an amazing grasp of the technology. With just fragmented information of what the actual system is, and with the most basic explanations of what GPS technology broadly was about, the drivers had woven together a rich and comprehensive account of its capabilities. That the TLC claimed most of these would not be implemented and that all this was just a "misinformation" campaign was beside the point.

The enormity of the change introduced by the GPS and the drivers' loss of power is difficult to characterize. There is a kind of epochal transformation at work here, epochal not in the sense of an active and violent revolutionary change but in a sense the exact opposite: all that was ephemeral has been brought under scrutiny and control. Thinking again about what precise loss Maninder was mourning, I was taken back to a moment in the Alliance's negotiations with the mayor's office. In the days immediately preceding the strike, at a negotiation meeting aimed at preventing the strike, Bhairavi spoke with utmost candor. "This is an industry," she said, looking straight at Jeff Kay, the most senior officer of the administration present:

> in which drivers have historically been at a disadvantage in relation to the brokers and the garages; where after twelve hours of working they find again and again that the brokers and garages have taken away most of the money. In such an industry, by putting the GPS on the meter and handing that data over to the garages and brokers you are arming them with more power in a situation that is already way out of balance. And yet, in spite of all the imbalances, in spite of all the inequities, drivers have continued to work because there is this sense of independence . . . that

they are their own boss, that nobody can check up on
them, that they decide what is good and bad for themselves, and they can stop when they want to and start
when they feel like. . . . And now with the GPS system, even that ephemeral sense of independence is
gone.

In both Maninder's and Bhairavi's comments the essential concept they seize is that of worker autonomy—a concept that is central to the very idea of labor organizing. One could go so far as to
argue that the goals of a typical labor organizing project—
increased wages, better working conditions, increased time off,
and so on—all derive from notions of worker autonomy. If we
are to theorize as to how and why the GPS system matters to taxi
drivers, we will have to think through the question of autonomy.

GPS AND THE FLEXIBLE SUBSUMPTION
OF LABOR

Something very specific is happening in the taxi industry with the
GPS system. In our earlier discussion of labor control in the taxi
industry (chapter 3) we outlined the failure of the Fordist model
as a regime of control over taxi drivers and the pioneering move
toward the post-Fordist form in the taxi industry in the late
1970s. The introduction of leasing where the owner collected a
rent up front and made, in formal terms, no further attempt to
control the work of the driver was a pioneering departure from
the accepted wisdom of labor control at the time. It preceded the
general change in direction brought on by neoliberalism where increasing numbers of workers were outsourced or downsized and
an ever expanding pool of contingent workers and independent
contractors was created. In other words, the taxi industry of the

late 1970s was, so to speak, on the cutting edge of a paradigm shift in how labor was to be repositioned in the neoliberal economic formation.

Most significant efforts at theorizing the labor process—from Marx to Braverman—grapple with the question of worker autonomy as capital organizes and reorganizes the labor process to facilitate the greater extraction of surplus value.[17] The historic archetype of worker autonomy in Marx is the independent artisan. Marx describes in detail the processes by which the "independent" artisan loses autonomy—as capital takes control over the credit and commodity markets. The loss of autonomy is specific— the artisan is constrained in as much as he loses control over the cost of input and the price of outputs, but the core labor process—the process of production—where the artisan crafts and fashions his product still remains fairly within the control of the artisan. This degree of loss of autonomy is what Marx refers to as the "formal subsumption of labor" to capital and the conditions under which absolute surplus value is extracted from the worker. It is not difficult to see the similarity between what Marx theorized as the condition of the nineteenth-century artisan/worker and the taxi industry where a fixed lease is extracted from the driver, as well as all the other industries that have used outsourcing, franchising, and other forms of externalized production. For instance, in fast food franchising, the multinational corporation that collects the franchise fee is structuring surplus extraction along lines of formal subsumption.

However, it would be unwise to settle with this comparison because there is more at work here. For the nineteenth and early twentieth century capitalist, the extraction of absolute surplus value through formal subsumption was never the end of the road. Leaving the entire labor process still within the control of the worker/artisan meant that the capitalist could never maximize the extraction of surplus. It is precisely this constraint that leads the capitalist toward a different idea of subsuming labor—what Marx calls the "real subsumption of labor."[18] Here, we see a marked change, what several theorists note as the paradigmatic change in the history of capital-labor relations. With the emergence of the factory and the Fordist system of production, labor is brought into a relation of real subsumption viz capital. Here, the worker is fixed in time and space, production is transformed into a revolutionary new process of socialized production, and the extraction of surplus value is no longer absolute but relative. The capitalist, in other words, seeks to control not just the external conditions of production but the labor process itself. To be clear, the emergence of real subsumption does not automatically mean that formal subsumption vanishes. The struggle over the length of the workday, for instance, continues. Capital continues to seek control over the workers' time, or as Marx puts it, capital continues to "fill the pores" of a worker's day. But what makes for real subsumption is the fact that once a worker yields control over a minute of his or her time, capital seeks to organize and reorganize that minute so as to increase productivity of that minute of labor time. Within the Marxian teleology this is indeed the pinnacle of the relation capital seeks with labor—fully and really subsumed. But it is also the mode that allows workers to take the struggle to a new level. The factory and real subsumption creates a new environment of socialized production—where hundreds, if not thousands, of workers are under one roof, engaged in tasks that are defined from the top, where their experiences of work are now entirely common. Such a reorganization of the production process is premised on a new technological interface between worker and capital—one that capital controls. For the first time, then, the worker has completely lost control over the means of production. But, capital has, so to speak, through the reorganization of the worker into a

socialized labor process set up the conditions where a sense of
worker unity and the strike as an organized form of action can all
emerge. Labor is thus organized for itself in the mirror image of
how capital wishes to organize it. It is under such conditions of
organization that collective bargaining emerges as the core form
of capital-labor negotiations. Collective bargaining is fundamentally premised on the real subsumption of labor under capital. The
very notion of collective bargaining is epistemically linked to the
idea of real subsumption of workers and their collectivization by
capital. Even as capital's intent is to extract maximum productivity
from each minute that the worker yields control over, so too the
core of collective bargaining strategy is one of seeking a portion
of the value extracted from each such minute yielded back for labor itself. It is thus that productivity battles become the core battles of the golden age of Fordism. But the schema of collective
bargaining is not just about the share of every dollar gained
through productivity increases. It is also about working conditions and the dignity of the worker. If in the early days of capitalism the complete lack of power in the hands of the worker
allowed the capitalist to dehumanize workers, the battle ever since
has been about the worker becoming human again and dare we
say "autonomous." And with the socialization of production,
with workers building a new spirit of united action, with industrial towns and cities emerging where workers define in significant
part its very cultural and social life, with every battle around dirt
and grime, safety and health won by workers, the worker becomes
human again. In prose and poetry that marks the rise of socialized
production, the worker emerges as hero too! From Upton Sinclair
to John Steinbeck, from Charles Dickens (in *Hard Times*) to
Charlie Chaplin and the anticolonial struggles described in Os-
mane Sembene to the worker–super hero represented by Amitabh
Bachchan in contemporary Bollywood cinema, the worker is the

hero of social change.[19] All of this constitutes not only a cultural framework in which workers' struggles are undertaken but also, most important, the ethical framework through which the worker emerges as human and hero.

And here is where the oddity that needs examination is inaugurated. With every victory won, every precedent set, the labor movement of the golden age set up its own demise, its own collapse. Having created the conditions under which labor's fightback produces the new regime of labor-capital relations, capital sought to minimize its disadvantages through law. This is no place to go into an elaborate analysis of what emerged as the structure of law that governs collective bargaining and unions in general, but the NLRA of 1935 and the Taft Hartley Act of 1947 and several other local, state, and federal laws do indeed form the limits of the labor struggle today.[20] If the collectivization of labor was inaugurated by the emergence of the factory, its future was doomed by the bourgeois legal infrastructure created between 1930 and 1960 in the period of the famous labor-capital partnership. For instance, the very definition of a worker crafted and enshrined in law during that era is so limited and constrained that today it leaves a mass of workers outside of the very definition of a worker. So also, the strike—the historic and central part of the workers' armory—was placed in a straightjacket which limits when a workforce would be allowed to strike and precluded the idea of a general strike. The list of constraints that labor ended up imposing on itself and those that capital managed to inflict on them is a long one. Not only had a legal framework ossified, but with the turn to business unionism by a large segment of the labor movement in the 1960s labor lost its ethical framework of worker as human and hero and instead embraced as its own an ethical principle that belonged to capitalism and would become the ruling ethical framework of neoliberalism—utilitarianism.[21]

All this then forms the historical context for what emerged not only in the taxi industry but in labor-capital relations more generally under neoliberalism. Capital changed the rules of the game and labor was left with the task of responding from within a constrained legal infrastructure and bankrupt ethical framework.

The move to independent contractorship so early in the taxi industry seems like a return to formal subsumption, but it is in fact far more complex. The TLC, created in 1972 under the auspices of a sympathetic and bureaucratized state, almost immediately inaugurated and then oversaw the return to leasing. The introduction of the electronic meters in the mid 1980s gave the ownership some degree of control, both in terms of information on driver earnings (so that the lease could be increased) and in terms of their capacity to program the meters to turn off at a specific hour on a specific day. Further, the TLC's legal infrastructure ensured that garages and brokers could do as they pleased with drivers. For instance, the broker could locate and confiscate a taxi anytime he wished to with no penalty. The growing rigor of the three-times-a-year taxi inspection and the new inspection facility at Woodside meant that not only could the TLC impose an exploding set of standards on the taxi but also could put a driver out of work for several days at a stretch, as was the case with OBD disasters between 2002 and 2007. In addition, the TLC grew into a large enforcement bureaucracy on the streets that was entirely focused on the drivers. Active policing aimed to ensure that drivers stuck to the standards being imposed—such as writing trip sheets, not taking fares off the meter, not "misusing" off duty, restrictions on the drivers' capacity to decide the route of travel, precise rules on the locking and unlocking of doors, to name just a few of the plethora of rules that govern the act of driving. Further, every rule violation allows the TLC to extract money from the drivers. All in all, the process in formation in the taxi industry since the

1980s has, with the GPS system, accelerated and extended beyond anybody's wildest imagination. It is not a simple case of either formal subsumption or real subsumption, but a complex hybrid of the two, tailored and crafted to the specifics of the taxi industry.

I call this flexible subsumption because its articulation not only uses, as in the example of the taxi industry above, elements of both real and formal subsumption, but more important because its uniqueness lies in the fact that similarly specific recombinations can be created for every industry. We have only to look around us to see the processes of combination at work. Whether it is security services, janitorial services, fast food franchises in the first world, call centers, or cotton farming using marginal farmers in India, we see the specific articulation of flexible subsumption tailored to that particular industry. Again, for instance, going beyond the taxi industry, in fast food franchising, while at a superficial level it seems that the relation of real subsumption is between the franchisee and the worker, this is hardly true. The MNC-principal sets the entire set of standards for production—equipment and prepackaged food, employee uniform and look and feel, the sales pitch script to the standard on number of orders per minute are all set in place by the MNC-franchiser rather than by the franchisee.

The question then is, what should labor's strategy be in the context of flexible subsumption?

A NEW ETHIC FOR THE WORKING CLASS: STRATEGIES FOR THE LABOR MOVEMENT

At the outset, it is critical to note that the following discussion on strategy is speculative. We do know that the last thirty years have belonged almost without question to the capitalist, and the victories of the working class that culminated in the emergence of collective bargaining are now a distant memory. This may be a moment when the tide can be turned, but if we do not experiment with new strategies and concepts we might condemn ourselves to many more years of defeat. We should begin by asking a simple question—What is it that we are fighting for? A narrow answer such as "wages" would immediately put us at a disadvantage. A broader answer—such as worker autonomy or class power—will place us in a different trajectory altogether.

Under conditions of flexible subsumption the worker is placed into two different relations—the first with those who control his or her income and directly extract surplus; and the second with those who structure the work that creates the conditions for extraction of surplus. In the case of the taxi industry, the garages and brokers collect leases thereby maintaining the conditions of formal subsumption (the extraction of absolute surplus value), but it is the TLC that creates the conditions of work and controls the very process of work. If the factory was the first form where production was socialized by the physical coming together of workers, the TLC's infrastructure of standards is the metaphorical roof that socializes production in the case of the contemporary taxi industry. The limiting condition of formal subsumption— that the driver be independent—is negated as much by the lease as by the array of rules the TLC imposes on the driver. Thus it is precisely the existence of brokers/garages on the one hand and the TLC and its standards on the other that make a driver a dependent rather than an independent contractor. The battle of first order then is to upset the independent contractor applecart by establishing through legislation the category of dependent contractor and creating an independent Work Rights and Contracts Board. The idea behind a Work Rights and Contract Board is to create a legally sanctioned forum where the target of flexible subsuption— the worker/dependent contractor (driver or fast food worker); the machinator of formal subsumption—the ownership (garage/broker or the franchisee); and the creator of real subsumption—the standard setting body (TLC or the franchiser/MNC) are brought into a periodically defined negotiation to organize/reorganize the conditions of the industry. Many aspects of such a vision are already embedded in the work of the Alliance. For instance, the emergence of the lease cap in the mid 1990s and the Alliance's strategic insistence that the lease cap be negotiable in the 2004 fare increase negotiations with the TLC is an excellent example of a move in this direction—without, of course, the requisite institutions, such as a contracts board, in place. The same is true in the GPS battle where drivers are attempting to negotiate with those who define their work, as the latter attempts to bring the driver under greater regulation. In the end, the sole reason the Alliance is still battling the GPS regime, instead of having already defeated it, is that no such legally defined contracts board is in place, and the TLC and ownership have no obligation to negotiate with the Alliance.

One strategy I would advocate is to look not simply at the relationship of employee-employer as we tend to do today but to ask who controls the work and then to force that institution along with the immediate exploiter into a combined framework of negotiations. Other strategies should become clear to us once we grasp the complexity of flexible subsumption. It is possible that some forgotten strategies such as worker cooperatives could be part of the picture. Here I am thinking, for example, of worker cooperatives (which have been revived in Argentina and other parts of Latin America) because the idea of cooperatives is located in the realm of worker autonomy and minimizing the control capital has over the producer.

We need to remember that the reason we are headed for such a renegotiation of the very categories of worker/dependent

contractor and standards is that the moment the labor movement entered into a phase of collective bargaining it fell into the
utilitarian ethic that capital promoted. Business unionism is in
that sense a natural outgrowth of collective bargaining shorn of
its ideals of formation—worker autonomy. The battle for redefinition is not just about the precise conditions of work and
wages; it is also about changing the ethical framework under
which we operate. Utilitarianism as an ethical framework has to
be defeated, and such a transformation needs to begin with the
working class itself. Workers across the world will first have to
be convinced that autonomy is a goal far more important than
immediate wages—the latter, it should be obvious, will come if
we are able to change the ethic. The labor movement as a whole
needs to begin investing in this change. Only a new ethic of autonomy will be able to alter the broader ethical framework of
society—utilitarianism and its attendant cultural forms of consumption and narrow self interest.

The "second working class" will be the one that is primarily in
charge of carrying such agenda items forward. They will be the
ones who will define the future of the labor movement as they
move toward redefining the very terms of what a "worker" will
mean in this new millennium.

NOTES

PROLOGUE: THE DISTANCE BETWEEN TWO VICTORIES

1. Henceforth to be referred to as the Alliance.
2. Yellow taxi drivers depend on the simultaneous working of multiple businesses and sites. The September 11 attack meant that a range of businesses—from Broadway theaters to the airports and the whole of downtown tourist attractions—all came to a standstill for several weeks. The downturn in business for drivers was thus compounded because all the sectors they rely on went down at the same time.
3. The UJC report, "Unfare: Taxi Drivers and the Cost of Moving the City," was executed in partnership with the Alliance. The UJC and the Alliance worked closely in designing and executing the survey, while the former took prime responsibility for the analysis of data and report writing.
4. *Daily News* editorial, January 5, 2004. The other very supportive editorial position came from *Newsday*. See "After 8 Years, Cabbies Really Do Deserve a Raise," *Newsday,* January 30, 2004.
5. "New York Cabdrivers Deserve Better," editorial, *New York Times,* November 11, 2003.
6. A detailed description of the May 1998 strikes, its effects, and the Alliance's campaigns that came out of the strikes are outlined in the first four chapters. What is important to register now is that the Alliance went into these strikes as a new organization with limited membership.

1. ROOTS OF VICTORY: THE TAXI STRIKES OF 1998

1. There are two such holding lots at LaGuardia Airport, one serving the Delta and US Airways terminals and the other serving the main terminal. At John F. Kennedy International Airport there is a single large holding lot serving all terminals. The waiting time in the lot is dead time for the drivers. At

LaGuardia, the terminals are immediately adjacent to the holding lots; thus the taxis that have lined up just roll down to the terminal column by column in a first-in first-out system. At JFK, the operation is more complex since the lot is located at some distance from the terminals. Dispatchers at each terminal communicate with the dispatchers at the holding lot and request a certain number of taxis anticipating loads based on the sequence of flight arrivals. It happens often enough, especially later into the night, that dispatchers make a wrong judgment and request too many taxis at a specific terminal. Only after the driver may have waited there for a good twenty minutes does the dispatcher reassign him to another terminal. Thus, driver waiting times at JFK include a lot of overhead: the drive from a terminal to the lot after a passenger has been dropped off; the wait in the lot itself, which depends on how busy the airport is on any day; the drive from the lot to the terminal and the wait at the terminal; and last of all, the reassignment to another terminal if necessary, causing another long drive through the large airport complex to get to the new terminal.

2. HORSE HIRING: ABOLITION AND RETURN

1. It often happens that a driver, after having spent several hours waiting for his turn at an airport holding lot, gets a "short" ride to a destination close by. The driver's wait in the lot will pay off only if he gets a ride back into Manhattan. The system set up to respond to this problem is commonly referred to as the "shorty" system. Per the shorty system, a driver who gets a ride to a destination close by gets a "shorty" ticket from the dispatcher that allows him to return to the airport, jump the regular line, and be allotted another passenger through a separate shorty line.

2. At the time of this writing, Mayor Bloomberg had just announced a plan to introduce 900 new medallions. The first auction of 300 new medallions was conducted in May 2004. If this sale of the remaining 600 medallions goes through, then the city will have just above 13,000 medallions in a few years.

3. The history of the New York City taxi medallion rendered here comes not from historical archives but from the recollections of older drivers. Today's immigrant driver workforce has little knowledge of this history. Kevin, Steve, and Leo, all older white drivers who were active in industry politics through 1950-1980, were my primary sources.

4. Between 1911 and 1921 New York City taxi drivers operated on a fixed salary. However, in 1921, this agreement broke down and the industry headed toward the commission system that would turn, as the times got worse, into horse hiring.

5. The medallions' naturalization as private property took well over a decade. In the period from the inception of the Haas Act to the mid to late forties, many owners did let their medallions lapse. It was only in the late forties that the number of medallions stabilized at around 12,000—the first signs of it becoming "valuable" as private property. Bruce Schaller records this trend in his "Taxi Cab Fact Book" (http://www.schallerconsult.com/taxi/fb/fb3.htm).

3. THE AGE OF GREED, OR WHAT'S NEOLIBERALISM GOT TO DO WITH IT?

1. Quoted in Charles Vidich, *The New York Cab Driver and His Fare* (Cambridge, MA: Schenkman Publishing Company, 1976).

2. This system of automatic dues collection lasted until 1998. Each of the MTBOT garages had a dues ticket machine into which drivers had to put $2 (later $3) and then get a ticket before they could go in and lease a cab for the shift. Drivers constantly referred to Local 3036 as the "two-dollar union."

3. Quoted in Vidich, *New York Cab Driver*.

4. Even as this book goes to press in late 2004, the value of the individual medallion has climbed past $300,000, while that of the fleet medallion has risen past $350,000. This spike in medallion values is part of Mayor Bloomberg's new medallion sales.

5. The lease rates quoted in this section are from December 2003. With the 8 percent increase in lease caps in 2004, the rates that owners charge currently are far higher. For instance, weekly rates for a single shift have gone up to the current lease cap of $667, or sometimes even higher. Similarly, daily lease rates have also changed. A Friday or Saturday night lease rate in most garages is currently at the lease cap of $129, or in some cases even as high as $132. Garages, after losing the battle with the Alliance during the fare hike–lease cap negotiations, have begun deploying a range of quasi-legal tactics—charging a sales tax that used to be rolled into the lease rate in the past, or in some cases charging a weekly lease rate far above the weekly cap by just adding up the lease caps for the daily rates. With the fare increase and the lease increases, the

specifics of the daily margins that a driver makes may have altered somewhat. I use the December 2003 rates because the post–May 2004 scenario and what it will finally yield is as yet unclear. In some part, how much the driver will ultimately make will be determined by how the battle around the owners' quasi-legal tactics will unfold.

6. The number of women drivers in the taxi industry currently is pegged at less than 1 percent. This is in comparison to anecdotal evidence that prior to the advent of leasing, close to 7 to 8 percent of the workforce were women.

7. The differential in the weekly rate payments between day and night drivers exists because overall the night shift is considered more lucrative. Also, it would seem that the partner of a DOV driver is the best positioned in the industry, since he gets to pay lower weekly rates and bears no liability at all. This is true except that the number of drivers who can be DOV operators' partners is limited by the number of drivers willing to be DOVs.

8. For a detailed understanding of the logic of Fordism, especially a rigorous theoretical discussion of Fordism as a regime of production under capitalism and the conditions of disempowerment it constitutes for workers, see Harry Braverman's *Labor and Monopoly Capital: The Degradation of Work in the Twentieth Century* (New York: Monthly Review Press, 1998). For a social history of the origins of Fordism through education and the pivotal figure of the engineer, and for the specific impact that the Fordist reorganization had on the U.S. labor force, see David Noble's *America by Design: Science, Technology, and the Rise of Corporate Capitalism* (New York: Oxford University Press, 1979). What is fundamental in understanding Fordism as explicated in these works is that Fordism as a regime of production was a response of capital to its inability to produce control over workers in earlier forms of organization of production. Also, Fordism brought into place the fundamental necessity that for labor to gain power it needed to organize as a unit—i.e, since Fordism homogenized workers in terms of their condition of absolute lack of control over their work, the only response left was collective struggle rather than individual acts of resistance.

9. I prefer the term "neoliberal economic practice" or "neoliberal economic organization" for its specificity. A host of terms, including post-Fordist, postindustrial, globalized, and informational, have been used to signify the nature of economic organization in the world after Fordism. Terms such as globalization are entirely unspecific, as they cover a range of phenomena from the globalization of certain cultural forms to the reorganization of finance and banking. The problem with terms such as post-Fordist or postindustrial is that

they fail to convey that Fordist production and regulation structures are very much part of what is called post-Fordist. Theorists such as Aglietta and Lipietz (of the French Regulation School, who were primarily responsible for the term post-Fordist gaining currency), Bell (postindustrial), and Castells (informational) seem to use these terms because of their perspective as theorists who are concerned entirely with the social organization of the Western capitalist world. It is indeed true that Fordism has significantly vanished in large parts of the Western capitalist world. However, it is just as true that neoliberalism is a global practice and Fordism as a regulatory structure is significantly part of this reorganization except it has been largely shifted to the Third World. For most of these theorists, the reorganization appears merely as part of the internal logic of First World capitalism. While it is certainly the case that the reorganization is fundamentally about the logic of capitalism, it is also true that the reasons that capitalism manages to reorganize in this fashion is because of historically produced imperialist relations, including the power to make war and dominate peoples across the world. In this sense, most of the theorists fail to see the continuities, and their sole focus on the Western capitalist world allows them access only to the discontinuities. For an excellent critique of the Fordism/post-Fordism thesis, see Gambino (1996).

Neoliberalism, on the other hand, allows us to keep in focus all the continuities while seeing the new. Just as Fordism referred to both a form of labor regulation and also the Keynesian compact at the level of larger economic organization, neoliberalism allows us to refer to practices of regulation at the level of a firm and simultaneously as forms of the economic reorganization of the world as a whole.

For a sample of the theorists mentioned, see Michel Aglietta, *A Theory of Capitalist Regulation: The U.S. Experience* (New York: Verso, 1979); Alain Lipietz, *Mirages and Miracles: The Crisis of Global Fordism* (London: Verso, 1987) and "The Post-Fordist World: Labour Relations, International Hierarchy and Global Ecology," *Review of International Political Economy* 4, no. 1 (1997). Also, for an excellent collection on post-Fordism, see Ash Amin, *Post-Fordism. A Reader* (Oxford: Blackwell, 1994); Daniel Bell, *The Coming of Post-Industrial Society: A Venture in Social Forecasting* (New York: Basic Books, 1973); Manuel Castells, *The Rise of the Network Society: The Information Age: Economy, Society, and Culture, Vol. 1* (Oxford: Blackwell, 1996); and Ferruccio Gambino, "A Critique of the Fordism of the Regulation School," *Common Sense*, no. 19 (1996).

4. THE REINVENTION OF THE YELLOW CAB

1. The details of the legislation are too dry and complicated to go into here. The idea that legislation is meant to make things more cumbersome and thus create a space for a driver to fight back is what is unique about this process. For instance, the TLC had created a rule that meant automatic suspension of the hack license if the driver gathered six points on his license over any two-year period. Intro 376A undercut this rule by creating a series of provisions for its implementation. First, it reduced the period of point accumulation from two years to eighteen months. Second, it made the counting of the eighteen months begin on the incident date rather than on the conviction date. Third, it made it possible for the TLC to count only one summons from a specific incident even if multiple summonses were issued. In other words, the space created through the legislation was one in which the TLC had to track so many different technicalities that even one minor oversight on its part could restore a cabdriver's license.

2. Robert Fitch, *The Assassination of New York* (New York: Verso, 1993), 135. (DLMA was the Rockefeller-run Downtown Lower Manhattan Association.)

3. Ibid., 159.

4. Ibid., 159–60.

5. Ibid., 166.

6. The rationalization of the livery industry was much needed because it had historically developed out of two trajectories—the early radio cabs and the "illegal" gypsies on the one hand and the newly emergent black car/limo industry. They operated in a liminal space. Their legitimacy in the late 1980s came from the fact that black cars operated on radio had legitimacy. As such, many of the petty capitalists who had invested in livery were concerned about whether they would be allowed to survive in the long run. Thus del Valle's efforts can be seen as the last chapter in the transformation of the taxi industry but also can be seen as a response to the worries of the small capitalists of the outer boroughs and upper Manhattan.

7. Richard Sennett, *The Hidden Injuries of Class* (New York: Cambridge University Press, 1977).

5. PUNISH AND DISCIPLINE: RACE IN THE NEW URBAN SPACE

1. The entry of the word "taxi" as a referent for sex work in daily street conversations, whether in Punjabi or Urdu, is simple to unpack. The reference is clearly

to the nature of "for hire" services. The metaphor, of course—once framed—is available to all sorts of further flights of fancy.

2. I owe much to Jay Shuffield for giving me the confidence and some of the terminology used in this section. I arrived at much of the analysis in early drafts of this section and then discovered the work of Shuffield. The sheer joy of reading him is difficult to describe. While I do not necessarily concur with Shuffield's elevation of "visual order" above all else, and with his reading of the limitation of Marx's notion of the annihilation of space, I clearly owe much to him in rewriting this section. Obviously, many of the concepts have long intellectual histories to which my easy use does not do justice. The idea of a space as a complex of the physical, social, and environmental owes much to the tradition of radical geographers such as David Harvey (*Paris, Capital of Modernity* [New York: Routledge, 2003]). Harvey's analysis of Paris and its transformation from medieval city to modern consumerist spectacle based in a bourgeois imaginary as against the other available vision of a "social republic" was truly inspirational. Similarly, a long tradition beginning with Marx's Grundrisse and its explication of the "annihilation of space through time" leads us to both Harvey's and Lefebvre's (1991) ideas of the production of space as well as the latter's concepts of domination and appropriation of space. For Shuffield, see his 2002 piece "Visual Order in Times Square: The Social Regulation of Urban Space," available at: http://www.urbanresidue.com/visual_order.html. For Harvey's analysis of Paris see *Paris, Capital of Modernity*. For Marx's "annihilation of space through time" see Karl Marx, *Grundrisse: Foundations of the Critique of Political Economy*, trans. Martin Nicolaus (New York: Random House, 1976). For the production of space see David Harvey's two books, *The Limits to Capital* (Chicago: University of Chicago Press, 1982) and *The Condition of Postmodernity: An Enquiry into Cultural Change* (Oxford: Blackwell, 1989). The concept is introduced first in *The Limits to Capital* and developed in the latter book. Also see Henri Lefebvre, *The Production of Space*, trans. Donald Nicholson-Smith (Cambridge, MA: Blackwell, 1991).

3. There are two of Sassen's exceptional contributions that I draw upon and which form, in some part, the underlying theoretical categories in much of the descriptions: the first is the idea of a "global city" as a space where some of the momentum of finance capital is both centralized and generated—a city among a small group of other cities that form the core network of the globalized world of finance capital. (See Saskia Sassen, *The Global City: New York, London, Tokyo*

[Princeton: Princeton University Press, 1991]). The second aspect I borrow from Sassen is her focus on "place and production." For Sassen a focus on "place and production" is the primary means through which she can make visible "the multiplicity of economies and work cultures in which the global information economy is embedded." (Saskia Sassen, "The Global City: Strategic Site/New Frontier," *Seminar*, July 2001, p. 1, http://www.india-seminar. com/2001/503/503%20saskia%20sassen.htm.) With these two points of departure Sassen is indeed able to capture the fact that a range of immigrant workers occupy and "produce" the global city. Sassen is primarily a political economist and hence pays little attention to the organization of the social/cultural in the global city (in the way for instance Zizek does in theorizing the culture of globalization). Thus, the effort in much of this and the next two chapters is to pick on Sassens notion of "places and production" and use it to understand the domain of cultural/social organization of a global city.

4. My point here is not that the Third World professional did not face racism but that their struggle against racism was conducted within the context of a class solidarity with the white middle class. Precisely because of the social and cultural capital that allowed them to migrate, they were already part of the white middle class before they left the shores of Bombay. Largely because of the question of class interests, where they do not see themselves outside of the white middle class imaginary of what it means to live in America, their struggles against racism are bound to be muted using strategies such as job shifts and private complaints in living room conversations rather than protest. Also, when I characterize the 1960s wave of migration as largely professional and middle class, this does not mean that there was no working-class migration until much later. All through the 1900s there were working-class migrations, such as those of the Afro-Caribbean tobacco workers and Chinese workers into the fast-growing Chinatowns.

5. My characterization of the Third World working-class migration as male is not to deny the emergence, especially in the late 1990s, of a significant female working-class migration into specific sectors such as care and domestic workers. However, two facts need to be noted: first, the ratio between male to female migration remains skewed as many more men still migrate than women. Second, the acceleration of female migration is a far newer phenomenon and therefore understudied. From my experiences within political organizing, the large part of the female worker migration seems to be from the Philippines and South Asia. In the United States, a large part of the South Asian domestic workers are from Bangladesh and India.

A large part of the organizing work among the South Asian domestic workers has been based on casework with large-scale and sustained mobilization against individual employers. These have often worked very successfully to reclaim the dues owed to a worker. However, because domestic work employment in the South Asian case is so often produced through entirely privatized networks, it has been very difficult to transform the organizing work into mass membership–based union formations. For information on such cases contact Workers Awaaz at 718-565-0081 in New York City. Workers Awaaz is one of the domestic worker organizing projects in New York.

In contrast, the Filipino community has seen more broad-based organizing efforts come to some fruition. Again, in large part this difference could be because of the numbers and the modes of employment. A significant segment of Filipina domestic workers tend to find their employment through classified advertisements, and since private employment agencies are involved, mass organizing becomes possible. Some of the largest Filipina domestic workers' organizations are found in Canada, where local legislation has allowed the hiring of such workers to be carried out on a large scale, especially as home-care workers.

Finally, there is a significant Sri Lankan domestic worker migration, in most part to the Middle East and Canada. For a documentation of the Sri Lankan case, see Nilita Vachani's 1995 documentary, *When Mother Came Home for Christmas,* Greek Film Centre ZDF Filmsixteen.

6. Published in the NACLA Report on the Americas, 2001, www.aclu.org/Drug Policy/DrugPolicy.cfm?ID = 10966&c = 2. Also see Vijay Prashad, *Keeping Up with the Dow Joneses: Debt, Prison, Workfare* (Boston: South End Press, 2003).

7. See Urbanfutures at http://www.urbanfutures.org/abstract.cfm?id = 45.

8. A limited understanding of biopower without getting into all of its complexities is difficult. Its conceptualization is part of a larger framework that attempts to explain modern structures of governmentality where the "subject" internalizes the rules of conduct, thereby producing the power of the state within his/her body. See Michel Foucault, "Technologies of the Self," October 1982 seminar, University of Vermont, in L.H. Martin, H. Gutman, and P.H. Hutton, eds., *Technologies of the Self: A Seminar with Michel Foucault* (Amherst: University of Massachusetts Press, 1988), and Foucault, "Governmentality," in Graham Burchell, Colin Gordon, and Peter Miller, eds., *The Foucault Effect: Studies in Governmentality* (Hemel Hempstead: Harvester Wheatsheaf, 1991), pp. 87–104. For a shorter piece, see Thomas Lemke, "'The Birth of

Bio-Politics'—Michel Foucault's Lecture at the Collège de France on Neo-
Liberal Governmentality," *Economy and Society* 30, no. 2 (2001): 190–207.

9. Once again in his second term in office, Giuliani began a defense of City Hall
Park. He banned the use of the park for protests and demonstrations, all done
under the guise of "security concerns." City Hall steps have long been a site of
protests and press conferences. In the last two years of his term, City Hall Park
suddenly went under construction, fueling speculation that it was yet again a
Giuliani tactic to win his petty battles.

10. Mohammed Baazi, "A Cabbie's Nightmare/Career in Jeopardy After Confrontation with Official." *Newsday* (combined editions), June 17, 2001, p. A5.

6. THE BORDERS OF GLOBALIZATION:
NEGOTIATING THE METROPOLIS

1. The Punjab Alienation of Land Act of 1902 was a typical colonial act, one
that was based on a rudimentary and flawed understanding of the colony and
its social structure as also one that served their material interests. The act defined certain "caste groups" (Jat, for instance) as farming castes and attempted
to mimic a permanent settlement of land for such castes so as to create strong
values of private property. A large number of the excluded castes, primarily
lower castes, became landless labor, and especially in Western Punjab (the part
that was to be in Pakistan after 1947) this became the condition of the majority of the population. For an excellent account on the Punjab Land Act, see
Gerald Barrier, *The Punjab Alienation of Land Bill of 1900.* (Durham, NC:
Duke University Press, 1966).

2. The green revolution that enveloped large parts of Pakistan starting in the late
1950s and Indian Punjab in the late 1970s and 1980s, can be seen as a forerun-
ner to the current regime of global agrarian economy, with large agribusiness
firms such as Monsanto and Cargill gaining significant control. Largely funded
in the case of Pakistan by the USAID and later by the World Bank, it brought
large-scale mechanization—such as tractors, harvesters, large dams, and canal
systems—and capitalization—such as hybrid seeds that farmers had to acquire
from large seed companies and pesticide systems, again to be bought from large
chemical companies. For an excellent analysis of the impacts of the green revolution on Pakistan, see Hamza Alavi, "State and Class in Peripheral Capitalism,"

in Hamza Alavi and Teodor Shanin, eds., *Introduction to the Sociology of "Developing Societies"* (London: Macmillan, 1982). For a detailed description of the connections between U.S. agrarian history, U.S.-based MNCs, and Third World green revolutions, see Jack Kloppenberg, *First the Seed: The Political Economy of Plant Biotechnology* (Cambridge: Cambridge University Press, 1988).

3. As was true all over the world, with the exception of slavery and indenture, travel beyond the boundaries of one's own country was mostly an elite practice till very recently. From within such a context Bhutto's "liberalization" of passports through the opening up of the passport office infrastructure in small towns all across Pakistan is a "break" from the past inasmuch as it is one of the factors that created the large-scale working-class migrations of the late twentieth century.

4. For a detailed documentation of the fate of the Cochon Creole or the Haitian pig, see the video documentary, *A Pig's Tale* by Leah Gordon and Anne Parisio (Crowing Rooster Films, 1997).

5. The year 1857 is a critical date because the First War of Independence against the British Indian empire was fought during this year—what the British called the Sepoy Mutiny—because large segments of the British Indian troops stationed in Northern India rebelled against the British authority and joined forces with the rebel armies (united under the symbolic authority of Bahadur Shah Zafar the last Mughal ruler of India) seeking independence from the British. After the uprising was brutally quelled, using in part British Indian forces from the Punjab, and Bahadur Shah was exiled to Rangoon, the British, in their typically uninformed way, identified the rebellion's base as located within certain ethnic/religious communities. Having arrived at this analysis, the British then began active recruitment for the army from communities that they saw as outside the rebellion. The Punjab was an area untouched by the rebellion and thus became a space for new recruitment. For a detailed account of the British recruitment from Punjab, see various essays in Partha Sarthi Gupta and Anirudh Deshpande, eds., *The British Raj and Its Indian Armed Forces, 1857–1939*. (London: Oxford University Press, 2002). See especially "Punjab and the Military Base of the Indian Army, 1849–1900" in this volume.

6. The lottery visa or the DV-1 category visa is a system where different countries are given quotas on migration to the United States based on how widely represented they are in the U.S. society and labor demand in the United States. Thus, Bangladesh has a significant quota that it fills each year through a lottery while

India has no quota at all because the Indian migration to the United States is seen as adequate. Of course, these levels are defined in an arbitrary fashion.

7. For the triumphalist narrative of capitalism, see Francis Fukuyama, *The End of History and the Last Man* (New York: The Free Press, 1992). For the Islam versus the West theses, see Samuel Huntington, *The Clash of Civilizations and the Remaking of World Order* (New York: Simon & Schuster, 1996).

8. Arjun Appadurai, *Modernity at Large: Cultural Dimensions of Modernity* (Minneapolis: University of Minnesota Press, 1996), p. 9. For an excellent critique of Appadurai that places a Lefevbrian reading on globalization, see Neil Brenner, "Global, Fragmented, Hierarchical: Henri Lefebvre's Geographies of Globalization," *Public Culture* 10, no. 1 (1997): 135–67.

9. Many economists argue that the restrictions to the mobility of labor is not of much significance in terms of how the relation between capital and labor is negotiated inasmuch as if one of the factors is free to move it will necessarily produce the same effects as if both were free to move. While this may be theoretically true, if we were to take the Harveyian notion of capital's spatio-temporal fix—as a constantly articulated series of fixes to deal with the contradictions of capital—then we can surely see the thickening of borders as an aspect of such a fix. See David Harvey, *The Limits of Capital* (Chicago: University of Chicago Press, 1982) and *The Condition of Postmodernity: An Enquiry into Cultural Change* (Oxford: Blackwell, 1989).

10. By locating the relationship between domestic violence and the class and race contradictions of American society, it is not my intention to either cast Third World societies as free of domestic violence or to place domestic violence as a solely middle-class phenomenon. The point simply is to put in perspective the idea that domestic violence, while firmly entrenched in cultures of patriarchy, precipitate and proliferate in relation to the pathologies of the public world that are carried into the private world of the home.

11. The idea that we are a union that welcomes "all" of a driver's life into the organization is something that we have discussed at great length in our meetings. For me, the idea of a more comprehensive organizational ideal rather than narrow economism is one that I draw from a significant number of social movements in India. The approach of the Chattisgarh Multi Morcha, the Mazdoor Kisan Shakti Sanghtan, or Kashtakari Sanghtan all come to mind as long-standing inspirations.

7. IMPERIAL AMNESIA

1. Eric Asimov, "$25 and Under; Driver, Follow That Cab (for Some Fine Indian Fare)," *New York Times,* August 9, 2000, p. F9.

2. Desi, literally means "of the desh" or "of the home country." Over the last decade it is a term that has found significant acceptance among South Asians as a self-descriptor for its numerous advantages. For one, it helps in moving away from the term "South Asian," which many recognize as a category that owes its origins to the Cold War–era carving up of the world by the American establishment intellectual. Further, it has an ambiguity to it inasmuch as it gets rids of all easy national references. If somebody in urban India uses this term it could refer to somebody from his village. Among diasporic populations, the term cannot uniquely refer to Indians or Pakistanis. Sometimes an Indian may use it to refer to other Indians and at other times to everybody from the subcontinent. When I first began working in the taxi industry, it was a term I heard only within the South Asian driver community. But over the years, it has found its way into South Asian middle-class liberal/left circles. While the term has by now some universal appeal, we must still recognize that for many desis from Sri Lanka or South India or Bangladesh, the term does not have the same resonance as it does in large parts of Central, West, and Northern India and Pakistan.

3. A search on the *New York Times* archives for references to Eat Again Deli is informative. There are two prior references before Asimov's column. First came an article on the conflict with residents, which detailed the complaint and then explained the settlement. Then someone wrote into "Metropolitan Diary" quoting a poster on the deli's wall, complete with malapropisms, as though it were a quaint piece of immigrant awkwardness. But the poster was quite clearly a list of stipulations that arose from the dispute—Andy and Mohinder Singh's effort to inform drivers what the effects of the dispute were. Finally, then came the Asimov piece, recommending the deli's food. All three ran in different sections of the paper and clearly were not read by the same editors. Together they really uncomfortably illustrate three angles on middle-class entitlement in New York. Working-class immigrants are a) dirty, b) cute, and c) a source of cheap authentic eats. See Asimov and David Kirby, "Neighborhood Report: Chelsea; Cabbies at a Deli Keep Neighbors' Anger Meter Running," *New York Times,* May 9, 1999.

4. Slavoj Žižek, "Multiculturalism, or, the Cultural Logic of Multinational Capitalism," *New Left Review* 225 (September–October 1997): 28–51.

5. In *No Logo,* Naomi Klein articulates the relation between product and consumer as one that has transformed dramatically in the post-eighties phase of corporate globalization. Klein, *No Logo* (London: Flamingo, 2000). See the conclusion, "Consumerism Versus Citizenship."

6. The consumer as a primary identity is, in my opinion, a phenomenon of the last three decades that coincides with such large-scale changes as the acceleration of suburbanization; the entry of technology into daily life, such as the emergence of fast food as the cheapest food (Eric Schlosser, *Fast Food Nation: The Dark Side of the All-American Meal,* (New York: HarperCollins, 2001); the neoliberal turn under Reagan that brought the idea of the market to a new level of common sense; and a postmodern relativization of culture. To say, however, that this subjectivity belongs to the last three decades is not to claim a complete discontinuity from the past. It is in this sense that the Wilsonian fetishization of "scientific America" that met the demand of an advancing industrial revolution and the civil rights "equal America" that met the demand of a Cold War claim to freedom that was unsustainable if America was itself internally "unfree" are both part of this said continuity.

7. For detailed documentation of the AFL-CIO and CIA connection, see the works of Robert Armstrong and Michael Sussman: Robert Armstrong et al., *Working Against US: The American Institute for Free Labor Development and the International Policy of the AFL-CIO* (New York: NACLA, 1990) and Michael Sussman, *AIFLD, U.S. Trojan Horse in Latin America and the Caribbean: A Joint Venture of the AFL-CIO, Department of State, U.S. Corporations and the CIA—The History of the American Institute for Free Labor Development* (Washington, DC: Epica, 1983).

8. In the 1980s various left-labor groups—from the AFL-CIO to the SWP and the CPUSA to the RCP—fell apart under the attack of the Reagan state. On the one hand was the internal repression and threats epitomized by the air traffic controllers' strike, and on the other was the aggressive pursuit of the Cold War. Many of those organizations lost their mass base when they pulled their cadre out of the workplace in response to the pressure. I offer this explanation not so much to create an "excuse" for various mistakes but to place it in context. That the Stalinist state must be understood as a primary cause for the collapse of the USSR cannot be denied if one were to simply acknowledge that the USSR collapsed without a civil war. If forces internal to the republic that represented the state had any mass appeal, then, under the pressure of the Cold War and with the breakup of the Communist Party, the least that would

have happened would have been some version of a civil war. That the whole Soviet bloc went without an internal whimper is evidence enough that there was something dramatically wrong inside.

9. Diwali is a Hindu festival that is very popular in the Indian community, while Eid is a generic word used to denote one of the two important events in the annual Islamic calendar.

10. William Fletcher, "Another World Is Possible: But How?," Socialist Scholars Conference, panel organized by the Brecht Forum, New York, 2004.

11. While I claim no clear correspondence with my use of the category of justice as a broad intellectual tradition, I do owe the idea to Walter Benjamin. His distinction between "divine" and "mythical" does leave in its wake a pessimistic imaginary where justice is not possible through the modern system of states. However, he does position the notion of justice as apriori to any contract or legal form. Walter Benjamin, *Illuminations*, ed. with an introduction by Hannah Arendt, trans. Harry Zohn (New York: Harcourt, Brace & World, 1968).

EPILOGUE: TRACKING TAXIS, WORKER AUTONOMY, AND NEW LABOR STRATEGIES

1. The United Taxi Workers of San Francisco is one of the oldest organizations in the taxi industry in the United States and has fought several landmark battles in the taxi industry including those related to permit (medallion) reform.

2. The East Bay Driver Association is a Teamster union; the San Jose union is sponsored by UDCW.

3. The decision to include "international" in the name of the International Taxi Workers Alliance was made after a discussion in the final session of the conference when driver organizations from New Delhi, Sydney, and Punjab had all called into the conference to express solidarity and long-term interest in the organization.

4. Ed Ott, "New Strategies for Today's Labor," with Bhairavi Desai, Brecht Forum, November 2, 2007.

5. One such driver, Shah Raza, was at JFK almost around the clock spreading ridiculous rumors about the Alliance in general and Bhairavi in specific. One such effort from him included carrying around a fudged computer printout claiming she received half a million dollars from Ford Foundation to ensure that Ford Crown Victoria remained the car of choice in the taxi industry.

6. This is in contrast to several brokers who had in 1998 given drivers a break on the lease for the May 13 strike. This closing of ranks where the brokers and the garage owners stood together this time is indicative of the level of opposition that NYTWA faced (and faces) through the GPS struggle.

7. Pete Donahue, "PA Data: Strike More Successful Than Mayor Claims," *Daily News*, September 7, 2007. . The news report looked at Port Authority data for September 5 and 6 and also conducted an independent survey of garages to pin down a figure on strike participation and concluded that the mayor's figures were wrong.

8. Patrick Arden, "On the Backs of City Hacks," *Metro New York*, September 10, 2007.

9. Tom Robbins, "Robes for a Rogue," *Village Voice*, September 4, 2007, focuses on Noach Dear's sordid history of special interest sell outs. Robbins followed this up with a second story on September 11, 2007, "Cabbies Get Taken for a Ride by the Taxi Commission, So You Don't."

10. Within weeks of the October 1 launch date of the program, NYTWA began a preliminary survey. The survey involved 150 drivers, and the data secured indicates a significant degree of equipment failure on the streets. The survey results are forthcoming and expected to be published. In addition, the NYTWA has set up a toll-free voicemail system for drivers to register complaints against the system. NYTWA was forced to do this because no agency of the city was accepting complaints from drivers on GPS equipment failure. The city's 311 system, which accepts complaints from any New Yorker on any aspect of the city's administration, was explicitly rejecting driver complaints. Within ten days of the toll-free line being set up, more than one hundred complaints had already been registered.

11. "Taxi Technology Files for Ch 11," *Forbes*, November 13, 2007.

12. "City Agency Sets Deadline for Philly Taxi Technology Fixes," *Philadelphia Inquirer*, January 25, 2008.

13. See chapters 3 and 4 for details of TLC chairmen and garage owners in scandals.

14. Recent articles in the New York City press indicate that a significant number of passengers are against the system. See for instance, Jacarino and Siemaszko, "Few Riders Hailing High Tech Screens," *Daily News*, October 21, 2007. . Also, Alessandra Stanley, "Taxi TV: As Brisk as the Traffic You are Stuck In," *New York Times*, December 15, 2007.

15. There is a much larger technological criticism to be made of the system. In short, the technology being sold is effectively one to two generations old. For

instance, most network technologies today are equipped with forward diagnosis of potential failure as network health is constantly monitored. No such feature is available. This can be considered basic failure.

16. The 5 percent cut on every credit card transaction is a straightforward wage cut for drivers. The absurdity of the 5 percent service fee is clear when one breaks it down. Approximately 2 to 2.5 percent goes to the credit card institution. The remaining 2.5 percent is grabbed by the vendor and the garage/broker. In other words at least 2.5 percent of service fee is being levied against the driver for no reason at all.

17. The distinction between absolute and relative surplus value as laid out in *Capital* (vol. 1, chapter 7) is a crucial distinction for us in understanding how contemporary labor is organized under sub contractorship structures.

18. See Marx's *Economic Manuscripts* of 1861–63. The concepts of formal and real subsumption of labor is introduced at the end of Part 3 on Relative Surplus Value.

19. My point here is not to claim that there is any essential unity between the works of such a disparate group of artists and writers but to show that in a wide range of spaces the worker emerged as protagonist.

20. There is not much written on the question of how American labor compromised with capital but for broader criticisms of business unionism. However, I find the work of Michael Burowoy (*Manufacturing Consent*, University of Chicago Press, 1982) to be most valuable as it departs from a materialist framework of subsumption of labor and asks the crucial question of capital's cultural hegemony over the worker.

21. While the issue of utilitarianism being the hegemonic value of neoliberalism is pervasive in many works that try to understand its success, it is rarely framed as the very core of the cultural logic of neoliberalism. I am deeply indebted to Vamsicharan Vakulabharanam and Sripad Motiram for their paper on microfinance, "The Ethics of Microfinance and Cooperation" (forthcoming) for laying out the logic of utilitarianism as central to neoliberalism so clearly.

INDEX

CPSIA information can be obtained
at www.ICGtesting.com
Printed in the USA
LVHW04s1828120618
580475LV00012B/210/P